Praise for *Pujols: More than the Game*

As a part of the great tradition of St. Louis Cardinals baseball, it is very gratifying to me to see a man of Albert's character enjoy the success that he has achieved. Leadership comes in many forms, but the constant quality that all great leaders possess is an unwavering dedication to personal values. The fact that Albert's Christian witness is such a visible part of his life, both on and off the field, has made him a wonderful model for fans of all ages to follow. His dedication to his craft and to God makes him the ultimate Hall of Famer.

Tommy Herr
St. Louis Cardinals' second baseman (1979–1988)

One of the challenges that comes with watching from the press box and writing the first drafts of a legend is being able to chronicle his feats while still capturing the complexities of Albert Pujols, the greatest hitter of his generation. Scott Lamb and Tim Ellsworth are able to do both, peeking behind the box scores, scraping beneath the statistics, and illuminating not just what drives Pujols in the batter's box, but what inspires him beyond it. By showing how a 13th round unknown blitzed baseball and became a potential first-ballot Hall of Famer, they reveal the person even as they highlight the player who, with each swing, can make history.

Derrick Goold
baseball writer *St. Louis Post-Dispatch*

I've long admired Albert Pujols' marvelous baseball talent, especially since I pitched so many hitters into the Hall of Fame throughout my career. But, more importantly, I've also admired his character, integrity, and enthusiasm in helping those less fortunate than he. Ellsworth and Lamb do a great job exposing the wonderful man beneath the uniform. Even if you're not a baseball fan, you can't help but fall in love with this quality guy.

Frank Pastore
former pitcher with the Reds and Twins,
and host of the most-listened to Christian talk show in America.

Pujols is full of nuggets. Given that the action in the famous poem "Casey at the Bat" starts with "Cooney died at first, and Barrows did the same," I enjoyed reading that Albert Pujols asks opposing runners at first base, "If you died today, where do you think you're going to go?" Lamb and Ellsworth lucidly describe both the season-by-season baseball exploits of Pujols and the impact he's having on some lives for eternity.

Marvin Olasky
Editor-in-chief, *World*

Pujols has mastered the ability to use one's platform for the glory of God. You will walk away from this book encouraged in your faith as you read of Pujols' steadfast commitment to God in the midst of obstacles.

FLAME
Christian rap artist

To millions of American sports fans and the people of his native Dominican Republic, Albert Pujols is a modern day hero. But just as he acknowledges God by pointing to the sky after every home run blast, Pujols points his fans, reporters, and even opposing players who land on his first base to Albert's own hero, the Lord Jesus Christ. Lamb and Ellsworth deliver a home run themselves in this fascinating and well-documented story of a young boy who began playing baseball using milk cartons for baseball gloves and now uses his platform as baseball's greatest player to proclaim the joy and strength he receives in walking with the Lord. Baseball fan or not, you'll enjoy this inspiring biography of a great man dedicated first and foremost to faith, family, and community as he lives out a great baseball career.

Les Steckel
veteran NFL coach and President/CEO,
Fellowship of Christian Athletes

Lamb and Ellsworth have given baseball fans everywhere a truly outstanding baseball book about the greatest player in the game today. In this well-written and readable introduction to the life of Albert Pujols, we learn about his early days, the shaping influences along the way, and various aspects of his amazing career. Baseball fans, especially, will love this book, the interpretation of Pujols's incredible statistics, and the powerful retelling of pivotal games and seasons. This book, however, is so much more than another fine baseball book and even more than a wonderful biographical portrait; it is an inspirational book about character, commitments, faith, and family. You will want to read this excellent book . . . and buy an extra copy for a family member or friend.

David S. Dockery
President, Union University

St. Louis Cardinal baseball is genetically imbedded into the DNA of kids born in Arkansas during the Baby Boomer generation. I still remember my teacher at Brookwood Elementary School letting us sit on the playground on a beautiful October day so we could skip class and listen on a cheap AM transistor radio as the Cardinals beat the Yankees in the 1964 World Series. I was a nine-year old kid, but the memory of that will live with me far more than any of the lessons we would have had.

Years later, when I had my own children, I would take them on their birthdays to St. Louis to see the Cardinals play in Busch Stadium. If we were really lucky, we'd catch a doubleheader.

I was in Busch Stadium in 2004 when the Boston Red Sox beat my Cardinals in game 4 of the World Series, and despite the sadness of the loss, I witnessed history both in the breaking of the "curse of the Babe" for Boston, but also to witness first hand the classiest sports fans in America—the people of St. Louis, who despite their disappointment, stood and gave a standing ovation to the Champion Red Sox as a show of sportsmanship that is unparalleled in any sport in any city.

It's not surprising that one of the games truly great players, Albert Pujols is a star for the Cardinals. A world class team in a world class city deserves a world class gentleman for their team. They have that and more in Pujols. He embodies the best of sports and of heroes. His Christian testimony, his commitment to God and his family are a reminder of what real stars are about. One thing about Pujols—he matches in his personal life the excellence that he demonstrates on the diamond. You will love this book and will love Pujols if you don't already. You may never love the Cards like I do, but there's hope for you!

Mike Huckabee
44th Governor of Arkansas, former Republican presidential candidate,
host of Fox News' Huckabee Show, best-selling author

Many of the greatest stories of human achievement come from the battlefields and the playing fields. I was reminded of that in reading *Pujols: More Than the Game* by Scott Lamb and Tim Ellsworth. A story emerges from a baseball field that points to something far greater. Readers will be drawn into the story of Albert Pujols and his understanding of the game, seen from the vantage point of one of the greatest players of our generation. But there is more to this story, and that is where Lamb and Ellsworth really help us to understand Albert Pujols, not only as the baseball player, but as the Christian. And in that sense, they help us to understand the gospel as well, and how, indeed, in the life of a great athlete, the gospel of Jesus Christ can become so visible.

DR. R. ALBERT MOHLER, JR.
PRESIDENT, THE SOUTHERN BAPTIST THEOLOGICAL SEMINARY

In today's dysfunctional world—whether business, politics, sports, or religion—we have become profoundly aware that all our heroes are profoundly broken. While his manager Tony LaRussa called him "a real-life hero," what Lamb and Ellsworth demonstrate is that Albert Pujols only serves as a hero as he lives out the reality of his faith in the True Hero, Jesus Christ. Far beyond the stats, MVP awards, and championships, this book shows what real heroism is: a life lived in the shadow of the cross, a life lived for others, a life lived for God's glory.

DR. SEAN MICHAEL LUCAS
SENIOR MINISTER, THE FIRST PRESBYTERIAN CHURCH, HATTIESBURG, MS

Pujols is a book about a man, his game, and his God. For too many athletes—professional or amateur—their game is their god. It is refreshing to read about a legendary athlete who openly declares that God is his highest priority and who wants to live as a biblical Christian both on and off the field.

DONALD S. WHITNEY
AUTHOR OF *SPIRITUAL DISCIPLINES FOR THE CHRISTIAN LIFE*

Baseball and great reading go hand in hand, and this book is no different. Christian sportswriters would all agree that idolatry is bad . . . but many of them go on to tell you all the reasons why you should idolize a particular athlete. This book honors Pujols without idolizing, and keeps the gospel where it should be—at the center of everything."

TED KLUCK
AUTHOR OF *THE REASON FOR SPORTS: A CHRISTIAN FANIFESTO*
AND *FACING TYSON: FIFTEEN FIGHTERS, FIFTEEN STORIES*

Having had the chance to partner with the Pujols Family Foundation, I have seen firsthand how deeply Albert believes there truly is more to life than baseball. His actions prove it. You will be inspired as you follow the journey of a man who uses every inch of the platform he has been given to care for the disabled, aid the less fortunate, and most of all, to shine a light on the giver of all good things.

MATTHEW WEST

THE PUJOLS FAMILY FOUNDATION EXISTS TO HONOR GOD AND STRENGTHEN FAMILIES THROUGH OUR WORKS, DEEDS AND EXAMPLES.

To learn more about the Pujols Family Foundation

Visit us on the web: www.pujolsfamilyfoundation.org

Like us on Facebook: www.facebook.com/pujolsfamilyfoundation

Follow us on Twitter: @PujolsFound

Email us: info@pujolsfamilyfoundation.org

Write to us: Pujols Family Foundation
111 Westport Plaza Suite 225
St. Louis, MO 63146

Peace to you,
Todd Perry
Executive Director/CEO of the Pujols Family Foundation

PUJOLS

MORE THAN THE GAME

SCOTT LAMB AND
TIM ELLSWORTH

THOMAS NELSON
Since 1798

NASHVILLE DALLAS MEXICO CITY RIO DE JANEIRO

Published in Nashville, Tennessee, by Thomas Nelson. Thomas Nelson is a registered trademark of Thomas Nelson, Inc.

Published in association with the literary agency of Wolgemuth & Associates, Inc.

Page design by Mandi Cofer.

Thomas Nelson, Inc., titles may be purchased in bulk for educational, business, fund-raising, or sales promotional use. For information, please e-mail SpecialMarkets@ThomasNelson.com.

ISBN 978-1-59555-517-5 (trade paper)

Library of Congress Cataloging-in-Publication Data

Lamb, Scott.
Pujols : more than the game / by Scott Lamb and Tim Ellsworth.
p. cm.
Includes bibliographical references and index.
ISBN 978-1-59555-224-2
1. Pujols, Albert, 1980– 2. Baseball players—United States—Biography. 3. Baseball players—Dominican Republic—Biography. I. Ellsworth, Tim. II. Title.
GV965.P85L35 2011
796.357092—dc22
[B]

2010037139

Printed in the United States of America

12 13 14 15 16 QG 5 4 3 2 1

For Daniel, Emmalee and Noah:
With hopes that you'll grow up to like baseball,
and prayers that you'll grow up to love Jesus.

Love, Tim

For Pearl:
Five kids and "Two Words"
were all brought to life,
By the hand of my God
and the heart of my wife.

Love, Scott

CONTENTS

FOREWORD

Albert Pujols has a chance to be known as the greatest player in the history of baseball. There are numerous statistical measurements to make the point, including the simple point that through age thirty he has more homers than Babe Ruth, more hits than Pete Rose, more RBIs than Hank Aaron, and more runs than Rickey Henderson did at the same age.

Yes, it's okay to think about that for a moment.

But Pujols' argument for greatest player ever isn't nearly as interesting or significant as the fact that there even *is* an argument. That's because perhaps the most amazing thing about Albert Pujols is that less than two years before he began one of the greatest rookie seasons in baseball history, he was a non-prospect. He was playing baseball at Maple Woods Community College, and though he was creating enough buzz that scouts actually came to see him (as you will see, he hit .466 with twenty-two homers in limited at-bats), he was not creating enough buzz to convince anyone that he could play in the big leagues.

Some questioned whether he would be able to play defense in the big leagues. Some questioned if his swing could hold up against the curveballs and sliders thrown at the big league level. Some questioned his body type. The local Kansas City Royals saw him several times and yawned. The Cardinals took him in the 13th round—only one other player in the round, Alfredo Amezaga, would get even moderate time in the big leagues.

Of course, there have been some other late-round picks who became big stars in the big leagues . . . but none of them are quite like Pujols. That's because Pujols didn't *become* a big star—he was *already* a big star. He was in the minor leagues for one season, dominated, went to spring training, won an Opening Day job, and then went on to hit .327 with forty-seven doubles, thirty-seven homers, 130 RBIs and 112 runs scored. It was one of the most remarkable debuts in baseball history. In the nine years since, he has been as good or better pretty much every year.

In fact, as a thought-experiment for a story I did on him for *Sports Illustrated* in 2009, I asked the question: What has been Albert Pujols' *worst* season? It may have been his second year, when he merely hit .314 with thirty-four homers, 127 RBIs, 118 runs, and finished second in the MVP balloting. It may have been 2007, when he hit .329 with thirty-two homers and, for the only time in his career so far, failed to score 100 runs (he scored ninety-nine).

Whatever year is his worst you can be sure that repeated ten times it would make Pujols a first-ballot Hall of Famer. And, again, that's referring to his *worst* season.

And beyond that, he just gets better and better at everything else in the game. He wanted to improve his defense—one of the big questions about his game—and he became one of the best first base defenders in the game. He wanted to improve his base stealing after a sluggish first five seasons, and since then he has averaged ten stolen bases a year and he is successful 75 percent of the time. He wanted to improve his strikeout-to-walk ratio and so, after striking out more than he walked as a rookie, he now walks forty or fifty more times a year than he strikes out.

How does a man develop that sort of consistency?

How does he repeat that sort of greatness year after year after year?

How does he find ways to keep getting better?

Some of the secrets are in this fine book by Scott Lamb and Tim Ellsworth. You will read about Albert's unshakeable faith. You will read about his wonderful wife Dee Dee and the depth of her support. You will read about Albert's childhood in the Dominican Republic, his not-always-easy adjustment to America, and how each shaped the way he attacks the game of baseball.

And you will read about how every single day Albert Pujols wakes up with that same purpose, that same drive to do one thing as well as anyone has ever done it.

The *Sports Illustrated* piece I wrote about Pujols was a lot of fun. I spent quite a bit of time with Albert and talked at some length with Dee Dee, and they were both wonderful. When the story came out I heard through various messengers that Albert and Dee Dee liked the story quite a bit, and while this is never the purpose of a writer, well, it is still a nice thing to hear.

A couple of months later, I went back to St. Louis to write a story, and while I didn't need to talk to Albert, I thought I would at least say hello. I stopped at his locker, where there was a large group of reporters. He talked bluntly and quickly—talking to reporters is not exactly Albert's favorite way of passing time—and when the conference ended he saw me and I reached out my hand to shake his. He walked right past me.

Well, that's okay. I know about Albert's singular focus. The next day, similar situation, I saw Albert, our eyes met, and he walked right past me again. Okay. So I thought maybe I had heard wrong; maybe he didn't like the story. Maybe he didn't have anything to say to me. So it goes. Like I say, as a writer you just try your best to write an honest story. If Albert didn't like it or me, well, he wouldn't be the first.

I didn't think about it again until the off-season. I was invited to go to the St. Louis Baseball Writers dinner. It was in a large ballroom—more than 1,000 people involved—and I was walking to meet someone when all of a sudden I heard, "Joe! Joe!" I turned around . . . and it was Albert Pujols, smiling and waving to me like a little kid. He could not have been happier to see me.

And that's when I understood: Albert Pujols wasn't ignoring me during the season. He may have been looking right at me in that locker room, but he didn't even *see* me. No, during the season, he sees baseballs. He sees them and he hits them. And he does it about as well as anyone who has ever walked on this earth.

Joe Posnanski

PART ONE

FROM SANTO DOMINGO TO SAINT LOUIS

CHAPTER ONE

THE HIGHWAY'S JAMMED WITH BROKEN HEROES

There was too much Albert Pujols today.

—Jim Tracy, Pittsburgh Pirates manager, September 3, 2006

The bronzed Latino approached the batter's box and performed the necessary rituals. Dug in with the right foot. Tapped the back of home plate with the bat. Glanced toward the small dirt mound just sixty feet to the left.

Another man stood atop that hill and worked through rituals of his own—groin-scratching, spitting, signaling, more scratching. He prepared himself for the sophisticated hurling of a small sphere made of cork, twine, and leather—otherwise known as a baseball.

A grizzled broadcaster looked down from the media booth where he sat behind his microphone, describing the on-field action with familiar terms and labels: fastball, changeup, curveball, slider.

But for the man at the plate wearing jersey number 5, the "perfect opportunity" pitch was the delivery he looked for, the delivery he knew would come. Only then would he swing his maple bat in an arc of geometric beauty and poetic power.

It was a Sunday game on the third of September, 2006. Gone was the sticky heat of the St. Louis summer, replaced with partly cloudy skies and temperatures in the mid-seventies. Early autumn made a perfect day for baseball, a fact not lost on the forty thousand fans who were soon to arrive.

This was the inaugural year of baseball in the red-brick home that some locals still called the *new* Busch Stadium, a reminder of past baseball glory and civic pride. On the tenth of April, Albert Pujols had become the first Cardinal to hit a home run in the new digs. He'd gone on to smash fourteen homers that month, a Major League Baseball record for April.

But now it was September, the last month of the grinding regular season. Just ten days earlier, the Cardinals had been locked in a tie for first place in the National League Central Division with the Cincinnati Reds. By the time the perennial cellar-dwelling Pirates came into town for a weekend series, the Cardinals had pulled away from the pack. A win today would put them a full six games ahead of the Reds. To get the win, though, they would have to beat Ian Snell, ace pitcher for the Pirates.

Pujols knew this day would bring special joy. It was Buddy Walk in the Park Day, when children with Down syndrome went on field during pregame ceremonies, rubbing shoulders and running the bases with big leaguers. Pujols walked around the field meeting countless numbers of children. While it would be fair to say these youngsters came to see a baseball game, in reality they came to see Pujols. Their joy would become his joy. Indeed, they were his buddies, and he was their hero.

Pujols stooped down and got on the level of a talkative ten-year-old boy, eye-to-eye and ear-to-ear, and listened to the exuberance of innocent baseball fervor.

Then the boy made his request—a home run. He wanted a home run from Pujols.

"I'll see what I can do," Pujols said with a smile.

Another child approached, leaned forward, and spoke into Pujols' ear.

It was the same request—just a home run. Today. Please. Thank you.

Pujols smiled big and assured each child he would try his best to hit one out today.

Although his response to the kids dripped with confidence, it didn't flow from pride in his abilities. Rather, Pujols simply knew from experience that when the stadium rocked with the cheers of thousands of children with Down syndrome, special things just seemed to happen.

Buddy Walk Day and Pujols had been good to each other in the past: In 2002, Pujols had hit a home run and driven in three runs. In 2003, he'd again hit a home run, this time in a dramatic thirteenth-inning win over Houston.

Did the kids understand just how hard it was to hit a home run off a major league pitcher? Probably not.

Nevertheless, even as they ran back to their parents and their peanuts and their Cracker Jack, they basked in a joy that can only come from meeting one's hero and asking him to smash the ball over the wall . . . "for me."

After the singing of "The Star-Spangled Banner," the first inning was underway. The last of the fans filed into their seats with a hot dog in one hand and a cold drink in the other.

Most of the crowd was clothed in Cardinal red, with a few Pittsburgh fans sporting grey, black, and gold. Some of these had "Clemente" stitched on their back—a noble name worthy of remembrance. Like those Pirates fans, St. Louisans appreciate baseball history and baseball heroes, especially their own: Musial, Gibson, Brock, Sutter, and Ozzie.

The Cards made quick work of the Pirates in the top half of the first—three up and three down—and headed back to the dugout for their turn at-bat.

On Snell's fifth pitch, Cards second baseman Aaron Miles grounded to the Pirates' first baseman, Ryan Doumit, for the first out.

Right-fielder Chris Duncan then stepped up to the plate and quickly fell into an 0–2 hole. He watched the next three pitches go by for balls, making it a full count. The next pitch looked like a gem, but Duncan swung through it for strike three.

So with two outs and nobody on base, Pujols walked up to the plate for his first at-bat of the day.

The first pitch was low; ball one.

Pujols readied himself for the second pitch. Though only the first inning, the stadium was electric in anticipation. Probably even a beer vendor or two twisted his neck to see the action on the field.

Snell wound and delivered.

A quick swing of the bat and seconds later the baseball landed 410 feet away in left-field seats. Pujols' fortieth home run of the season gave the Cards an early 1–0 lead.

Dozens of delirious Buddy Walk kids simultaneously had the same thought—Albert Pujols hit *me* a home run!

And so he did. Because heroes do heroic things—for others.

Vin Scully, Hall of Fame broadcaster for the Los Angeles Dodgers, once quipped, "Statistics are used much like a drunk uses a lamppost: for support, not illumination."

That is, statistics don't provide the full measure of an individual baseball player's impact on his team or on his era. For that, you need stories—lots of stories. You get the stories from loving the game, and this love affair demands faithful watching, listening, playing, and reading. And this is a romance with multigenerational rewards, for these are the stories you will tell your kids, and your kids will tell your grandkids.

If you don't own any of these stories yet yourself, then just listen in on guys like Scully or Cardinals broadcaster Mike Shannon and borrow some of theirs. They won't mind.

Pujols hustled around the bases. No showboating. No Jeffrey Leonard "one flap down." Pujols knew all too well that even great baseball players with a batting average of .300 will still fail at the plate seven times out of ten. This time up he got the big hit, but the next three times he could just as likely produce an out.

Did you notice what just happened? Right there, in the very act of telling a good home-run story, we ended up talking statistics and batting averages—and for good reason. Though the stories *do* illuminate, it *is* the stats that give support to phrases like *one of the all-time greats*.

If baseball math isn't your thing, then go ahead and skip the next page or two. But, if you like your baseball heroes smothered in a thick gravy of amazing stats, then Pujols is your man, and this section is for you.

It's no wonder Pujols routinely tops the list of the greatest players in modern Major League Baseball. Even before turning thirty, he had accrued batting totals that most players only hope to gain over the course of an entire career.

Among all major leaguers who ever played the game, Pujols already ranks in the top twenty in batting average, slugging percentage, on-base percentage, and on base plus slugging (adjusted for league and ballpark effects). In simple terms, he is already one of the twenty greatest offensive players in baseball history.

Pujols hit 201 home runs in his first five seasons, placing him in second place all-time for the most homers hit during a player's first five years. Not stopping there, in 2009 he reached the 350–home run mark at a younger age than anyone except Ken Griffey Jr. and Alex Rodriguez. By doing so, he also surpassed the record for most home runs in the first nine years of a career, breaking the mark established by Hall of Famer Ralph Kiner way back in 1954.

And speaking of nine seasons, Pujols now stands as the only player ever to begin a career with ten consecutive years of thirty home runs and a hundred runs batted in.

Take a deep breath. We're just getting started.

Pujols owns the Cardinals franchise record for most career grand slams, having surpassed a guy known as Stan the Man.

When compared to legends of the game, Pujols stands alongside Stan Musial, Ted Williams, and Joe DiMaggio as one of only four players to have less than five hundred career strikeouts and a career batting average over .330 at the time they hit their three-hundredth home run.

Yankee hero Lou Gehrig posted nine consecutive seasons with thirty doubles, a .300 batting average, thirty home runs, and one hundred runs batted in. Has anyone else accomplished this feat? Nobody except Pujols, and he has now accomplished this feat for ten consecutive years.

In more than one hundred years of National League baseball, nobody ranks ahead of Pujols in extra base hits (744) within the first 5,000 career at-bats. He gets around a lot.

He has led the Cards to postseason play year after year, and to the World Series twice, winning it all in 2006.

And what about individual awards?

Pujols is a three-time National League MVP (Most Valuable Player), a three-time winner of the ESPY Award (best MLB player), and a nine-time NL All-Star. In 2003, he won the NL batting title and subsequently won the Hank Aaron Award (given each year to only one player in each league) for hitting prowess. On defense, he won a Gold Glove in 2006. He has earned

Player of the Month honors six times, won the NL Silver Slugger award six times, and was the NL Rookie of the Year in 2001. In 2009, a sports columnist placed Pujols' offensive stats in historical perspective when he wrote, "If Pujols plays only nine more years and simply averages the numbers he put up in his worst season to date, he would retire at 38 with a career average around .330 and rank fifth on the all-time list in home runs (659), fourth in RBIs (2,035) and in the top 10 in runs (2057) and walks (1,792). Only Babe Ruth has done better."

Those kinds of stats both illuminate *and* support.

It was the bottom of the third inning, and the Cardinals still led 1–0.

After fighting off several pitches, Aaron Miles swung for strike three. One out.

Next up was Chris Duncan.

Chris is the son of Dave Duncan, the revered pitching-coach guru for the Cardinals. Dave played eleven seasons as a catcher before turning to coaching and has worked with Cards manager Tony La Russa for nearly three decades and on three different teams. So, Chris had been around a lot of baseball in his life, and a good portion of it had come in proximity to his father.

For Pujols and his "Papá," Bienvenido, the father-son relationship worked itself out a little differently. Pujols didn't see him all that much, being raised instead by his grandma América, alongside aunts and uncles who shared common living quarters there in the Dominican Republic.

But when it came to baseball, Pujols knew he wanted to be like his father. Bienvenido was known throughout the island for his pitching prowess and great passion for the game. In like manner, from the earliest days of childhood, Albert played ball whenever and wherever he could. Yes, he would be like Papá.

Duncan singled on a line drive that dropped in front of right fielder Xavier Nady. From the dugout, Dave took fatherly pride in his son's accomplishments. With Duncan on first and only one out, Pujols walked up to the plate for his second at-bat. Snell strategized how to go after him this time around. He made his decision, and he then made his pitch.

The loud crack of Pujols' bat echoed off the shining steel of the Gateway Arch and killed some pigeons in flight. Well, maybe not, but it *was* a thunderous *thwack*.

As Yogi Berra said, "It's déjà vu all over again." The Pirates certainly felt that way as Pujols hit his second home run of the day over the same left field wall. Into the stands went the ball, and onto the scoreboard went two more runs. The Cards now led 3–0.

With two home runs in two at-bats, Buddy Walk Day was going very well indeed.

As Pujols again rounded the bases and crossed home plate, he pointed to the sky, acknowledging God as the source of all athletic skill and talent. Then, as he glanced up into the stadium at the fans celebrating with him, he saw families having fun—enjoying the game and enjoying one another.

Being a hero to large numbers of baseball fans must feel great. Being a hero to buddies with Down syndrome must be even better. But being a hero to your own family—nothing beats that.

So, what *does* it mean to be a hero to your own family?

To Pujols' wife, Dee Dee, being a hero means fidelity, honesty, abiding love, and friendship. To his children, being a hero means time, talk, and taking interest.

To Pujols' father, grandma, and the extended family that helped raise him, being a hero means upholding the family's standards of integrity, instilled in him by word and "whoopin'." Pujols once explained why he had never used steroids, saying that his family would be "embarrassed and disappointed because it would be stupid." He said, "That's not the way I grew up. Papá would give me a whoopin'. I can't make you believe what I stand for. I can only tell you my story."

Pujols' story is of one being a hero in his own home. Because heroes do heroic things for their families.

As the bottom of the fifth rolled around, the scoreboard still displayed 3–0 in favor of the Cardinals, and Snell remained on the mound for the Pirates.

Once again Duncan singled, and once again Pujols walked to the plate.

But Pujols didn't want to become too predictable. Rather than hitting a home run to left field, this time he sent the ball over the center field fence. Sometimes you've just got to shake things up a bit.

Snell was a great sport about the shellacking he took from Pujols that day. During the postgame interview he said, "I hung it, and he banged it.

I thought it was going to hit the St. Louis Arch out there. I wanted to go high-five him. That's unreal. That's like Superman playing baseball."

Many fans, especially the young ones, dream about living the life of a baseball superstar, imagining the pleasures of stockpiled fortune and fame. Albert and Deidre Pujols have given clear testimony, however, that Jesus Christ is at the center of their lives, providing meaning, purpose, and direction. They talk and walk their Christianity and their commitment to faith, family, others. Pujols writes:

> People have said to me, "Albert, I would give anything to be able to play baseball like you." They may look at my abilities and think that being a great baseball player is the goal of my life. Believe it or not, baseball is not the chief ambition of my life. Becoming a great baseball player is important to me, but it is not my primary focus. Because I know the Hall of Fame is not my ultimate final destination. My life's goal is to bring glory to Jesus. My life is not mostly dedicated to the Lord, it is 100% committed to Jesus Christ and His will. God has given me the ability to succeed in the game of baseball. But baseball is not the end; baseball is the means by which my wife, Dee Dee, and I glorify God. Baseball is simply my platform to elevate Jesus Christ, my Lord and Savior.

When Albert and Dee Dee Pujols talk about *faith*, it is a word loaded with real content. In a day and age when churches and denominations seem afraid to speak unequivocally about doctrinal commitments, a first baseman in the MLB comes forth with a ten-point statement of faith nearly four hundred words long.

Pujols' faith is neither a vague spirituality nor an improve-your-morals campaign. Rather, the core of his faith is in Jesus Christ, defined in his foundation's statement of faith as "God's only Son, [who] lived a perfect life of obedience to the Father and substituted Himself as the perfect sacrifice for our sins. He became our mediator to bridge the gap between mankind and a Holy, Sinless God."

Hear what Pujols says when asked why faith in Christ is of such crucial importance: "The answer simply is because our faith in Jesus Christ is the central point of our individual lives, our marriage, family and Foundation.

Take Jesus Christ and faith in Him out of the equation, and all those other things would not exist."

And Pujols' faith includes a commission to tell others. Pujols believes that he lives under a divine mandate to be a representative for God. He says, "At the end of the day as long as I glorify Him and those 45,000 people know who I represent out there every time I step out on the field, that's what it's about. It's about representing God."

A Christian hero points people to an even greater hero, directing them to Christ and calling on them to believe—to have faith.

It was the bottom of the seventh, and the score remained 5–0. Pujols walked to the plate for what would be his fourth and final at-bat of the game. Would he become only the sixteenth player in MLB history to hit four home runs in one game?

The broadcaster called out, "Pujols hits it deeeeep to center . . . all the way back to the warning track . . . where it is caught just short of another home run for Albert."

Bruce Springsteen famously crooned, "The highway's jammed with broken heroes on a last chance power drive." Pujols is no broken hero. He has not jammed the highway. He has not been weighed in the balances and found wanting. And for that, we can be thankful—because he is a hero to take joy in, to tell the stories of, and to share with our children.

When the heavy stench of cynicism lifts away, if even for a moment, our antihero culture rediscovers the pleasure of breathing the fresh air of belief. But if you read this story and consider Albert Pujols to be the greatest hero, you will have missed the point entirely.

Pujols believes devotion to Jesus Christ is what has fueled him to excel in baseball. It's what has driven his philanthropy and generosity to those less fortunate. It's what has bolstered his integrity and kept him humble in an occupation that often places personal glory above all else. It's what prompts him to talk about Jesus Christ regularly, no matter the setting and no matter the question.

Pujols says, "The kids look at me, 'Ah, you're my hero.' I want to teach those kids. 'Hey listen, God is my hero. He died on the cross for my sins, and He's the one. That's how I want to live—like Him and I want you guys to do the same thing. They look at me and say, 'What does Albert have in his heart or in him that I don't have?' I want them to see this Jesus that I have in me."

Our hope for you in reading this book is that you will develop a deeper admiration and respect for Albert Pujols and what he has achieved. But more than that, our prayer is that you will leave this book with a greater sense of awe and wonder at the majesty, grace, and glory of the Lord—the God who created Albert Pujols and gave him such incredible abilities; the God who is truly mighty to save.

CHAPTER TWO

WE HAD EVERYTHING BUT MONEY

God made me older.
—*Albert Pujols*

Decked out in a miniature white St. Louis Cardinals uniform, sunglasses, and a necklace, nine-year-old A. J. walks with his dad and the rest of the players from the team clubhouse to practice field number one on a warm, breezy March 2010 day at Roger Dean Stadium in Jupiter, Florida. The players take up their positions in left field to start the day's spring training activities with stretching and warm-ups, and A. J. joins right in. He is the only kid out there among a group of adults playing a kid's game.

The team trainer barks out instructions—"Right hand up!"—and the players obey, twisting and contorting their bodies, with right hands held aloft, to get loose. His white uniform makes A. J. stand out from the rest of the ballplayers, who are wearing red practice jerseys and white pants, accessorized by red belts, red hats, and red shoes. Last names in white block letters adorn their backs: RASMUS. PENNY. WAINWRIGHT. FREESE. GREENE. LUDWICK. And PUJOLS.

As he stretches, the young A. J. talks with his dad, Albert, for a bit, before Albert becomes engrossed in a conversation in Spanish with teammates Julio Lugo and Felipe López. A. J. moves on to a more interesting exchange with team shortstop Brendan Ryan, a nine-year-old trapped in a twenty-eight-year-old's body. "One time I sneezed and there was this big snot bubble," Ryan tells A. J., holding his hands in a soccer-ball-sized circle in front of his nose. A. J. laughs, as any boy would.

"Right knee out! Left hand up!" the trainer calls. "Straighten it out!"

By this time Cardinals coaches José Oquendo and Joe Pettini have started playing catch along the left field foul line, the baseball popping in their gloves as the chatter continues behind them.

"Who are we playing today?" someone asks.

"Mets," comes the reply.

A. J. has had enough of the stretching, and Pettini begins hitting him a few ground balls. A. J. is a lefty, and on one grounder makes a diving stop to his right. "Nice," Pettini tells him.

Sufficiently stretched out, the players begin their running, jogging from the left field foul line several yards into the outfield, then walking back and doing it again. A. J. moves from fielding grounders to playing catch with Oquendo. A few minutes later, infield practice starts for the Cardinals. As Pettini smacks ground balls their way, A. J. stands next to him and catches the throws coming in from the fielders. He tosses a ball to Pettini, snags a throw from his dad or Skip Schumaker, and then repeats the drill. Over and over.

The morning progresses in similar fashion until Albert and A. J. leave the practice field and head toward the stadium for batting practice. A. J. plants himself in right field to shag balls being sprayed about by the hitters. Albert stands with him until it's his turn to bat. During lulls in the action, father and son squat together in right center field, side-by-side, and talk, enjoying each other's company and the opportunity that baseball provides for them to be together.

For Albert, the scene must bear a striking resemblance to his own childhood. Oh, the peripherals are different—the fields on which A. J. plays with him are more manicured, the players more skilled, the stakes higher. But the basics are much the same—a young Albert Pujols tagging along with his dad, a professional softball player in the Dominican Republic, to watch him play.

"I always liked to go with my dad wherever he was going," Pujols told the *St. Louis Post-Dispatch* years later. "I wanted to be there when he was playing."

It's what came after the games that Pujols could have done without, and what he has pledged that A. J. will never have to endure.

The crack of a bat rings out in the steamy afternoon hours on a makeshift baseball diamond in the heart of Santo Domingo. A scorching fastball pops into the catcher's mitt near a sugarcane plantation in a rural *batey* (a village where sugar workers live). The chatter of the players across the entire country—as they take their cuts, fire the ball across the infield, and dig hard for second base—forms the soundtrack for the youth of the Dominican Republic as they meander through childhood and adolescence, honing their skills and dreaming of the day when the game they love will love them back.

Roman Catholicism claims as its adherents 95 percent of the ten million residents of this Caribbean nation, but baseball rivals it as the true religion. The sport may be the national pastime in the United States—in the Dominican Republic, it's the national obsession. Soccer in Brazil has nothing on baseball in the DR.

Sharing the island of Hispaniola with Haiti (from whom the DR won its independence in 1844), the Dominican Republic is about the size of Vermont and New Hampshire combined. Santo Domingo, the capital, is the oldest continually inhabited European city in the Americas. Details of baseball's origins in the country are sketchy, but it seems that the Dominican Republic has Cuba to thank, as refugees fleeing the Ten Years' War scattered across the Caribbean Sea in the late nineteenth century, taking baseball with them. Other islands may have adopted the game, but the Dominican Republic consumed it with wholehearted devotion.

Sugarcane plantation owners promoted the sport because it gave their laborers something to do with their time when they weren't working. The impoverished workers embraced it because it provided a much-needed distraction from the harsh realities of life. Children played baseball because their dads played baseball and their granddads played baseball. As part of the local tradition, parents of baby boys often put a little baseball glove in their child's crib. And so the sport became a way of life, ingrained in the fabric of Dominican culture as much as Coke or apple pie is in the United States.

That was before the promise of riches came from Major League Baseball, once it opened its doors to nonwhites. Jackie Robinson did much more than break the color barrier for black Americans—he broke it for Hispanics too. In 1956, Ozzie Virgil Sr. became the first Dominican-born player in the majors when he signed with the New York Giants. Virgil, who had actually moved to New York as a child, played parts of nine seasons in the big leagues in an otherwise unremarkable career, but he smoothed the way for hundreds to follow—many of whom would be quite remarkable on a baseball diamond.

From Julián Javier and the Alou brothers—Felipe, Matty, and Jesús—in the 1960s, to Manny Mota, Julio Franco, "One Tough Dominican" Joaquín Andújar, George Bell, Pedro Guerrero, Pedro Martinez, Vladimir Guerrero, David Ortiz, and Manny Ramirez, the Dominican Republic has churned out its share of star baseball players. Juan Marichal was the first Dominican elected to baseball's Hall of Fame. Sammy Sosa became the first to hit five hundred home runs.

With the rise of such stars who could play their way to fame and fortune, baseball took on another identity altogether in the Dominican Republic: savior. Major league scouts began blanketing the Dominican cities and countryside looking for the next unknown superstar. In the 1980s, major league teams began opening their own baseball academies in the country to teach the sport—and to have the inside track on promising young players. No longer was baseball just a diversion for Dominican youth. Now it was a way out and a hope for a better life. Going to school and getting an education couldn't yield the rewards that baseball could offer.

When he was born January 16, 1980, in the dangerous and crime-filled Santo Domingo neighborhood of Cristo Rey (Christ the King), José Alberto Pujols had little chance to escape the baseball hysteria that held nearly the entire population of the Dominican Republic in its tightly clenched grip. Born to a father who was a standout softball player in his own right, young Albert was almost entirely predisposed to love the game as much as his dad did, and as much as everyone else around him did. That love began manifesting itself when Albert began playing with sticks and balls at age two. By six, he was playing the game in the streets at every opportunity and tagging along with his father, Bienvenido, as the elder Pujols pitched regularly for local softball teams.

Bienvenido was a painter by trade, and not a steadily employed one. Sometimes he would be away from home for long periods of time pursuing work wherever he could find it. The family moved from Cristo Rey to Villa Mella, a safer, yet still impoverished part of Santo Domingo, sometime early in Albert's childhood, which was shaken by his parents' divorce when he was only three years old. Though his mother played virtually no role in his upbringing after that point, Albert's dad continued to remain—however intermittently—a part of his life. Albert idolized Bienvenido, and the young Pujols often wore his dad's jerseys, proud of the fact that his dad's abilities left him in high demand from many different teams across the country.

As much as Pujols enjoyed watching his dad play softball, what came after the last out was typically a nightmare. Bienvenido was an alcoholic, and often spent hours after games drinking heavily with his teammates and friends. By the time Albert was nine years old, he was regularly hoisting his drunken father across his shoulders and dragging him home late at night.

Albert's experience with an alcoholic dad made a significant impact upon him, he once told the *St. Louis Post-Dispatch*'s Bryan Burwell. "Can you imagine what that's like, man?" Pujols asked Burwell. "I'm a kid, you know, and I'm draggin' him home and putting him to bed drunk. And every night I did it, I kept thinking to myself, 'I can never do this to my son when I grow up.' There's no way a kid should have to go through that." On another occasion, speaking to Joe Posnanski of *Sports Illustrated* about the trials he endured through his father's alcoholism, Pujols said simply, "God made me older."

Despite his father's failures, Pujols continued to revere the man, and still speaks highly of him. "My dad always supported me," Pujols told *USA Today*. "Sometimes we didn't have anything to eat for breakfast, but if we could eat lunch and dinner, we weren't poor."

Bienvenido's inability to secure a consistent job forced him to move in with his parents by the time Albert was six. With work taking Bienvenido away for long periods of time, Albert's grandparents, Papá and América, became his primary caregivers. The couple had ten other children as well, who—though Albert's uncles and aunts by blood—became like brothers and sisters to him. Living arrangements were cramped, often with an amalgam of ten or twelve aunts, uncles, and cousins living under Papa's and América's roof. But America devoted herself to instilling in her grandson a strong sense of morality and a diligent work ethic. Her influence, more than any other person, was largely responsible for shaping the man Albert Pujols would become.

Most of the population of the Dominican Republic lives in what U.S. citizens would consider to be poverty. These days, the average household income in the DR is about $7,500. Pujols is quick to say that his family wasn't poor—but poverty can be a moving target, depending upon your frame of reference. For Pujols, the fact that he ate at least one meal a day—probably a combination of beans, rice, and some kind of meat—meant he wasn't poor. The poor people in the Dominican Republic were those who went days or weeks without eating a meal and who drank grimy water from the river. But despite his insistence that his family wasn't poor, they certainly weren't rich—often relying on government aid—and financial struggles were common. Sometimes he lived in homes with dirt floors and no plumbing. Shoes were a luxury he often didn't have.

"He showed me a couple of shacks that were comparable to the way he grew up, and it's very sad," says Todd Perry, executive director of the Pujols Family Foundation, who has accompanied Pujols on several mission trips to the Dominican Republic. "When we go down there, some of the things that we see are very shocking to me. But for Albert, it's very natural. I've never seen him surprised, even when we encountered a man with leprosy. There's compassion and pity, but for him, it's just a way of life."

Financial difficulties meant Pujols seldom had proper equipment to play the game he loved. He improvised the best he could, often using limes as baseballs, sticks for bats, and fashioning gloves out of milk cartons. He and his friends played for hours in the streets of Santo Domingo, usually in the sandlot located a few miles from his home. Pujols would regularly make the long walk to the sandlot to play ball when he wasn't in school.

As he grew older, Pujols learned more about the intricacies of the game and about fellow Latinos who had made it to the big leagues. It was increasingly common in the Dominican Republic, during the 1980s when Pujols grew up, for nearly everyone to have some kind of connection to the major leagues. Pujols was no different—his cousin Luis Pujols debuted with the Houston Astros in 1977. Though he didn't hit well (his career batting average was .193 over nine seasons), Luis had proven to Albert the possibilities that could be attained.

Sometimes during his childhood, Pujols had regular access to TV and was able to watch Major League Baseball occasionally, especially the Atlanta Braves in the 1990s. "They had (Fred) McGriff, Terry Pendleton, Alejandro Peña, (David) Justice, and all that pitching," Pujols told *USA Today*. "They were the team to beat."

His favorite player was Julio Franco, also a native Dominican, who began his career with the Philadelphia Phillies in 1982 when Pujols was just two years old. Franco went on to play twenty-three seasons in the big leagues, retiring after the 2007 season when he was forty-eight years old. Other favorites of the young Pujols were Sosa and Raúl Mondesí. He also was familiar with Roberto Clemente and Tony Pérez.

During his teenage years, several of Pujols' family members had moved from the Dominican Republic to the United States, in an attempt to make a better life for themselves. Pujols, his father, and his grandmother joined the movement themselves when Albert was sixteen, leaving their native land and moving to New York City.

They hadn't been there long when Pujols, on a trip to the grocery store, witnessed a shooting. His grandmother quickly decided that the violent (and expensive) city was no place for Albert and the rest of her family, so they packed up and settled instead in Independence, Missouri, to which other extended members of the family had moved in previous years for work. The home of Harry S. Truman, Independence was the Queen City of the Trails, the starting point in the mid-1800s for millions of westward-bound pioneers, treasure hunters, and settlers who journeyed from the city on the Sante Fe, Oregon, and California trails.

For Pujols, Independence proved to be the starting point for his own trail to baseball immortality.

CHAPTER THREE

THE BASEBALL GODS WERE SMILING

He wasn't the normal eighteen-year-old.

—Chris Francka, teammate and friend, Fort Osage High School

Ryan Stegall was miffed for giving up a home run to Chris Francka of Fort Osage Senior High in a matchup between two of the Kansas City area's best high school baseball teams on a spring day in 1997. Fort Osage had advanced to the state semifinals the year before, and Stegall's Liberty High School was intent upon challenging the Indians' supremacy.

The Blue Jays had the talent to do it, and Stegall was one of the reasons why. A junior in 1997 and a standout both as a pitcher and as a shortstop, Stegall would go on to play at the University of Missouri before being drafted by the Houston Astros and spending four years as an infielder in the Houston farm system. But it was this day on Stegall's home field when he would make history.

The two-run Francka homer had given Fort Osage a 4–0 lead. Now Stegall would have to deal with Albert Pujols, who, though playing in his first season of high school baseball, had already earned a reputation as a fearsome hitter. Stegall and his Liberty teammates certainly knew about him.

"He was an absolute monster," Stegall said. "He was dang near the same size that he is now. I'm sure he's added a lot more muscle, but his legs were as big as all of our waists. He was a horse."

Angry at himself for serving up a round-tripper to Francka, Stegall tried to put some extra mustard on an inside fastball to Pujols. That was a mistake—a big one, and one that would earn Stegall fame in Liberty for years to come. Pujols didn't just hammer the pitch. He annihilated it. The ball rocketed through the sky in left center field, way over the left field fence. Beyond the fence, about forty to fifty feet back, loomed the two-story Liberty High School building. An air conditioner unit sat atop the building, probably twenty or thirty feet from the edge, and had just become target practice for Pujols. The home run traveled five hundred feet, easily.

"He hit a ball that pretty much never landed," Stegall said. "And he was using one of the cheapest bats ever. We all remember that. He had an old Black Magic, which was outdated by that time. But it didn't matter what he had. It didn't matter."

After Pujols' blast, Stegall's catcher, Shannon Blackburn, sauntered to the mound to give his pitcher a new ball, and a needed word of encouragement. "You suck," Blackburn said. "I've never seen a ball hit that far."

The mammoth home run earned Stegall, now a teacher and an assistant baseball coach at Liberty, a spot in local lore. "It hasn't gone away, and it never will," he said. "When I'm coaching, every year the guys bring it up. I don't know how they know. They probably weren't even born. But everybody knows. And everybody who was there has their own story about how it happened."

That includes Fort Osage coach Dave Fry, who also remembers what was probably the longest home run he's ever seen from a high school player. "That was one of those where both the Fort Osage crowd and the Liberty crowd, when he hit the ball, it sounded like somebody let the air out of the whole crowd," Fry said. "Just a super home run."

The shot may have surprised Fry, but not by much—because by this time, he had gotten used to seeing what Pujols was capable of doing on the baseball field. Shortly after arriving in Independence, Pujols found himself sitting in Principal Steve Scott's office at Fort Osage Senior High School to register for classes. He spoke no English and relied upon his cousin Wilfredo to interpret for him.

"Do you have any questions?" Scott asked, as they completed the registration process.

Pujols had just one: *"Tiene un equipo de béisbol?"*

"Yes," Scott replied. "We do have a baseball team. But usually it's the seniors who get most of the playing time. You might have to wait a while before making the team."

Pujols remained undeterred, and had Wilfredo take him to see Coach Fry. Fry taught seventh grade life science and eighth grade earth science in the Fort Osage Junior High, but was the baseball coach for the high school. One day after school, Wilfredo introduced him to Albert.

"Coach Fry, this is my cousin Albert," Wilfredo said. "He wants to play *béisbol.*"

Fry looked up and saw Pujols, a "good-looking big kid," smiling from ear to ear.

"That's great," Fry said. "We start tryouts in February. You need to get a physical and report for tryouts."

That meeting was the first time Fry had ever seen Pujols, and he liked what he saw. Pujols certainly looked like a baseball player, standing six-foot-two and weighing in at 190. But Fry had no idea what kind of skills he possessed—because he could barely communicate with the kid.

"He didn't hardly say anything, just kind of shook his head," Fry recalled. "Back then the language barrier was the main problem."

So Pujols went about his business for the next few weeks, going to class, adjusting to a new life in Independence, learning to speak English, until baseball tryouts rolled around. Fry was expecting to have a strong team returning after Fort Osage's run to the state tournament during the 1996 season, so he was not anticipating an unknown teenager from the Dominican Republic who spoke little English figuring into his plans for the 1997 season, especially when Pujols told him that he played shortstop. Fry told him that he already had a starting senior he was expecting to play at that position—Chris Francka, who had been an all-state player the year before.

"Albert says that I told him he probably wouldn't make the team," Fry said. "I don't remember if I did or not."

What Fry does remember is when he first saw Pujols hit a baseball. The tryouts were held in the gymnasium, with Fry hitting ground balls to some of the players downstairs while his assistant coach Chris Walker worked the batting cage upstairs. The players took a few swings the first couple of days so the coaches could evaluate them and determine who had the ability to make the team. Walker watched Pujols take a few swings, and rushed downstairs.

"Coach Fry, come here," he said. "You've got to see this."

"I go up there, and we've got the Jugs machine set up—you know, intermediate, we're not trying to blow anybody away or anything," Fry said. "And Albert's just crushing the ball. Every one he hits is almost tearing out the end of the net."

Gee-man-ee, Fry thought. *Where'd this kid come from*? Pujols was making solid contact with every pitch, tearing the ball up, and proving to Fry and everybody else that despite the fact that he was the new kid, and despite the fact that he couldn't speak English very well, he knew what he was doing on the baseball field. Suddenly Fry began to get excited about the possibilities for his team in the season ahead.

Pujols' emergence moved Francka to third base, but Francka didn't mind a bit. As a senior and one of the leaders on the team, he knew he had a responsibility to help Pujols fit in with the rest of the team as much as possible, so Francka did more than become his teammate. He became his friend.

"You're coming from another country to play baseball in the US, I can imagine it being quite a culture shock," Francka said. "It was right of me to take him under my wing."

The friendship between Francka and Pujols didn't end in high school, as the two have remained close over the years. What impresses Francka—and humbles him—is how Pujols, even when he's in the middle of a playoff race and the crunch of the baseball season, always finds time to call and check up not just on Francka, but on Francka's family as well. In the fall of 2009, Francka's mother had cancer and was going through chemotherapy treatments.

"Albert's the type of guy that, as much as he has going on, every time we talked he never forgot to ask about her: How's she doing? What's the latest?" Francka said. "He never forgets a name and never forgets what's going on in your life. He's always conscientious of that and thoughtful enough to ask every time."

As a newcomer, Pujols' work ethic, which he demonstrated early and which hasn't waned over the years, earned him the respect of Francka and the rest of the team.

"He had to work extra hard to fit into the system that Coach Fry had for us. That's what impressed me about him," says Scott Hanna, who played with Pujols during the 1997 season. "You could always tell that he was trying hard. He'd always be one of the first ones there and one of the last to leave."

As his Fort Osage teammates began figuring out ways to communicate with Pujols, Fry was doing the same thing. He sometimes spoke to Pujols through an interpreter, and sometimes he used the universal language of baseball, by taking his hands and showing Pujols what he wanted him to do with the bat, or with the glove. Fry found the young Dominican to be a workhorse obsessed with improving his game.

> When it came to the baseball, Albert was so intense. And Albert still today has a sixth sense about baseball—in the fact that even though he's not that fast, he's a good base stealer. As a big man, he does a lot of things that only smaller people can do. But he understands and he knows the game so well. Even as a student, he wanted to excel, and he wanted to do good. He would wear you out. He would stay out there at shortstop and take ground balls all night. It would get dark. Same thing in the batting cage. He would come up there in that cage, and he would hit and hit and hit and hit.

But despite his skills, and despite Fry's efforts to teach and instruct, communication proved to be a challenge, sometimes with amusing results. Fry tells the story of a hit-a-thon the team held every year to raise money for the baseball program. The players would solicit pledges, take ten swings and collect donations based on the distance of their farthest hit. Some players might have pledges of two cents a foot, or eight cents a foot, or twenty cents a foot if they really worked at it. Pujols, however, didn't understand the concept, because Fry was unable to communicate it to him.

"Albert, how many cents per foot do you have pledged?" Fry asked when it was Pujols' turn to hit.

"No, no cents. *No comprendo*," Pujols replied.

"Well, there's really no need for you to bat, then," Fry informed him. "Go on out to the outfield and shag some flies."

That directive didn't go over well.

"He really got mad," Fry said. "Because he knew that he could hit the ball farther than anybody else on the team."

By the next year, Pujols better understood what the hit-a-thon was about, and he collected pledges totaling one dollar per foot, enabling him to raise some serious cash for the team. Pujols was learning to understand more English, and Fry remembers one time when he burst into his office.

"Coach Fry, Coach Fry! Come here, come here!"

"What's up, Albert?"

"Come here and look. I've got a jellotoyta!" The words sped from Pujols' lips.

"A what?"

"A jellotoyta!"

So Fry went outside and quickly saw what had Pujols so excited: a yellow Toyota.

"It was an older car, but it ran, and he enjoyed driving it around and was quite proud of his first car," Fry said.

On the field, Pujols made an immediate impact on the team at the season's start. Described as a poor man's version of Alex Rodriguez by the *Kansas City Star*, Pujols knocked five hits in the Indians' first two games, including what the *Star* called "an epic home run" that cleared Fort Osage's thirty-foot fence in left field and sailed over a house beyond the fence. But that was just a start. Pujols would go on to hit .471 with eleven home runs and thirty-two RBIs during his sophomore year, when Fort Osage went 21–7 and won the school's first state championship since 1991.

"I remember down at state him having so much fun playing Playstation in the hotel," Hanna says. "It's kind of weird because he was playing MLB '96 or whatever, and now he's on the cover."

That summer he played American Legion baseball, again with Francka as a teammate. Pujols would always come to Francka's house before their Legion games, and the two would travel together. Francka's home sat on about ten acres, with a baseball field in his yard, and to Francka's amusement, Pujols had a habit of arriving two or three hours earlier than necessary. Sometimes, Francka would be taking a nap. He'd wake up and find Pujols out on his baseball field, hitting balls off a tee and working on his game.

"He wasn't the normal eighteen-year-old," Francka says.

In sixty games that summer, Pujols hit twenty-nine home runs, setting an American Legion record. Francka finished second in the league with twelve homers. The next summer, Pujols would outdo himself, smashing thirty-five home runs in sixty-one games to break his own single-season record, while driving in 124.

In his junior year at Fort Osage, Pujols continued to pound the ball when he had the opportunity, but those opportunities were coming much less frequently. Opposing coaches were wise to Albert by now, and many chose to walk him instead of letting their pitchers challenge him. Some pitched around him as a form of vengeance. They were skeptical that Pujols was only eighteen years old during the spring of 1998, so they lodged their complaints by giving him a free pass to first base.

"A lot of the other coaches always gave me a bad time," Fry says. "They wanted to see his birth certificate. And I had seen Albert's birth certificate, and I knew he was sixteen years old [in the fall of 1996, when he enrolled at Fort Osage]. And when you were around him day in and day out, he acted like a kid. He would do things with the other kids. He would tease, and he would jest. He'd shove and push. He was one of the guys, that's all he was. And he'd act like a sixteen-year-old. He didn't act like he was twenty-one or anything like that."

No, Albert's success didn't come because he was older than everyone else. It came because of his God-given ability, and because he was determined to work harder than anyone else.

"He was so driven to be such a good baseball player," Fry says. "I think that's the secret to Albert's success—his personal motivation, and how he has made himself a good ballplayer. God has blessed him, don't get me wrong, because he's given him really good eyes and a really good hand-eye coordination. But he's given him a desire where even if he had lesser tools, I think he'd still be a good ballplayer."

Though just a junior in terms of athletic eligibility, Pujols had enough academic credits after the fall semester in 1998 to graduate from high school. The way he had been pitched the previous season—or, perhaps more accurately, the way he hadn't been pitched—helped make the decision an easy one for Pujols. He would leave Fort Osage a semester early and take his game to the next level.

CHAPTER FOUR

DEE DEE

She's the best wife out there.
—Albert Pujols

As she walked into the hospital room to visit her friend Keisha, who was having a baby, Deidre Pujols experienced a type of déjà vu. But it was deeper than that for the wife of Albert Pujols. It was more meaningful and more powerful than simply a sense that she had been there before.

"I just felt that God, by his grace, brought me back to that place to kind of hold my hand and say, 'Do you see how far we've come, when you trusted me that day in this room?'" Deidre says.

Ten years before—to the day—Deidre herself had checked into that same hospital, into that same hospital room, to give birth to her first child, Isabella. At the time, Deidre was unmarried and unsure of her future—especially after discovering that Isabella had Down syndrome.

But God used that event to draw her to himself. As she walked into that room again to see her friend, Deidre couldn't help but think back over the past decade. So many things had changed. Her world was completely different.

In the years since she was a patient in that room, she had met her husband and watched him become one of the biggest stars in baseball. She had welcomed two more children—A. J. and Sophia—into the world (and later added another son, Ezra in February 2010). She had helped to establish a foundation that ministers to impoverished children, as well as families and children who live with Down syndrome. She had become a role model for single mothers and an encouragement to countless women of faith.

So for Deidre, that room was, in a sense, a monument of God's faithfulness to her and her family.

Deidre, or Dee Dee to her friends, grew up in a Roman Catholic family. As a child, she often attended other churches with her friends. Her friend Keisha, the same one she visited in that hospital room, invited her to church when she was sixteen.

"I really enjoyed it, and I started going a lot," Deidre says. "It pulled me away from the Catholic religion, because I realized that I'd had no growth in that. It was actually in church where I studied the Bible and I learned scripture and I incorporated it into my life. It wasn't just hearing something that happened two thousand years ago. I got to learn how to put that in my own life."

Dee Dee soon responded to an invitation and made a profession of faith. Looking back, however, she now realizes that it was only that—a profession. Dee Dee admits she lived promiscuously during her teenage years, also characterized by drug and alcohol abuse. At twenty-one, she was pregnant with Isabella.

"She did not come from a church family," recalls Jeff Adams, pastor of Kansas City Baptist Temple. "She went off to Boston University and became pregnant. Then she came back to Kansas City to have the baby, and started going to church again."

"The day I gave birth to Isabella, it was the encounter that I needed with God to really decide to repent and change and try to live like a new person in Christ," Dee Dee says. "The moment that I laid eyes on her, and she laid eyes on me for the first time, just as you and I are having this conversation, God spoke to me that way."

The reality of facing life as a single mother—and as a single mother of a daughter with Down syndrome—was what Dee Dee needed to turn to God for help. "That's really where my journey with God began, because it put me in such a needy position," she said. "I really did trust God and held onto him for everything, and wanted to start knowing more about him and deepening my relationship with Christ."

Shortly after leaving the hospital, however, Deidre was back out in the clubs, dancing and drinking. She was dangerously close to slipping back into her previous life when she met and started dating eighteen-year-old Albert. The two had met at a salsa club, and Pujols was immediately interested. He would grow increasingly so as he got to know Deidre.

"I think Deidre's maturity and grown-up attitude were very attractive to me," Pujols says. "I was so young when we met. I was new to the United States. My English was just okay, and I needed someone to take care of me and direct me. She was that person for me. We were very excited about each other on our first date at the Cheesecake Factory on the Plaza in Kansas City."

As it turns out, those feelings Albert had for Deidre were mutual.

"I call Albert my earthly savior," she says. "He didn't drink. He didn't smoke. He didn't have tattoos. No earrings. He spoke a little English and he loved baseball. I guess seeing that example, it started to change my heart. As I was deepening my relationship with Christ, I was also deepening my relationship with Albert, and just started to draw away from some of those things."

She and Albert had conversations about spiritual matters, and they started attending church together at Kansas City Baptist Temple. Albert became a Christian shortly thereafter (see chapter 6), and the couple started growing in their walk with the Lord (see chapter 12).

"It's been a slow process in our personal relationship, but I feel like God has so much to do with us, that he's sometimes waiting for us to catch up," Deidre says. "We just have to stand back and be faithful in our call in obedience."

She recognizes the blessings of God on her family's life, and understands that they are stewards of those blessings. Such a life can lead to various materialistic temptations, but it also provides something that Albert and Deidre wouldn't have had without it.

"Albert and I are on such a platform, where we actually are sharing the gospel of Jesus Christ so much that we have such a huge audience of accountability," she says.

"Dee Dee is really the one who keeps Albert between the white lines," Adams says. "She is passionate about sharing the gospel—it's a real deal to her."

Adams tells the story of an opportunity Dee Dee had to travel to Cuba, to visit and assist the family of a stateside Cuban friend. "Albert didn't want her to go because he was afraid for her, but she was going," he says. "She wanted to be able to take in literature to help Cuban pastors. So she went to the trouble and expense of getting a religious visa to get into Cuba, which is very hard to do. We loaded her up with all types of literature and materials for discipleship and for pastors." Dee Dee made the trip safely and was able to deliver the materials and minister to the people.

Life in the Pujols home can be hectic—but not that much more hectic than most homes. On home stands during the baseball season, Pujols sleeps in after getting home late from his game. Deidre wakes the kids, gets them fed and off to school. She'll spend her mornings doing various household chores and running errands, or she'll go to the Pujols Family Foundation office to work in her role as the organization's president.

Of course, for Deidre, being the wife of a major leaguer does have its perks. "There are also times when I travel, and I get to wake up and go to the gym or have a massage," she says. But then the kids are always a quick reminder about the less glamorous matters in life.

"Next to the Lord, family is the most important thing to Dee Dee," says Todd Perry, the foundation's executive director. "I don't think there's anything that's even a close second. She's a very doting mother. She's all about taking care of business with her husband and kids. Not until Sofia was born in 2005 did they actually bring in a part-time housekeeper."

Perry notes that fact with admiration. "Here's a woman with two preschool children, one of them with Down syndrome. Her husband played baseball 162 games a year, traveling to about twenty different cities in the process. And she managed the household without any external assistance. It's just amazing to see how she was able to keep all that in check and all that in balance for as long as she did."

Or, as Pujols once said, "She's the best wife out there."

Dee Dee realizes the importance of her responsibility as a wife and a mother. And because of the platform God has given her, she wants to encourage and empower other women who share some of her struggles. She urges young, single women to stay sexually pure until marriage.

In a radio interview with James Dobson, Dee Dee related stories of women, both young and old, with whom she has had opportunity to share about Christ and sexual purity. One woman e-mailed Dee Dee to let her know how attractive she thought Pujols was, and how she lusted for him. "My immediate reaction was not a very nice one," Dee Dee recounted. She prayed, collected her thoughts, and discovered that she actually hurt for the woman. "There was a time in my life where I would've written a happily married a man a letter about how hot he was. So I wrote her back and shared Christ with her and told her that I would be praying for her. I ached for her."

For women with families, she stresses the importance of feeding their own faith and raising their children for God's glory and not their own satisfaction. "We can get so worn out as wives and mothers and bill payers and housecleaners," Deidre says. "There's so much that we're responsible for. But we have to take the time out that's required for us to get fed with God's Word, to get fed with his music, to make sure that the small time we have for ourselves that we're refueling with our faith."

Her main message to other women and mothers is simple: whatever they're doing, wherever they are, whomever they are with—Christ is the focus.

"We're going to have problems from the day we're born until the day we die," Deidre says. "There are times we slip up, because we're human. But I'd be twice the mess if I didn't have Christ. If we can stay Christ-centered and Christ-focused, man, our problems are so minor for what the big purpose is."

Deidre remembers some of those problems—problems that seemed so major at the time—when she thinks about that hospital room where she gave her life to the Lord years ago. She has seen clearly how God took the trials in her life and wove them into something beautiful. And she wants others to know he can do the same for them.

"I could sit here until I'm blue in the face to tell you how many miracles God has done in our own lives, but until a person has a personal encounter with God themselves to know how much God loves them and wants from them, then a person can't be different," she says. "We basically plant seeds, and pray that God would water those seeds however he chooses, and that people would be drawn to him. That's the goodness of it."

CHAPTER FIVE

RAISING STOCK AT MAPLE WOODS

This kid had a work ethic that I've never seen.

—Marty Kilgore, baseball coach, Maple Woods Community College

Marty Kilgore remembers one of the best Christmas presents he ever got—a gift that has kept on giving. It was December 1998, and Kilgore, then the pitching coach for the baseball team at Maple Woods Community College in Kansas City, knew something was brewing. Chris Mihlfeld, then the head coach, told him the coaching staff might have a surprise Christmas gift coming.

When Kilgore met Albert and Deidre while they were on campus for a recruiting visit, he knew what the surprise was all about—Albert Pujols, the heralded high school baseball star, would be playing at Maple Woods.

The Maple Woods coaching staff had known about Pujols, and had the chance to see him play a few months earlier when his summer league team, coached by Dave Bingham, visited Maple Woods to compete against the junior college team. The doubleheader ended with Pujols left in the on-deck circle, but Bingham came over to Mihlfeld and Kilgore with a request—à la Ernie Banks' famous "Let's play two" quote.

"Albert would like to play a few more innings," Bingham said. "Is there any chance that we could?"

"That kind of got all our attention," Kilgore recalls. "Here we've got a kid out here who has been phenomenal playing. He was playing shortstop for them, and it didn't take very long to tell he was a very, very special baseball player. He had some talents and some instincts that you don't normally see from a kid that age and that size."

Pujols decided to forego his last year of eligibility at Fort Osage for a couple of reasons. For starters, he had enough academic credits to graduate early. Some scouts had also advised him to get to the college level as soon as he could, since opposing high schools, terrified at the prospect of facing Pujols at the plate, largely chose to pitch around him. Moving to the next level would allow scouts to better evaluate his skills, and would give them a chance to see him swing the bat more frequently.

So Pujols chose Maple Woods as the next stop on his baseball journey. Mihlfeld left the college for a strength and conditioning position with the Los Angeles Dodgers before the start of the season, and Kilgore became the head coach.

"This kid had a work ethic that I've never seen," Kilgore says of Pujols. "We would hit three times a day. We would hit anytime he had a break between his classes. We would hit after practice. I could throw BP [batting practice] to him, and I'd do that all day long, but I did not know that much about hitting. So when he would ask me things about, 'What can I do to get better?' I really felt worthless and helpless."

Scouts also had advised Kilgore to leave Pujols alone and not do anything to mess him up. Not that Kilgore had to do much to help him, as Pujols already had a grasp on hitting that far surpassed that of his peers. He showed as much in the team's first practice on a cold winter day in mid-January. At that time of the year, the team didn't use regular baseballs for batting practice, but used composite rubber baseballs instead. The rubber balls didn't travel as far—probably 90 percent of the flight of a regular baseball—but you can hit them in the mud, wipe them off, and they're as good as new. Landon Brandes, the team's third baseman, noticed what Pujols did to those balls.

"We would always take a lot of batting practice with those balls, and

I remember he would hit those things like it was a regular baseball—and more—compared to the rest of us," Brandes says.

In his collegiate debut, Pujols hit a grand slam at West Arkansas Community College (now the University of Arkansas–Fort Smith). And playing shortstop in that game, with men on first and second base, he started a triple play when he dove for a line drive, tagged second base for the second out, then threw to first to nab the runner there.

Word of that performance quickly spread. As Kilgore awoke the next morning in the hotel, his assistant coach Kyle McCune came in with a report.

"You've got to go downstairs, man," McCune told Kilgore. "There's about twenty scouts down in the lobby."

"So we went down there, and sure enough, there were quite a few scouts," Kilgore says. "It was quite a little frenzy and a little buzz. We were familiar with the scouts and them being around, but we knew there was somebody very special that we were around and watching play."

Pujols went on to hit .466 for the Monarchs that season, with twenty-two home runs and seventy-six RBIs in only 193 at-bats, and proved to be invaluable not only for his statistical contributions, but for his maturity and the way he provided leadership to the team. He didn't typically hang out with the players, preferring instead the company of the coaches. That was fitting, because with his knowledge of the game and his baseball instincts, Pujols was like another coach on the field. He knew where everyone was supposed to be and where everyone was supposed to go.

"He was always helping the hitters, trying to explain to them what to look for or how to make adjustments," Kilgore says. "He was always trying to help. He was serving even from the first time I met him."

Although things were going well for him on the field, Pujols had his share of hardships off it. Much of the difficulty stemmed from the way he was treated by his teammates.

"The other players were very jealous of him," Kilgore says. "They were jealous of all the notoriety he was getting and all the scouts that were coming to watch him. They were very jealous of the fact that he was so gifted and he made the game look so easy. He had a lot of that stuff to deal with."

It wasn't the first time for Pujols to deal with criticism from others. Throughout high school, opposing fans had questioned his age, sometimes not very politely. That continued in college, and those questions even persisted after Pujols had established himself in St. Louis. But like Dave Fry, his high school coach, Kilgore had seen his birth certificate and all the documentation proving his age.

"You knew that hurt his feelings," Kilgore says. "That's where I got very protective. Get off him. You don't know what this kid's been through. You don't know what his heart's like. He's a very, very special person, not just a great baseball player. This kid's got things that most eighteen-year-old young men don't have and don't bring to the table."

Brandes concurred with Kilgore's assessment of the situation.

"With him coming in with as much exposure as he had previously, there was definitely a lot of jealousy," Brandes says. "It's a small community college in Kansas City, and 90 percent of the players are from the Kansas City area. So they've heard of him, they've played against him in high school in previous years through high school and summer ball competition. I was from outside of Kansas City, so I didn't really know that much about him.

"I think they kind of felt overshadowed by him," he continues. "He was kind of the next Babe Ruth, if you will, of the area and received all the exposure. A lot of jealousy and stuff stemmed from that. He had kind of a hard time gelling with the players, and that's really all it came down to, it was jealousy on their part. He'd stolen the spotlight in the past, and he comes in and he's probably going to steal the spotlight again. It obviously wasn't him stealing the spotlight, it was just him trying to play to the best of his ability and use his talents to play as well as he could. Some of the guys didn't like that."

Many of the players, though they were not openly hostile to Pujols (because Kilgore wouldn't have tolerated it), muttered things about him under their breath and behind his back. When Pujols hit a home run, they didn't bolt off the bench to congratulate him. They wanted to see him flop rather than succeed.

In the midst of such hostility, one of the bright spots for Pujols that year, and a seeming answer to prayer, was Brandes. A third baseman who had redshirted at Maple Woods the year before, Brandes was expected to be the Monarchs' anchor in 1999. When he found out that Pujols would be a part of the team, Brandes didn't respond with petty jealousy. He was grateful, because he knew Pujols' presence would take some of the pressure off him. Brandes also figured he might be able to learn something from Pujols that would aid his own development as a player.

Though they shared a connection through baseball, they didn't find out until a couple of years later they shared an even stronger bond through Jesus Christ. Pujols may not have known that Brandes was a Christian—about the only time they spent together was on the baseball field, not usually a setting for deep conversations about life and faith (though Pujols would later change that)—but he definitely saw the fruits of a Christian life in Brandes. While many others on the team tried to veil their disdain for Pujols, Brandes befriended him, and the two have remained friends through the years. The Cardinals selected Brandes in the 2000 draft, and the two players were roommates during spring training in 2001, allowing them to renew—and deepen—the friendship they began at Maple Woods.

"It was more of an accountability thing, and not letting each other get wrapped up in this whole thing of baseball, and keeping our foundation where it needs to be and our eyes focused on Christ first and baseball second," Brandes says. "Even though you're in the middle of spring training and the days are so long, sometimes you've got to refocus and say, 'Hey, it's not all about baseball.' You've got to step back and look at what's really important. We were able to have some good conversations, and he was just a great guy to be around."

Through the trials Pujols endured that semester, Kilgore said he became acutely aware of how tender Pujols' heart was. He was sensitive toward other people's feelings, and never wanted to show anybody up on the field. Though he was confident in his skills, he wasn't arrogant. Kilgore may have thought himself to be helpless when it came to teaching Pujols about baseball, but he was able to provide a listening ear at a time in Pujols' life when he needed a friend.

"I'll never forget our talks in Florida," Kilgore says. "He wouldn't hang around the players. When we were on our spring trip, he would hang out with the coaches. That's how we got to know him so much. He would hang out in our room. We'd say, 'Aren't you going to go out with the rest of the guys?'"

"I've got a game tomorrow," Pujols would reply. "I've got to get ready to play."

Their conversations also revealed Pujols' love for Deidre.

"He wanted to hang out with us and talk baseball," Kilgore says. "He didn't want to go out and look at girls and chase girls. He had Deidre as a girlfriend and he loved her with all his heart. So that was not an option. He knew what he was here for. He was here to try to move on with the baseball, and to be the best he could be."

As he did in high school, Pujols often left his mark at the different fields where he played. At Highland Community College in Highland, Kansas, he hit a ball out of the park, over the street, over a house, and off a tree in the yard behind the house. To this day, every time Kilgore goes to play there, Highland coach Rick Eberly brings it up: "Marty, I've never seen a ball hit that far."

Led by Pujols and Brandes, Maple Woods won the state title for junior colleges. In one of those playoff games, Pujols went deep off Mark Buehrle (now with the Chicago White Sox), who was pitching for Jefferson College. After taking the state championship, the Monarchs advanced to a three-game series against perennial baseball powerhouse Seminole Community College—the winner of the Oklahoma/Kansas title. In a three-game series, Seminole blew out Maple Woods in the opener. The Monarchs rebounded to win the second game, but lost the deciding contest. A victory in that final game would have meant a repeat trip to the Junior College World Series.

Though Pujols was only at Maple Woods for a semester, he and Kilgore formed a bond that has endured beyond that 1999 spring season. Pujols regularly invites Kilgore to St. Louis for events like Christian Family Day and his children's birthday parties.

"It really means a lot to me that he keeps me in that loop," Kilgore said. "Me being so much older than him, he looks at me as more of an uncle-type or something like that. I understand where I fit into the piece and where my role is and stuff like that. I'm very thankful and blessed that we have a relationship that I'm able to call him and talk to him."

Maple Woods retired Pujols' number 33 in 2002, after his Rookie of the Year season with the Cardinals. But that was still a long way off. The more immediate question, as that semester at Maple Woods came to a close, was what the Major League Baseball first-year player draft would hold for the emerging star.

CHAPTER SIX

MORE THAN THE GAME

By your blood you ransomed people for God
from every tribe and language and people and nation.
—*Revelation 5:9*

Jeff Adams remembers the first time he met the "enormous guy." Adams, pastor of Kansas City Baptist Temple, had wrapped up the evening Bible study and was milling around talking with church members. He relished these opportunities to keep in direct contact with them.

"I'm the pastor of a somewhat larger church, so I don't know everybody," Adams says. "But I remember very distinctly the night Dee Dee came up to me after the Bible study. Standing beside her was this enormous guy. She said, 'Pastor, this is Albert. I think I led him to the Lord, but I'm not sure. Could you talk to him in Spanish and make sure that he really understands what he's doing?'"

If you're wondering why Adams is fluent in Spanish, it isn't from leftover lessons learned in school. Rather, there is a gospel explanation. Adams became a Christian in college after reading Billy Graham's book *Peace with God*. He married and settled in Kansas City in early 1971. Then he did what every comfortable, middle-class Midwesterner thinks to do—he moved his family to Central America.

After first working in Nicaragua and Costa Rica, the Adamses settled in El Salvador during that nation's brutal civil war. Bono, of the music group U2, saw these same conditions firsthand—"I feel a long way from the hills of San Salvador"—and the experience led him to write the powerful song, "Bullet the Blue Sky." Bono spoke of the sky being ripped open and the rain pelting the women and children. Such violent imagery accurately described the turmoil of the nation, and yet, the San Salvador church Adams pastored experienced remarkable growth during these times.

In 1984, Adams returned to Kansas City to serve as the pastor of his home church. But though stateside, Adams' missionary impulse has never left. He has led his congregation to be a multicultural, mission-minded church that trains and sends out others for the work.

This brings us back to the story about Pujols. Dee Dee, knowing very little Spanish, brought Albert, knowing very little English, to Pastor Adams to talk about Jesus, of whom the angels sing: "by your blood you ransomed people for God from every tribe and *language* and people and nation" (Revelation 5:19, emphasis ours).

Dee Dee told her new boyfriend she wanted "to be serious with God." He was glad to have the opportunity to go to church with her, and since Pujols' family worked on Sundays, Dee Dee picked him up.

"I pretty much grew up non-Christian in the Dominican Republic," Pujols says. "I went to church probably once—it was just all baseball down there. My family never had the time or the opportunity to share with me."

Dee Dee recounts, "After a couple of weeks of going he said, 'What are they doing when they walk down the aisle at the end of the service?' It gave me an opportunity to share with him about Christ and what it meant to have him in his life."

"Her Spanish was not that good and his English was not that good at that time," Adams says. "She was looking for me to talk to Albert in Spanish and make sure he really understood what he was doing. So I started talking to Albert in Spanish. Didn't talk very long, and he was giving me all the right answers. I said, 'Dee Dee, I think he really understands what he's doing. I think you did a good job.'"

Indeed, from Pujols' perspective, Dee Dee was the key to his coming to faith in Christ. "One Sunday, she just invited me to church, and she just walked with me and told me how much Jesus loved me, and about two weeks after that, I gave my life to Christ," Pujols says. "And I can tell you something, guys—that was the best moment of my life, the best decision that I made in my life."

Pujols was baptized, and joined as a member of Kansas City Baptist Temple.

"From that time forth, every Monday night they were there for Bible study, and every Sunday morning, they were there for worship," Adams says. "They were just as faithful as could be. After so many Bible studies, Albert would come up with your typical 'new Christian' questions—'What about this?' and 'What about that?' From the very beginning, his faith seemed to be genuine and profound. Albert is very much his own man. He's not the type of guy who's just going to swallow something because you tell him that. So he would ask all the typical questions that you would expect a new Christian to ask."

What did Adams think about ministering to a young baseball player with so much potential for greatness and fame?

"I had no idea he played baseball," Adams says. "Nobody here at the church had any idea he played baseball. They had been coming for probably a year and a half, and they had no money to live on. But I can remember the shock that I had one night when Albert came up and said, 'Hey, pastor, I just got drafted by the St. Louis Cardinals. I'm going to be going to Peoria."

Adams was elated for Pujols, but found even greater joy in hearing him ask, "Do you know of a good church in Peoria?"

CHAPTER SEVEN

DRAFT DODGING AND JAYHAWKING

I don't think any of us knew the ability he had to adjust. And that's the name of the game.

—Dave Karaff, former St. Louis Cardinals scout

June 2, 1999, was the day for which Albert Pujols had been waiting, dreaming, and preparing for a lifetime. It was the day for Major League Baseball's amateur draft, when hundreds of young baseball players hold their collective breaths and sit by the telephone for hours, waiting to receive the call announcing they have been selected by a big league team.

Pujols was no different, and was hopeful that the day's events would be the launching of his professional career and would set him on firm financial footing. He had reason to be hopeful. During the course of his high school career and his semester playing at Maple Woods Community College, no shortage of scouts had followed him and analyzed his baseball ability. New York Mets scout Larry Chase was one of those who liked what he saw in Pujols. Fernando Arango, a scout for the Tampa Bay Devil Rays at the time, had been bullish on Pujols ever since he began watching him play in high school.

"He could really hit the ball," Arango told the *Tampa Tribune*. "In high school and college, it wasn't fair with him using an aluminum bat. When he hit the ball, it sounded like thunder."

Another scout who had noticed Pujols was Dave Karaff of the St. Louis Cardinals. Karaff lived in Kansas City and had heard about Pujols for some time before finally seeing him play in an American Legion game. The first thing Karaff observed was Pujols' power and strength. But Karaff also thought Pujols was "heavy-hipped" and worried that he might gain too much weight to be an effective big leaguer. Though Pujols was playing shortstop at the time, Karaff knew that he didn't have the body to play at that position professionally.

As Pujols advanced, however, and moved on to play at Maple Woods, he slimmed down a bit, and Karaff continued to be intrigued by his potential. Karaff envisioned him as a third baseman in the future, thanks in part to Pujols' arm and his excellent hands. With 5 being the average Major League scouting score, the Cardinals' scout had rated Pujols' arm a 6 and his power a 6 or 7 on a scale of 1 to 8. He projected Pujols as a fourth- or fifth-round selection.

"But he had some things I didn't know if they were correctable in his hitting," Karaff says. "He was a lunger, and that was a question mark."

Other organizations also began to have some of their own questions. Prompted by Arango, Tampa Bay had brought Pujols down to Florida for a special workout at Tropicana Field a few days before the draft—the only club to do so. But the workout didn't go well for the nineteen-year-old Pujols. Perhaps it was nerves. Perhaps it was just a bad day like everyone has once in a while. Whatever the reason, Pujols didn't showcase the power that Arango had seen from him previously. In fact, Dan Jennings, the team's scouting director at the time, called it "just an ugly workout." Arango may have considered Pujols to be a second- or third-rounder, but those calling the shots in Tampa had dropped him way down their list.

As draft day began, the Rays took Josh Hamilton with the first overall pick, and the Florida Marlins followed by grabbing Texas high school pitcher Josh Beckett. The Cardinals drafted pitcher Chance Caple with the thirtieth selection, and in supplemental first round picks claimed Nick Stocks and Chris Duncan. More names came and went, as the second, third, and fourth rounds passed. The Cardinals filled their draft roster with players such as Josh Pearce, B. R. Cook, Ben Johnson, Jimmy Journell, Melvin Williams, and Josh Teekel. The marathon day continued with rounds five through twelve, and still Pujols had not received a phone call informing him that he had been picked. Prior to the draft, Pujols reportedly was looking for a signing bonus of at least $350,000, but that dream had died as more and more players found homes with major league clubs while Pujols had not.

Karaff was sitting at home when the phone rang. At the other end was Mike Roberts, a national cross-checker for the Cardinals, and also Karaff's brother-in-law.

"Dave, we're in the eleventh round, do you think we can sign Albert there?" Roberts asked.

"I don't know for sure, Mike," Karaff replied. "He wanted better money than that."

"Well, give him a call," Roberts said. "And call me back."

Karaff tried to reach Pujols, but got Dee Dee instead. She told him Albert was out taking batting practice.

"Have him call me as soon as he can," Karaff asked her.

He called Roberts back with the news.

"Don't worry about it," Roberts said. "We took him in the thirteenth round."

Moments before, as his St. Louis colleagues considered their pick in the thirteenth round, Roberts pled Pujols' case, arguing that whatever negatives Pujols might carry, his power potential made him a player the team shouldn't bypass yet again. So the Cardinals staked their claim to Pujols; he was player number 402 to be picked. For whatever reason, despite the stats he had posted in high school and college, despite the fact that his coaches lauded his work ethic, despite the tremendous power potential he displayed, teams passed on Pujols 401 times.

The reasons for that have been explored many times over the years, as twenty-nine teams have kicked themselves for not taking Pujols earlier. Some may have had questions about what position he would play. Some stories have circulated that scouts weren't interested because of their concern over his weight. But Maple Woods coach Marty Kilgore doesn't buy that.

"He wasn't like he is now, but the kid wasn't out of shape," Kilgore says. "It wasn't like they made him out to be."

Karaff has his own theories about why Pujols fell so far in the draft. "Here's the thing about Albert," he says. "I don't think any of us knew the ability he had to adjust. And that's the name of the game. You have to be able to adjust. He adjusts from pitch to pitch. He adjusts from at-bat to at-bat."

The Cardinals initially offered Pujols a ten-thousand dollar signing bonus, which he quickly rejected, saying he might return for another season at Maple Woods if the club didn't come through with a better offer.

"I was really excited about getting drafted," Pujols said in the *Kansas City Star*. "It all depends on what the Cardinals want to do."

In the meantime, Pujols headed west to Hays, Kansas, to spend the summer playing for the Hays Larks in the Jayhawk Summer Collegiate League, one of the premier college summer leagues in the country. The Larks have a long history, going back to 1946, when the squad was a town team playing games against surrounding communities. The Summer Collegiate League took control of the team in 1977, and Frank Leo assumed the reins as head coach a few years later. He was still there in 1999 when Pujols adorned his roster. The Larks were no strangers to major league talent, as Lance Berkman played there in 1995, and B. J. Ryan and Jack Wilson were part of the 1996 team.

At only nineteen, Pujols was one of the youngest players in the league, but his performance on the field and his approach to the game quickly caught Leo's eye. "He was a very mature, intense, hardworking player when I had him," Leo says. "That impressed me for his age, and how he carried himself at that age. He had a very good understanding of the game."

Halfway through the season in a home doubleheader against El Dorado, Kansas, Pujols drove in a run with a sacrifice fly in the first inning, then added another RBI on a single in the third that pushed the lead to 4–0 in a game Hays won 5–2. In the second game, the Larks completed the sweep, 5–4, with Pujols driving in two runs in the fifth to give his team a 4–2 lead. A few games later, Pujols gave the Larks a quick lead with a two-run homer in the first and added a solo blast in a three-run sixth inning to lead Hays to a 14–3 win over the Salina Blaze. Late in the season, Pujols drove in the game-winning run in the eleventh inning against the Midwest Wolverines in the National Baseball Congress Midwest Regional, a 7–6 Hays win in which Pujols had three hits and three RBIs.

Leo recalled one game in El Dorado when Pujols launched a mammoth shot over a shed beyond the outfield fence. Even today when the Larks play in El Dorado, that home run is a topic of conversation during batting practice. Pujols played solid defense at third base, impressed Leo with his baserunning skills, and hit about .380 during the two-and-a-half–month season that ended in mid-August.

"And it wasn't a soft .380," Leo says. "When he hit, there was that thud off the bat. You had line drives in the gap, none of these little bloop-type doubles. You could tell there was something special there. Nobody can predict how quick a player's going to rise to the top, but you could tell that he was going to get there someday."

Off the field, Pujols lived with Leo and his wife Barb for the summer. He spent many hours playing RBI Baseball on their Nintendo with the Leos' twelve-year-old daughter Abby, and at night after ballgames would sit on the couch with Frank watching baseball highlights on *SportsCenter*.

"Someday I'm going to be watching you on those highlights," Leo told him one night. He remembers Pujols' response: "Just as humble as he could be, he said, 'You really think so, coach?'"

With games in the evening, Pujols typically lifted weights in the morning at the high school gymnasium. For a few weeks, he helped Leo with baseball camps that the coach ran. Sammy Sosa was the big star in baseball at the time, and the campers quickly began calling Pujols "Sammy." He didn't have transportation, so he spent many hours simply hanging around the Leo home. Deidre often came to visit that summer, bringing Bella with her, and stayed with the Leo family as well. Sometimes she'd bring home-cooked Dominican food from Pujols' grandmother, América—a special treat.

"He was so polite," Leo says. "His room was picked up every day. His bed was made. He thanked Barb after meals. He just became part of our family."

All the time he was playing in Hays, Pujols continued to have conversations with Karaff about signing with the Cardinals. Finally in August, as the season in Hays was coming to an end, player and team came to an agreement: a $65,000 signing bonus (which included money for his education) for Pujols, who was now officially a member of the St. Louis Cardinals organization.

"I didn't get what I wanted, but it doesn't matter," Pujols told the *Peoria Journal Star* the following year about his signing bonus. "It doesn't matter what round you go in either. What matters is how hard you work and how much you improve."

It was too late for Pujols to be assigned to a minor league team at that point in the season, so the club sent him to instructional league in Florida. The second day Pujols was in Florida, Karaff got a call from the Cardinals' John Mozeliak, now the team's general manager, who reported to Karaff that Pujols had smashed a couple of doubles off the wall, homered, and driven in five runs. That was just a small sampling of what many in the St. Louis organization would see on a larger scale the following year, when Pujols began his minor league career in Peoria, Illinois.

Karaff and Pujols continued to stay in touch in the months and years ahead, as Pujols rocketed through the Cardinals' farm system, then quickly made his mark in St. Louis. But the relationship soured in the aftermath of a reshuffling of the St. Louis scouting department in 2004 that left Karaff without a job with the team. Unable to get back into baseball, the sixty-something Karaff took a job at Wal-Mart, where he still works. Pujols expressed his irritation at Karaff on more than one occasion in the media.

"How can you draft a guy and say you don't know if he's going to make the big leagues?" Pujols said in *USA Today*. "All of a sudden, the next year [I'm] in the big leagues, and he wants to take all the credit."

Karaff still isn't sure what sparked those kinds of remarks from Pujols. But he wonders if Pujols may have gotten some bad information, and been told inaccurately that Karaff said he didn't know if Pujols would succeed in the major leagues.

"I never once said he couldn't play in the big leagues," Karaff says. "I had reservations about whether he was going to *hit* in the big leagues. You can hit .240 and play in the big leagues. I was very hurt at the time, and a lot of people who have known me for years were very upset. I couldn't fight him, and I didn't want to fight him. I'm still proud to sign him, of course, and I've never ever said one derogatory remark about him."

Those kinds of comments were painful for Karaff to hear, and for all of Pujols' positive traits, his lashing out at Karaff remains one of the few blemishes on an otherwise praiseworthy reputation. The confidence Pujols has in his own ability is commendable, as is his determination to succeed in the game of baseball. But the fact that he was drafted in the thirteenth round, after 401 other players were taken, provides ample evidence that lots of baseball scouts and player development experts had plenty of doubts about Pujols' prospects of success at the big league level. Karaff was firmly in Pujols' corner as he pushed the Cardinals to draft him, and certainly played a role in beginning Pujols' professional career.

Despite the fractured relationship, Karaff seems to hold no hard feelings. He still raves over Pujols' ability, his work ethic, the improvement he showed early in his career, and the kind of person he is.

"It's just an unfortunate situation," Karaff says. "Someday I hope I can reconcile with him and just sit down and tell him how much fun it's been watching him play."

CHAPTER EIGHT

WILL IT PLAY IN PEORIA?

He was sort of a streaking star through Peoria. A supernova or something. He just lit up the night for a few months there and he was gone.
—*Dave Reynolds,* Peoria Journal Star

The smell of barbecue floated through the stadium and music from B. B. King's Blues Club on Beale Street echoed in the distance as nearly twelve thousand fans remained at AutoZone Park to gut out the marathon ballgame on a September night in 2000. Their hometown Memphis Redbirds were gunning for the city's first league title since the Memphis Chicks had captured the Southern League crown ten years before. Now the St. Louis Cardinals' Triple-A affiliate, the Memphis team was facing the Salt Lake Buzz in the best-of-five series for the Pacific Coast League championship.

The Redbirds led the series 2–1 and were poised to celebrate a title in the ninth inning, holding a 3–1 lead after a two-run homer by Darrell Whitmore in the eighth. But Salt Lake refused to go quietly, scoring twice to send the game into extra innings. The tenth inning passed, the eleventh, then the twelfth. Now in the bottom of the thirteenth with one out, twenty-year-old Pujols came to bat against Salt Lake's David Hooten.

Pujols had barely had enough time to unpack his suitcase in Memphis. He had spent most of the year in Peoria, then Potomac, before the Cardinals promoted him to Memphis late in the season for the playoff drive.

"I've been enjoying it," Pujols told the *Commercial Appeal* about his time in Memphis. "I never thought I was going to get called up here. I should be at my house right now. But I guess I got called up because they needed people up here. The guys are pretty nice to everybody. They've been treating me all right. It's like I'm one of their brothers right now."

He played in only three regular season games before the postseason started, but made his presence felt in the playoffs, collecting three hits and driving in a run in the Redbirds' win against the Buzz in the first game of the PCL championship series. Pujols homered in a losing effort in game two, as the Buzz tied the series. Memphis bounced back to win the third game, and now Pujols had his chance to give the Redbirds their first PCL title. On a 2–2 pitch with one out, Pujols lined a laser over the right-field fence off Hooten, handing Memphis a 4–3 win and setting off a party at AutoZone that would far surpass the festivities on Beale Street.

The win meant Memphis would go to Las Vegas and the Triple-A World Series against the International League champion Indianapolis. With confetti raining down on the crowd, fireworks exploding in the late night sky and Pujols' teammates swarming him at home plate, Elvis Presley's "Viva Las Vegas" blasted over the public address system. Elvis may forever be the King in Memphis, but on this night, the city crowned Pujols as *El Rey*.

"The people in Memphis had really embraced the team," club president Allie Prescott says, "and then they fell in love with Albert those limited number of games he was with us."

The 2000 season had begun for Pujols seven months earlier when he reported to the Cardinals' spring training home in Jupiter, Florida. Because he had signed too late in the 1999 season to be placed on a minor league club and due to his youth, Pujols could have been destined for the Cardinals' rookie league team for his first season in professional baseball. Instead the Cardinals slated him to begin the season with the Single-A Peoria Chiefs in Illinois.

Dave Reynolds, a reporter who covered the Chiefs for the *Peoria Journal Star*, was in Jupiter that year and remembers the first time he saw Pujols play.

"That first day I was checking out the minor leaguers, because that was going to be my beat," Reynolds recalls. "I went down and watched their game. The Peoria team was playing against the Double-A team in a scrimmage game, and Albert comes up to bat—first time I'd seen him. About the second pitch, he lines a double down the left-field line. The next time up he hits one into the gap in right-center field for a double. And now he's got my attention."

Pujols quickly grabbed the attention of others in Peoria as well. After belting a three-run homer against the Vero Beach Dodgers in the Chiefs' first exhibition game of the year, Pujols and his Peoria teammates soon headed north to open the regular season at Kane County (Illinois). Coming to bat for the first time as a professional baseball player, Pujols doubled on the first pitch he saw from Josh Beckett. He also homered in that game and drove in three runs in a sparkling debut performance.

He cranked a two-run homer in the first inning to lead the Chiefs to an 8–1 win over South Bend in another early-season game, then later in the series drove in the only run of the game with a first inning single in a 1–0 Peoria shutout. Facing the Wisconsin Timber Rattlers in May, Pujols stroked three hits and drove in three in a 4–2 victory.

In an April 30 matchup against the Lansing Lugnuts (the Single-A affiliate of the Chicago Cubs), Pujols scored the game-winning run in the ninth inning on a wild pitch from José Cueto with two outs. An inning earlier, the game was delayed for several minutes by a massive brawl between the two clubs that stemmed from a hard-nosed play at home plate. Peoria's Shawn Schumacher had doubled in the seventh inning off Matt Bruback, and after advancing to third tried to score on a ground ball. Lansing catcher Casey Kopitzke tagged him out in a brutal collision at the plate in which Schumacher broke his left tibia and lay on the ground for fifteen minutes before an ambulance took him to the hospital. Kopitzke's reaction angered Pujols and his teammates.

"While he's laying there, their catcher stands there laughing at him," Pujols told the *Peoria Journal Star*. "I can't believe that. Our guy broke his leg. Their catcher acted like he'd hit a cow or something."

When Kopitzke came to the plate the next inning, Peoria pitcher Trevor Sansom drilled him in the ribs with a pitch. The Chiefs then came to bat in the bottom of the eighth, and Bruback sent a pitch sailing over the head of Danilo Araujo. After being warned by home-plate umpire Jason Venzon, Bruback plunked Araujo in the back on the next pitch. Araujo responded by punching Kopitzke behind the plate, and both benches emptied for an ugly melee that resulted in twenty three players being suspended and forty-eight being fined. Pujols received a hundred-dollar fine and a one-game suspension.

The fine was especially painful for Pujols, who was bringing home only about $125 per week on his measly Class-A salary. "We were truly living on love," Deidre has said. "We ate a lot of macaroni dinners in those days."

Pujols continued to hit throughout May and June. He tripled, homered, and drove in five in an 8–5 win over the West Michigan Whitecaps, and in mid-June was fifth in the Midwest League in hitting (.322), to go along with nine home runs and thirty-nine RBIs. His first-half performance earned him a spot in the Midwest League All-Star Game. Before the game, Pujols won a hitting competition in which he was paired with Hall of Famer Tony Pérez.

"He was very humble about it when I talked with him after," Reynolds said. "The thing he was most excited about was he got to meet Tony Pérez. He was kind of bubbly about that."

Pérez had spent twenty-three seasons in the big leagues, most of them with the Cincinnati Reds, where he was a member of the Big Red Machine in the 1970s. He hit 379 career home runs and drove in 1,652 runs before retiring in 1986, when Pujols was six years old.

"That was nice to be able to meet him," Pujols told Reynolds. "He's still in great shape."

By July 10, Pujols was tied for the league lead in RBIs with sixty-nine. He added to that total when he drove in two runs in the first inning that day to give the Chiefs a lead against Kane County they would preserve. In August, *Baseball America* named Pujols the best third-base prospect in the Midwest League, and on August 10, the Cardinals promoted him to high Class-A Potomac, just outside the nation's capital. He finished his season in Peoria with a .324 average that led the league, seventeen home runs, and eighty-four RBIs. Even though he didn't complete the season there, his numbers were still good enough to earn him the league's MVP award.

"He was sort of a streaking star through Peoria," Reynolds says. "A supernova or something. He just lit up the night for a few months there and he was gone."

Pujols' debut for the Potomac Cannons in the Carolina League was much like his debut in Peoria. With St. Louis Cardinals general manager Walt Jocketty in attendance, Pujols singled and drove in a run in his first at-bat, then scored the team's second run on a sacrifice fly. He lined another RBI base hit in the fifth inning as Potomac beat Frederick 4–1.

"I didn't try to do too much up there, because I know what I can do," Pujols was quoted in the *Washington Post*. "I just have to see the ball and hit the ball and I know I will be fine."

Against the Winston-Salem Warthogs on August 30, Pujols drove in Bo Hart in the tenth inning to win the game for the Cannons. He added another RBI the next day on an infield single and came around to score, but the two runs were all Potomac could muster in a 6–2 loss. Pujols played in twenty-one games with Potomac, hitting .284 with two home runs and ten RBIs. But his time there was at an end.

The Memphis Redbirds had lost Ernie Young to the U.S. Olympic team. That the Olympics just happened to be taking place at this point in Pujols' career is coincidental to some, but providential to those who share his faith. Also, Eli Marrero, Eduardo Pérez, and Thomas Howard had joined the parent club in St. Louis when the rosters expanded September 1. With a postseason berth locked up, the Redbirds needed some bodies for the playoffs, and some offensive firepower would be an added bonus.

"We needed another bat," says Galen Pitts, then the Memphis manager. "They gave me a choice of two or three players, and [Pujols'] name was one of them. But he was in A-ball. You don't usually call a guy up from A-ball. You have guys in Double-A that are ready to come up, and you usually go that route."

Pitts turned to Mitchell Page, the Cardinals' minor league hitting instructor that year, for advice on whom to select.

"Take this guy, Pujols," Page told him. "He might be in A-ball, but he's better than these other players right now, and he'll help you offensively."

Pitts took Page's advice. Though Mike Jorgensen, the Cardinals' director of player development, was reluctant to promote Pujols that far that fast, Pitts prevailed upon him, and Jorgensen relented.

With Lou Lucca firmly entrenched as Pitts' third baseman, the Memphis manager needed Pujols to play in left field, the first time he had ever played that position. "It was impressive to see a young kid come up and make the adjustments at that level right away, and even more impressive was the way he handled the outfield after not ever playing there before," Pitts says. "He made all the plays out there and threw to the right base. He didn't miss a beat."

Pujols went 0-for-5 in his Memphis debut September 2, but drove in his first run the next day and added another RBI September 4 in a seven-run ninth inning that propelled the Redbirds to a 9–7 win over Oklahoma. Just like that, the regular season was over for Pujols, with the playoffs coming next. The Redbirds took five games to beat Albuquerque in the best-of-five series in the first round. His heroics against Salt Lake sent the Redbirds to Las Vegas and the Triple-A World Series against Indianapolis, a series Memphis lost in four games.

Even though his time in Memphis was short—as it had been in Peoria and Potomac—Pujols made an impact on those with whom he interacted.

"He wasn't here long," says Woody Galyean, the Baseball Chapel leader for the Redbirds. "What I remember about Albert is number one, he never missed chapel. We actually did some extra chapels that year because we were in the playoffs. As I recall, he never said a lot. But we've had other guys like that, and I look at them and go, 'Well, they're not saying much, but they're listening.'"

Galyean said it was easy to see that Pujols worked diligently at his job, and in the years since the slugger left Memphis, Galyean has watched Pujols from a distance and been impressed with what he has seen.

"It's nice to see a guy like Albert who, number one, is a great ballplayer," Galyean says. "To me the more exciting thing is his walk with the Lord and how he serves. You never hear anything negative about him. It's kind of like you never hear anything negative about Billy Graham. They walk the walk and they live their life the right way."

After the whirlwind 2000 season, the Cardinals sent Pujols to the Arizona Fall League for more playing time. One of his teammates in Arizona was Mike Maroth, who would go on to pitch for the Detroit Tigers and for a brief time in 2007 would be Pujols' teammate again in St. Louis. Though Maroth didn't get to spend much time with Pujols that fall in Arizona, he did go to chapel with him regularly, and he did notice the young slugger's ability.

"Some of the things he did on the field were impressive," Maroth said. "Even in the Arizona Fall League, you could tell he was going to be a great player."

Fast-forward to 2007, when Maroth found himself pitching for the Cardinals and again sharing the clubhouse with Pujols. He was pleasantly surprised by what he discovered in Pujols that year.

"Playing with him before he became such a great player—back in the minor leagues and the Arizona Fall League, when he was just at the time a prospect—to seeing him after many years of success and being one of the best players at the major league level, he was the same guy," Maroth says. "Nothing changed. A lot of guys get caught up in the success of playing in the major leagues. He is one guy I can say—especially with all that fame and the success he's had in the game—for him to be the same person in 2007 says a lot about his humility and to be able to stay grounded."

For Maroth, the grace of God that he sees in Pujols' life is evident. "He's not afraid to share and talk about God, even in the clubhouse and even to other guys," Maroth says. "He's not overbearing in any way, but he definitely shows where God stands in his life."

But even when he's not directly talking about the Lord, Maroth said that Pujols displays Christian virtues just by the way he lives his life—always in a good mood, always smiling (though some in the media would later take issue with this description), always willing to talk to those who want to interact with him, and working hard at his craft.

"Even with that work ethic of constantly working, I've seen him talk to the media for a long time," Maroth said. "I've seen him talk to teammates. Through all that time that he puts in, you would think that a guy like that would not have time for anybody, but he always makes time. You constantly see him talking to different guys, from the media to teammates to guys on the other team, to other teammates' families. That's Albert. His demeanor just shows where he stands from a faith basis. You can tell there's something different about him by the way he lives his life and what he shares with people."

Once the Arizona Fall League ended (Pujols hit .323 with four home runs and twenty-one RBIs in twenty-seven games), Pujols and Deidre returned to Kansas City, where they lived with Deidre's parents for a few weeks. To make some extra money, Pujols worked at Meadowbrook Country Club that off-season, helping with catering duties. In January, the couple had their first son, Alberto José, whom they call A. J.

"He's really excited about having this little baseball player," Deidre told the *Post-Dispatch*. "We videotaped when we had him. Albert didn't know what to think, he was so much in awe. That was probably one of the best moments in his life. If he accomplishes anything, moments like that still will be considered the best."

With his family now a bit bigger, Pujols returned to Florida in February for his second spring training experience with the Cardinals. After finishing the season in Memphis, Pujols knew that was the most likely destination for him to start the season in 2001, and Pitts was likewise expecting Pujols to be his regular third baseman that year. They were both wrong.

CHAPTER NINE

PUT ME IN, COACH, I'M READY TO PLAY

He's almost too good to be true.
—Tony La Russa

Spring training was winding down for a twenty-one-year-old Pujols in 2001. Though the Cardinals had invited him to participate with the big league club in their training camp in Jupiter, Florida, nobody expected him to compete for a job. But it was March 27, and Pujols hadn't been cut yet. He hadn't given the Cardinals reason to cut him. He was hitting well over .300 for the spring and had impressed team management, players, and fans with not only his hitting ability, but also his maturity and his overall baseball smarts.

With less than a week of exhibition baseball left, Pujols stepped into the batter's box in the top of the ninth inning against the Atlanta Braves at their spring home at Disney World. Matt Whiteside was on the mound for the Braves, who held a 5–4 lead. The Cardinals' Eli Marrero had just blasted a long homer off the scoreboard in left-center field to pull St. Louis to within one. Not to be outdone, Pujols crushed a Whiteside pitch and sent it flying *over* that same scoreboard to tie the game at five.

"That's beautiful," Cardinals hitting coach Mike Easler said. "That was amazing. It just shows what the kid is going to be like."

But was it enough to propel Pujols, with all of one year of professional baseball experience, onto the Opening Day roster?

The Cardinals certainly didn't seem to need Pujols as the players trekked to Jupiter in February for the start of spring training 2001. The team had won the division in 2000 before falling to the Mets in the National League Championship Series, and the core of the roster had returned intact as the 2001 season dawned.

St. Louis had a stout offense with single-season home run king Mark McGwire at first base, Jim Edmonds in center field, J. D. Drew in right, Edgar Renteria at shortstop, Ray Lankford in left, and Fernando Viña at second base. Veteran catcher Mike Matheny would manage a pitching staff that included promising youngsters Matt Morris and Rick Ankiel and veterans like Andy Benes, Woody Williams, and Darryl Kile (a twenty-game winner in 2000). The off-season saw the departure of third baseman Fernando Tatis, traded to the Montreal Expos in exchange for Dustin Hermanson and Steve Kline, so third base was one of the few question marks on the team. But the St. Louis management expected Craig Paquette and Placido Polanco to do an adequate job keeping the hot corner warm until Pujols, the team's prized prospect, was ready to claim the position in 2002.

After that stellar season in the minor leagues in 2000, Pujols had earned this invitation to the Cardinals' training camp as a nonroster player. The St. Louis brass had been intrigued by what they'd seen of Pujols' meteoric rise through the farm system the year before, and they wanted to get a closer look at what the future might hold. In his only year of professional baseball, Pujols was the Cardinals' Minor League Player of the Year. He'd hit .314 on the season, with nineteen homers and ninety-six RBIs, and was the MVP of the Pacific Coast League playoffs after his promotion to Triple-A Memphis.

"It was an unbelievable year," Pujols said during the 2001 training camp. "But it's already in the past. So you need to come through this year and try to do the same thing, only better. I'm concentrating on this year. What I did last year was a blessing from God. I didn't get hurt, I stayed strong until the end. Now it's up to me to work as hard as I can to take the next step."

But despite his heroics in 2000, nobody in his right mind envisioned Pujols making the team in 2001. From the start of camp, Pujols was ticketed to begin the season with the Memphis Redbirds for more seasoning. He wore number 68 on his jersey, and they don't assign you number 68 if they think you have a chance of making the roster. Unless you're a tackle.

Pujols may have been in the wrong sport to wear number 68, but his physique would have made many linebackers jealous. From the moment he arrived at camp, his teammates, his coaches, and even the training staff noticed him.

"He was the most impressive physical specimen I saw," said Dr. Ken Yamaguchi of the Cardinals medical staff, who helped administer physicals to the players. "He was like a rock."

Training camp for first-year players can be a time of immense pressure and challenges, especially for highly touted prospects like Pujols. Even without an open competition for a spot on the roster, professional athletes want to do well, and spring training provides them with an opportunity to showcase their talent to the right people.

"Everybody wants to make a good impression," says Ben Zobrist of the Tampa Bay Rays. "You want to show the manager and coaches that you can play at that level. It can be a very important time for a guy trying to break in."

Pujols handled the pressure well. Coaches began to observe not only his ability on the field, but also his maturity and his no-nonsense approach to the game.

"He has presence, and a heck of a lot of talent," Cardinals manager Tony La Russa said. "This is the first time I've seen him, and there's a real personal strength to him that's very impressive. With some young players, there's a tendency to view this as a spring vacation. They need time to grow up. But Pujols has it figured out. He has a serious, mature approach. He's almost too good to be true."

La Russa didn't realize his clairvoyance, as Pujols had yet to show all he could do with a baseball bat. But he began to foreshadow what was to come. In an intrasquad game before the exhibition games began, Pujols tripled and cranked a two-run homer to lead his team to a 6–3 win. In a March 10 exhibition against the Mets, Pujols hit his first home run of the spring and drove in another run on a groundout. Two days later, he tagged another homer, this one a two-run shot. Against the Expos on March 17, he doubled twice. The next day, he had two more hits and scored a run.

"This guy is going to be a star," Coach Easler said. "And I don't mean a little star, either—I mean a big star. Don't tell him I said this, but he's going to be another Edgar Martinez."

Pujols earned Easler's admiration almost immediately, and Easler didn't even have to watch him hit. All he had to do was listen to the sound of the ball coming off Pujols' bat.

"Only a few guys can make that sound," Easler later told *USA Today*. "Willie Stargell, Dave Parker, Dave Winfield, Mike Schmidt. I'm talking about guys like that. The ball just explodes off his bat, and he's talented enough that he can take his power swing and make adjustments and go the other way for a base hit."

The first round of cuts to the St. Louis roster came March 12, with nineteen players being reassigned to minor league camp. Pujols was not one of them, and by now the whispers were getting louder. Perhaps Pujols is good enough to make the team after all, fans began to think. Though Paquette and Polanco were also having solid springs, that platoon at third base didn't energize Cardinal Nation the way Pujols did. But La Russa remained skeptical.

La Russa didn't want Pujols to break camp with the team if he didn't have a place to play regularly. The Cardinals' skipper thought Pujols would benefit more from regular playing time in Memphis than he would sitting on the bench in St. Louis, and it's hard to argue with the logic of that. Still, Pujols was hitting well over .300 on the spring. He was driving in runs and hitting with power. He was playing adequate defense. Pujols began to convince some of the players that he deserved a spot on the team.

"I don't think you can lose either way with him," McGwire said. "If you send him down, you're not going to lose anything. If you keep him, you're not going to lose anything. But the most logical thing is to have him go to Triple-A and get off on a good foot and then if something happens, bring him up."

Even in late March, Pujols seemed destined for Memphis. La Russa and Cardinals general manager Walt Jocketty, however, kept finding it difficult to make the move. It seemed as if every time they were close to sending him to Memphis, Pujols would do something—like slam a game-tying home run over the scoreboard—to make them think twice about the wisdom of that decision. He followed that display the next day with a two-run single off Montreal closer Ugueth Urbina. After the game, the Cardinals informed Pujols that he'd be heading to the West Coast with the team for the final three exhibition games before the start of the season. In typical Pujols fashion, he had two hits in the first game in Oakland.

Pujols displayed not only his offensive prowess during spring training, but also his versatility. He played third base. He played left field. He played right field. He played first base. He even played shortstop. The St. Louis coaches jokingly accused La Russa of playing Pujols in a position where he would fail, thus giving La Russa an excuse to option him to Memphis.

As spring training wound down, Pujols was in the mix with John Mabry and Bernard Gilkey for the final spot on the roster. La Russa was enamored with Pujols' ability and work ethic, but continued to wrestle with the question of whether he could get the playing time necessary for his skills to continue to develop.

Then something unforeseen happened. Bobby Bonilla, signed by the Cardinals in January as a free agent and a lock for the Opening Day roster, pulled a hamstring and would begin the season on the disabled list. At the risk of over-dramatizing a hamastring injury, never has such a seemingly inconsequential ailment had such drastic implications for the history of the game—unless you count Wally Pipp's fictional headache that opened the door for a young kid named Lou Gehrig to take over at first base for the Yankees in 1925.

The injury to Bonilla meant that the right-handed Pujols would be a viable option to get considerable playing time in left field in the opening few games of the season, since St. Louis was scheduled to face several left-handed pitchers. Anyone who knows anything about La Russa knows he's a major proponent of playing the matchups. Suddenly, La Russa had all the reason he needed for Pujols to stay with the team for the start of the season. Worst-case scenario, Pujols would get some at-bats with the big league club for a few days and then get sent down to Memphis for more seasoning once Bonilla returned to health.

La Russa explained as much to Pujols when he broke the news to the young slugger on Sunday, April 1, that he had not only made the team, but that he would be in left field for the Cardinals' opener against Colorado.

"There are so many conversations that are painful," La Russa said, referencing the times he has to tell players they haven't made the team. "You have ten bad ones for every good one, so you'd better enjoy that one good one."

As much as La Russa enjoyed relaying the news, Pujols was even more thrilled. But he wasn't about to consider his mission to be accomplished.

"I'm still working hard every time I come to the ballpark," Pujols said at the time. "They told me I made the club, but I've still got to work hard to stay here the whole year."

The unseen hand of divine providence seemed to be pushing him onto the next level. Pujols didn't know what the future held, but he knew God had given him a tremendous opportunity, and he planned to make the most of it.

The Albert Pujols era in St. Louis had begun.

PART TWO

PUJOLS IN THE MAJORS

CHAPTER TEN

ROOKIE OF THE YEAR

There's a new hero in town.
—Jack Buck, legendary St. Louis broadcaster

The Big Unit peered in from the mound to get the sign from catcher Damian Miller in game two of the 2001 National League Division Series. At six-foot-ten-inches, southpaw Randy Johnson is intimidating in almost any circumstance. Johnson had gone 21–6 for the Arizona Diamondbacks in 2001, with a 2.49 ERA and a whopping 372 strikeouts—good enough for the Cy Young Award.

Bestriding the mound like a colossus, Johnson now towered against the Cardinals at Bank One Ballpark in Phoenix with the Diamondbacks already holding a 1–0 lead in the series. Curt Schilling had seen to that the day before, allowing only three hits and shutting out St. Louis in a 1–0 squeaker.

The rookie Albert Pujols stood in the batter's box staring up at the lanky Johnson. Though Pujols had put together one of the best rookie seasons in baseball history by this point—and had hit Johnson well that year—this was no longer the regular season. This was the playoffs. And Pujols had struggled in recent games, collecting only four hits in his final twenty-one at-bats to end the season and wearing the collar in four at-bats in game one.

With two outs in the top of the first inning, Edgar Renteria took his lead from first base, the beneficiary of a rare Johnson walk. Pujols, hitting cleanup, initially seemed headed for a similar outcome, as Johnson had hurled three straight balls to the Cardinals' first baseman.

Pujols then took a called strike, and fouled off the next pitch from Johnson to run the count full. Renteria would be in motion from first base, but the Big Unit had strikeout on his mind to put an exclamation mark on the first inning and set the stage for the rest of his outing. He wound up and fired a 97-mph fastball toward home plate. But the location was off—up and out over the plate. Pujols hammered the Johnson pitch 352 feet down the right field line for a two-run homer to give St. Louis an early 2–0 lead.

It was all the run support St. Louis starter Woody Williams would need, as the Cardinals answered with a 4–1 win to even the series at one game apiece. "It was big," Williams says of Pujols' home run. "For him to come up and hit a line drive down the right field line in a playoff game of that magnitude, with a sellout crowd and one of the best pitchers of all time up there, it said a lot for his character."

"Strong kid," Johnson said after the game about his matchup with Pujols. "Bad location."

"Just try to be aggressive, look for my pitch, and hit the ball hard somewhere," Pujols told reporters about his approach against Johnson. "I don't try to overpower anything. I trust my hands and do the best I can with the pitch."

St. Louis manager Tony La Russa, meanwhile, wasn't sure what to say about the decisive home run by Pujols.

"He's gotten so many clutch hits, I would hate to disrespect some of the other huge hits that got us here," La Russa said. "I would hate to put this hit ahead of the others because he's gotten so many others."

That's a statement La Russa didn't expect to make at the start of the season. Yes, the phenom Pujols—based in part upon his strong showing in spring training, and in part upon the injury to Bobby Bonilla—had made the Cardinals' Opening Day roster, and was in the starting lineup for the season opener against Colorado on a St. Louis team that was high on confidence as the 2001 campaign began. But the arrangement was supposed to be temporary, and the Cardinals fully expected to send Pujols back to Memphis upon Bonilla's return to health. Even the *St. Louis Post-Dispatch*, in its player capsules at the start of the season, declared matter-of-factly about Pujols: "More seasoning at Memphis is in his immediate future."

Pujols, however, planned to stay. Now wearing a more respectable number 5 on his uniform, he singled off Mike Hampton in the seventh inning of that first game against the Rockies for his first big league hit. That was the only noteworthy item that day for the Cardinals, who lost 8–0. One of the fans in attendance that day for Pujols' first game in Colorado? Stan Musial, who just happened to be in town, and decided he wanted to watch the ballgame. The next two days brought two more St. Louis defeats, as Pujols went 0-for-5 in his second game and failed to reach base in his only at-bat as a pinch hitter April 5. The Rockies swept the Cards to open the season.

The sweep wasn't what St. Louis fans had envisioned to start the new year. And things didn't look too promising the next day as the Cardinals traveled from Denver to Phoenix for a three-game set with Arizona, with slugging first baseman McGwire out of the game with a gimp knee, and center fielder Jim Edmonds on the bench with a sore big toe. Those two had combined for seventy-four home runs in 2000 and were expected to provide most of the punch in the lineup in 2001.

The rest of the team, however—including Pujols—picked up the slack. Starting in right field, Pujols smacked his first hit of the game off Armando Reynoso in the second inning. In the fourth, Pujols came to the plate with Ray Lankford on first base and one out as the Cardinals trailed 2–0. Reynoso hung a curve ball, which Pujols promptly deposited into the left field stands for his first major-league home run to tie the score.

One inning later, with the Cardinals trailing 4–3, Pujols whacked his third hit of the night, a double to left field that scored Lankford to tie the game. Pujols then scored on a single by Mike Matheny as part of an eight-run inning that keyed a 12–9 St. Louis win. The next two days were more of the same. After two hits and three RBIs on April 7 in an 8–4 win, Pujols found himself hitting cleanup against Johnson in the series finale. The Big Unit struck Pujols out in his first at-bat, but couldn't duplicate that outcome in the third inning. Pujols dug in against Johnson with the score tied at 2, two men on and two out—what longtime St. Louis broadcaster Mike Shannon would call "deuces wild." Pujols drove a Johnson pitch deep to center for a two-run double that gave St. Louis a lead it wouldn't lose, as the Cardinals swept the Diamondbacks to pull to .500 on the season.

The Arizona series was a coming-out party of sorts for Pujols, who led the Cardinals' offensive assault by hitting .500 (7-for-14) with a home run and eight RBIs in the three games.

"[Pujols] is a winning player," La Russa said during the series. "He acts like he's been around but that's not how he comes across to the players. He doesn't have all the answers and he has total respect." The Cardinals skipper later described Pujols as "like the team pet."

"These guys love Albert Pujols," La Russa said of the Cardinals players. "They would hurt somebody badly if they messed with him on the streets."

Pujols' breakout against Arizona may have saved his spot on the roster. With Bonilla set to come off the DL in time for the April 9 home opener against Colorado, the Cardinals had to make a roster move to create a spot for Bonilla. All along the plan was for Pujols to return to Memphis upon Bonilla's return. But after Pujols displayed an indispensible bat in the heart of the lineup, the Cardinals shipped John Mabry to the Florida Marlins for some cash. Pujols' spot on the team was safe for the time being.

The wisdom of that roster move was immediately apparent. Playing before a home crowd in Busch Stadium for the first time, Pujols took Colorado's Denny Neagle deep in the second inning for a two-run homer that gave St. Louis a 2–0 lead. The homer was the first by a Cardinals rookie in a home opener since Wally Moon did it in 1954. The St. Louis faithful responded by demanding Pujols' first curtain call. Legendary Cardinals broadcaster Jack Buck christened Pujols "a new hero in town."

Pujols came up in the ninth with nobody out and men on first and third in a 2–2 game. The Rockies, however, chose to walk him intentionally to load the bases. With Eli Marrero at the plate and one out, Colorado pitcher José Jiménez unleashed a wild pitch that allowed Lankford to score the game-winning run.

Cardinals fans were beginning to get a sense of things to come with Pujols. And they liked what they saw.

"It was kind of amazing how he went from A to B as a player," Cardinals broadcaster Rick Horton says. "That's the thing that struck me about him. He was a minor league shortstop for my friend Tom Lawless, who managed him in A-ball. He was a good player. But then we went from that, to this drive to become a guy that all of a sudden made the team out of spring training that nobody thought he would make. And he wasn't an infielder anymore. He was an outfielder, and then he became a third baseman, and then he became a first baseman. Just to see him grow as a player was really my first impression of him."

But more than just his skill on the field, Horton—and many others—noticed something else about Pujols and the way he approached the game.

"He seemed to be very gregarious and friendly and overjoyed about playing baseball, and that's a trait that he continues to have," Horton said. "He brings a lot of passion to playing baseball. It's awful hard to get excited about playing baseball every single day, but he does."

After going 3-for-4 with two runs scored on April 15 against Houston, Pujols was hitting a hefty .429 on the young season, tops in the National League. A week later, also against the Astros, he hit two homers and drove in all three Cardinal runs in a 4–3 loss. When Houston held Pujols hitless in four at-bats on April 21, it snapped a thirteen-game hitting streak that Pujols had begun the fourth game of the season. Unfazed, the next day Pujols cranked two home runs against the Astros to begin another hitting streak that lasted nine games.

That streak included three games at April's end with the New York Mets, the first time for the two clubs to meet since New York had ousted St. Louis from the playoffs the year before. Pujols slapped two hits and drove in three in the first game of the series, a 9–0 clubbing by the Cardinals. The next day, he hit his eighth homer of the season, tying Kent Hrbek for the most home runs in April by a rookie. Hrbek set the mark in 1982.

"I'm just trying to do my job," Pujols said at the time. "I don't care about the record."

What Pujols did care about was winning and being a consummate teammate. He displayed his tenacity and his spunk during that first game with the Mets. With the Cardinals holding a large lead late in the game, Pujols, playing at third base, took umbrage with a comment made by third base umpire Mark Hirschbeck, who at one point muttered to himself, "Throw strikes."

Pujols interpreted that comment as a slam against the St. Louis pitcher, and yelled at Hirschbeck, sparking a brief spat between the two. They met before the next game and cleared the air, but the outburst from Pujols showed him to be a player willing to stand up for his teammates, even as a twenty-one-year-old rookie.

Pujols won Rookie of the Month honors in the National League in April. But the Cardinals finished the month three games out of first and in fifth place in a bunched-up National League Central division. They had fallen to four and a half games behind on May 7 before ripping off a ten-game winning streak that launched them into first place by a game on May 17. During that stretch, Pujols continued to destroy National League pitching: he went 15-for-35 (.429) with five home runs and twelve RBIs. Three of those home runs came in consecutive games. He was now firmly entrenched in the St. Louis lineup, and again was named Rookie of the Month for May. Thoughts about sending him to Memphis for more seasoning had melted into oblivion, and Pujols was in St. Louis to stay.

In addition to Pujols' permanence in the St. Louis lineup, he was also beginning to win the hearts of the St. Louis fans and emerging as the heir apparent to McGwire as a St. Louis icon. Though McGwire's reputation suffered in later years as pundits and baseball fans linked him to the steroids scandal that blackened the sport, at this point Mark McGwire *was* baseball in St. Louis. He had electrified the sport in 1998 with his home run showdown with the Cubs' Sammy Sosa, rocketing seventy homers to crush Roger Maris's single-season record of sixty-one that had stood since 1961. As an encore in 1999, he racked up sixty-five more home runs. Mark McGwire jerseys were omnipresent in St. Louis, especially at Busch Stadium, where fans flocked to watch him take *batting practice*. The Missouri legislature had even renamed a five-mile stretch of Interstate 70 in St. Louis "Mark McGwire Highway."

Though hampered by injury during the 2000 season and limited to only eighty-nine games, McGwire still managed to knock thirty-two home runs while hitting .305 in the cleanup spot. But the omens foretelling the big slugger's demise were becoming more significant. McGwire was supposed to be healthy for the 2001 season, but in mid-April a bum knee sent him to the disabled list, where he would spend the next six weeks.

In his absence, La Russa found himself turning regularly to Pujols to fill McGwire's slot batting fourth in the St. Louis lineup. And the St. Louis fans found themselves becoming more and more enamored with the potential of the rookie, and with the way he played the game and carried himself off the field. A *St. Louis Post-Dispatch* poll of more than four thousand fans in May asked the question, "With first baseman Mark McGwire out of the picture for now, who's your favorite position player on the Cardinals?" Pujols was the top choice of 40 percent of the voters, with Jim Edmonds a distant second at 24 percent.

Pujols enjoyed a homecoming in June as the Cardinals traveled across the state for a three-game series in Kansas City. Friends, family, former teammates, and coaches all swarmed to Kauffman Stadium to get a glimpse of Pujols in a major league uniform. He had once lived within walking distance of the stadium and often sat as a spectator watching the Royals play. Now, only three years removed from high school, he was no longer observing from the stands. He was on the field as one of the top rookies in the game.

"As I sat there and watched him, it just gave me goose bumps to realize that at one time I had penciled his name into my lineup, and now I look out there on the field and here he is," Pujols' high school coach Dave Fry says. "I'm so proud of him."

Pujols didn't disappoint those who had come to watch him play. In the opener against the Royals, he smashed three hits, including a home run off Chad Durbin in the ninth, and drove in three runs. But it wasn't enough, as the Cards fell 7–4. The next day, Pujols had another hit in another St. Louis loss, and in the series finale, he went 3-for-5, but a home run by Mike Sweeney in the bottom of the thirteenth inning sealed the sweep for Kansas City.

Against the Reds on June 26, Pujols took Chris Nichting deep for his twenty-first home run, tying Ray Jablonski for the Cardinals' rookie record. Jablonski set the mark in 1953. Pujols broke the mark July 14 and claimed the record all for himself with a two-run shot off the Tigers' José Lima.

His stellar performance in the first half of the season earned Pujols a spot as a reserve on the National League All-Star team. Pujols became the first St. Louis Cardinals rookie to make the squad since third baseman Eddie Kazak did it in 1949. In the midsummer classic at Seattle's Safeco Field, Pujols walked in his only plate appearance and played defense at second base—a position he hadn't played all season—in the eighth inning.

"That's great," Pujols said about his selection to the team. "There are a lot of guys who didn't make it that deserved to make it. I've got good numbers and I think I deserve it. But, like I said, it really didn't matter if I made it or not."

Despite those good numbers from Pujols, the Cardinals couldn't hang onto their lead in the division. They had slipped to second place, two and a half games behind Chicago, at the end of May. A continued skid in June and July left St. Louis eight games back at the All-Star break in the middle of July, and they dropped another game behind after a loss to Detroit in the first game of the second half.

As July wound down, the Cardinals had some decisions to make about their plans for the remainder of the season. The July 31 trade deadline was approaching. Would they be buyers or sellers? Would they try to add a key player or two to get them back in the race, or would they unload some veterans in demand from other teams jockeying for playoff position? General manager Walt Jocketty seemed to answer that question on July 31, when he traded left-handed relief specialist Jason Christensen to the Giants for minor leaguer Kevin Joseph, indicating that the season seemed to be a lost cause.

Pujols, meanwhile, was struggling at the plate for the first time. During a month-long stretch from the end of June through the end of July, Pujols saw his average drop from .354 to .318. He hit a paltry .209 during that time frame, including a 2-for-35 skid, with only three home runs and eight RBIs. Perhaps he was wearing down. Perhaps word of his weaknesses was spreading around the league, allowing pitchers to exploit them. How much lower would he go?

Pujols answered those questions with a 3-for-5 performance on July 28 that seemed to be a sign of life in his sleeping bat. Two days later, Pujols started a streak that would forever quiet any naysayers. He embarked upon a seventeen-game hitting streak that spiked his average to .332 on August 16. From July 31 to September 5, he hit safely in thirty-four of thirty-six games.

"It was amazing that when we went over how to play him in meetings, it was as if he was in the league for fifteen years already," says former Phillies and Cubs outfielder Doug Glanville. "We had few answers on how to pitch him from the first time we faced him. Years later, I am retired and they still don't have answers for him."

The resurrection of Pujols fueled a resurgence in the Cardinals. Trailing the Cubs by eight games on August 8, St. Louis peeled off eleven straight wins to pull within two and a half games of the first-place Astros, who had overtaken Chicago in the standings, on August 19. But the Cardinals still couldn't seem to get over the hump. They lost five of six in late August, and after a September 2 loss to Los Angeles, fell to seven games behind division-leading Houston, with only a month left to play. Pujols may have been compiling one of the best rookie seasons ever, but the Cardinals, despite the optimism at the season's outset, seemed destined to spend October on the golf course rather than in the playoffs.

But the Cardinals refused to stop fighting. They swept a three-game series in San Diego, in which Pujols collected six hits and homered in all three games (including Bud Smith's Labor Day no-hitter) to bring his season total to thirty-four. He drove in five runs, bringing his RBI total to 109. Pujols was closing in on both the National League rookie home run record (thirty-eight, set by Wally Berger of the Boston Braves in 1930 and matched by Frank Robinson of the Cincinnati Reds in 1956) and rookie RBI record (set by Berger with 119 in 1930).

After losing to Los Angeles 7–1 on September 7, the Cardinals won their next nine games to move into second place, three and a half games behind Houston. Over that nine-game span, Pujols hit .400 (14-for-35) with two home runs and seventeen RBIs, surpassing Berger for most RBIs ever by a National League rookie. Following a six-day interruption of the season after the September 11 terrorist attacks on the World Trade Center, Pujols drove in the game-winning run in the Cardinals' first game back September 17. The next day, he enjoyed his first five-RBI performance.

St. Louis lost to Pittsburgh September 23 and fell to Houston the next day, but then won five straight to pull to within a game. On October 2, Pujols was all over the bases. He slapped three hits, including a double, walked once, and scored three runs as the Cardinals beat Milwaukee 6–1 for their sixth consecutive win. With a 4–1 Houston loss to San Francisco, the Cards and Astros now sat tied atop the division with five games left to play. The September rally also meant the Cardinals were close to locking up the wild card, even if they didn't win the division, holding a four-game lead over the Giants.

In the end, the wild card is what St. Louis had to accept. The team held a one-game lead over Houston, setting the stage for a three-game showdown with the Astros in St. Louis in the last regular-season series of the year. In the opener, despite seven shutout innings from Woody Williams (acquired from the Padres in exchange for Ray Lankford in early August), the Cardinals managed only one run off Houston pitching, and the bullpen coughed up a 1–0 lead to give the Astros the win. St. Louis rallied to win the second game, pulling ahead of Houston by a game in the standings once again, but the Astros pounded Darryl Kile for seven runs in the season finale to snatch the win. Both teams ended the season with a 93–69 record to tie for the division lead, but Houston held the tiebreaker by winning the season series with the Cardinals 9–7. The Astros were officially the division champions, but the Cardinals were playoff bound thanks to the wild card.

Despite a 2-for-12 (.167) showing in the final series with Houston, Pujols had put together one of the greatest rookie seasons in baseball history. In 161 games played (Pujols sat out only one game all season), he finished with a .329 batting average (sixth in the National League), 37 home runs (tied for tenth) and 130 RBIs (tied for fifth). His slugging percentage of .610 was seventh in the league, and his OPS (on-base plus slugging) of 1.013 was eighth.

Consider the performances by other position players who had standout rookie seasons:

- Fred Lynn, Boston Red Sox, 1975. At the time, Lynn was the only player to win both the Rookie of the Year and MVP awards in the same season. He hit .331 with 21 homers and 105 RBIs and led the league with 103 runs, 47 doubles, a .566 slugging percentage, and a .967 OPS.
- Mark McGwire, Oakland A's, 1987. McGwire set a major league rookie record with 49 home runs. He drove in 118 runs and led the league with a .618 slugging percentage, while hitting .289.
- Frank Robinson, Cincinnati Reds, 1956. Robinson, only 20 years old, tied Wally Berger's National League rookie record of 38 home runs, and drove in 83. He hit .290 and led the league with 122 runs.
- Wally Berger, Boston Braves, 1930. Berger hit 38 homers, drove in 119 runs and hit .310.
- Mike Piazza, Los Angeles Dodgers, 1993. Piazza hit .318 with 35 home runs and 112 RBIs.

- "Shoeless" Joe Jackson, Cleveland Indians, 1911. Jackson had played briefly in each of the previous three seasons, but the 1911 season at age 21 was technically his rookie year. He hit .408 with an OBP (on-base percentage) of .468 and stole 41 bases to go along with seven homers (in the dead ball era) and 83 RBIs.
- Ted Williams, Boston Red Sox, 1939. Williams smacked 31 homers and drove in a major league rookie–record 145 runs while hitting .327, with an OBP of .432 and a slugging percentage of .609.
- Dick Allen, Philadelphia Phillies, 1964. Allen hit .318 with 29 home runs and 91 RBIs, while leading the league in runs with 125 and triples with 13. But he also struck out a league-high 138 times.

In the American League, Ichiro Suzuki was also putting up incredible numbers. Though a veteran of professional baseball in Japan, Suzuki made his major league debut in 2001 at age twenty-seven. Suzuki hit .350 to lead the league, amassed 242 hits and stole fifty-six bases, good enough for both Rookie of the Year and MVP honors, making him and Lynn the only two ever to accomplish the feat.

So Pujols certainly fit in with the top rookie seasons of all time. He did it with only one season of professional experience. And he did it while playing four positions regularly (third base, first base, left field, and right field). He was a shoo-in for National League Rookie of the Year. Some were even touting him as the league's MVP.

But all of that was secondary for Pujols, who all season long had insisted that individual statistics and records meant little to him if the Cardinals didn't win. Right now Pujols' attention was directed toward the Diamondbacks, whom St. Louis would face in the National League Division Series.

One of baseball's two newest teams (along with Tampa Bay), Arizona was an expansion team added to the league in 1998. After finishing in an expected last place in 1998, the Diamondbacks made a splash by signing Randy Johnson as a free agent following the season. His addition paid immediate dividends, as the Diamondbacks won the National League West in 1999 (losing in the National League Division Series to the Mets) before dropping to third in the division in 2000, despite the midseason pickup of another star pitcher in Curt Schilling.

In 2001, the Diamondbacks had returned to dominance. They grabbed the division lead in mid-August and held off San Francisco (led by Barry Bonds and his seventy-three–homer season) the rest of the way. Led offensively by Luis Gonzalez (.325, fifty-seven homers, 142 RBIs in 2001), Reggie Sanders, and Mark Grace, the Diamondbacks held their most powerful hammer in Johnson and Schilling, especially in a short series. The two had combined for forty-three wins, 665 strikeouts and a 2.74 ERA in the regular season, one of the most potent one-two combinations baseball has ever seen.

After Schilling shut the Cardinals down in game one and Pujols took Johnson deep in game two, helping St. Louis to even the series, the venue shifted from Phoenix to Busch Stadium. The Cardinals held a 2–1 lead before Arizona scored four runs in the sixth inning off Darryl Kile and Mike Matthews pitching in his relief. St. Louis couldn't overcome the deficit and now stood on the brink of elimination.

Rookie pitcher Bud Smith kept the Cardinals' hopes alive, however, by pitching five strong innings in game four and giving up only one run. Fernando Viña and Jim Edmonds provided most of the offensive firepower for St. Louis and led the team to a 4–1 win to force a decisive game five. Pujols went 0-for-3 for the second straight game.

Though Matt Morris pitched brilliantly for St. Louis in the finale, giving up only one run in eight innings, Schilling matched him practically pitch for pitch. In the bottom of the ninth, with the score tied 1–1, Tony Womack drove in the winning run for the Diamondbacks, who went on to defeat Atlanta in the National League Championship Series and the Yankees in the World Series.

Although Pujols again went hitless in game five, and finished the series with only two hits in eighteen at-bats, his postseason struggles did little to tarnish the brilliance he had displayed all season long. As expected, he was the unanimous choice for National League Rookie of the Year. And though he was certainly the MVP of the Cardinals in 2001, leading the team in average, home runs, RBIs, doubles, runs, and total bases, he couldn't overcome Barry Bonds and his record-breaking season to earn National League MVP honors. Pujols finished fourth in the voting behind Bonds, Sammy Sosa, and Luis Gonzalez.

"I'm excited, I'm glad; it's a blessed year," Pujols said about his ROY award. "This is a pretty good honor. You can only win it one year. I'm honored I got it."

Pujols' Rookie of the Year selection was a foregone conclusion as the season ended. What wasn't known was McGwire's status with the Cardinals. Big Mac returned to the St. Louis lineup at the end of May after a stint on the DL, but he was a shell of his former self, still bothered by a sore knee that sapped his power at the plate. The once mighty McGwire still managed to hit twenty nine home runs in limited action, but his batting average was a woeful .187, and he struck out 118 times in only 364 at-bats. So lost was McGwire at the plate that in the ninth inning of game five of the National League Division Series, with Edmonds on at first, nobody out, and the game on the line, La Russa used reserve outfielder Kerry Robinson to pinch hit for McGwire—the man with 583 career home runs. The situation called for a sacrifice bunt, and Robinson was more capable than McGwire of getting one down, but still, that was a move La Russa never would have made just two years earlier.

It proved to be an ignominious end to a storied career. In November, McGwire would announce his retirement from the game. His body simply wouldn't allow him to play the game at an elite level anymore. So with the leader and face of the franchise now relegated to history, the time was ripe for Pujols to assume McGwire's mantle. He had just completed one of the best rookie seasons baseball had ever seen. What would he do for an encore?

CHAPTER ELEVEN

a TIME TO LAUGH, a TIME TO CRY

I ask that you say a prayer for the St. Louis Cardinal family.
—Joe Girardi, Chicago Cubs catcher

Chicago Cubs catcher Joe Girardi stepped to a microphone in front of the home dugout at Wrigley Field to deliver a cryptic message to a restless crowd. On a sunny Saturday afternoon June 22, 2002, the Cardinals and their hated rivals were scheduled for a nationally televised showdown.

St. Louis sat in first place in the National League Central, with the Cubs in a distant fifth place, ten games behind. Standings, however, matter little in the Cardinals–Cubs rivalry, and every matchup between the two teams is big, with an atmosphere resembling a playoff game. But the anticipation this day had turned to curiosity, as game time drew near, and then passed, with no indication that baseball would be played. As Girardi approached the microphone, his Chicago teammates, donned in their bright home uniforms, formed a background behind him three rows deep.

"Thanks for your patience," said the visibly emotional Girardi. "I regret to inform you that because of a tragedy in the Cardinals' family, today's game has been canceled."

He paused, and then resumed his remarks in response to some boos that began trickling down from the stands.

"Please be respectful when you find out eventually what has happened," Girardi continued. "I ask that you say a prayer for the St. Louis Cardinal family."

What Girardi and the rest of the Cubs knew was that the Cardinals had lost one of their teammates. Thirty-three-year-old pitcher Darryl Kile had been found dead in his hotel room that morning. It was the second death in the St. Louis baseball family in less than a week, as longtime Cardinals' broadcaster Jack Buck had passed away June 18. But Buck's passing at age seventy-seven was more expected. He had been declining physically, and everyone knew the end was near. News about the death of Kile—a healthy athlete in the prime of his life—was abrupt and packed a powerful punch.

"Darryl was always there," Pujols said of his fallen teammate. "We'd be down four or five runs and he was still there encouraging everybody. It's hard for us. We loved this guy. He never missed a start. He was there for his teammates. He would do anything for anyone here. It's going to be tough."

The deaths of Kile and Buck were defining moments for the Cardinals in 2002 and tested the mettle and makeup of a team that had begun the season with a gaping hole in the middle of its lineup. Mark McGwire, the team's leader and slugger, had shocked the team during the off-season by announcing his retirement from the game. Stepping into his spot in the batting order would be Pujols—in just his second season. That much was sure. But where would Pujols find himself on the field, after bouncing around among third base, first base, left field, and right field during his rookie year?

Tony La Russa answered that question before spring training even began. The Cardinals had signed free agent Tino Martinez to play first base, and the St. Louis manager announced that Pujols would be the team's regular third baseman in 2002. Though Placido Polanco had played well enough to claim that role, La Russa wanted him in a supersub role, filling in at both infield and outfield positions and spelling the everyday players. La Russa was projecting Pujols as a longtime third baseman in the big leagues, and figured inserting him into that position on a regular basis would hasten his development there.

But the available evidence suggested that La Russa's decision may have been a bit hasty. Pujols' defense at third base in 2001 was shaky at best. Despite his outstanding performance at the plate, Pujols sported a fielding percentage of only .938 while playing third base, where he committed ten errors in fifty-five games. Those trends continued in the early going of spring training in 2002. In his first ten exhibition games at third base, Pujols committed four errors, providing plenty of ammunition for La Russa's critics.

La Russa, meanwhile, was hoping someone would emerge to claim the vacant left field position. But judging by the lackluster performances, none of the candidates for the job seemed to want it very much. So with a week left in spring training, La Russa reversed course and said Pujols would play primarily in left field, with Polanco holding things down at the hot corner.

"I was totally surprised," Pujols told the *Post-Dispatch* at the time. "I had no idea that was his thinking. I'm not angry or upset by it, because it helps the team. But I am surprised."

In addition to the spring drama over where Pujols would play, Pujols also had to deal with contract negotiations with the Cardinals. Though the team had the rights to him and could have assigned him a salary for 2002, it's typically not wise to insult one of your organization's prime commodities. So after a bit of haggling, Pujols and the Cardinals agreed on a one-year contract worth $600,000, plus an additional $50,000 bonus if Pujols made the All-Star team. It was the richest deal in team history for a second-year player.

With the salary settled and the position question nailed down, Pujols could turn his attention to the field, where the Cardinals were again expecting to contend for the National League Central crown. McGwire may have been gone, but others were waiting to step up and fill the void. J. D. Drew had shown flashes of brilliance in his young career, and had blasted twenty-seven home runs in only 109 games in 2001, while hitting .323. Jim Edmonds was still an offensive and defensive force; the Cardinals returned a veteran rotation featuring Matt Morris, Andy Benes, Woody Williams, and Kile; and the team had fortified its bullpen by signing Jason Isringhausen in the off-season.

Then there was Pujols, who had fired the imagination of St. Louis fans during his rookie season. A sophomore jinx is a baseball cliché, but most of Cardinal Nation agreed with the assessment of *Post-Dispatch* columnist Bernie Miklasz: "If there's such a thing as a sophomore jinx, the guess here is that AP will take a bat to it and bust it up. He didn't coast after a superb rookie season; his head is on straight. He's hungry for more."

Indeed, on Opening Day against the Rockies, with the Cardinals holding a 2–1 lead in the fourth inning, Pujols came to the plate with the sacks jammed and drove a Mike Hampton pitch into right field for a bases-clearing double. He went 2-for-4 on the day, with three RBIs and three runs scored in the 10–2 St. Louis win, and seemed to pick up right where he left off in 2001.

A few days later, with the Cardinals in first place in the NL Central, Pujols had the chance to face off with the Big Unit for the first time in the 2002 season. For Randy Johnson, it was second verse, same as the first. Pujols cracked two hits off him, including his second home run of the season, but it wasn't enough for St. Louis to pull out the win.

"This is a team that has good at-bats against me and has a game plan and executes," Johnson said after the game. "Pujols has great at-bats against me. I'm still trying to figure a way to get him out."

Johnson never did figure it out. Pujols owns a .458 career batting average against the future Hall of Famer, with five home runs and thirteen RBIs in twenty-four at-bats.

"I have a lot of respect for that guy," Pujols said. "He's an incredible pitcher. Because he throws so hard, you have to be relaxed against him. You can't muscle up and try to overpower a guy who throws 97 or 98 [mph]. There's no way. You have to be quick."

Seventeen games into the season, Pujols was hitting .308. His power numbers had dropped somewhat, with only three homers, but he was still driving in runs (fifteen). Over the next couple of weeks, however, Pujols experienced a slowdown at the plate. By May 7, his average had dropped to a season-low .267, with five homers and twenty-one RBIs.

"I'm a little upset at my approach," he said early in the season. "I haven't really been consistent. But I'm pretty sure at some point I'll be happy where I'm at."

Sure enough, Pujols proceeded to hit safely in eighteen of his next twenty games to raise his average to .289. And the power started to return. On June 4, he homered for the second straight game, giving him twelve on the year, and drove in two as the Cardinals beat division-leading Cincinnati to pull to within one game of the division lead. Two days later, Pujols returned to

Kansas City, where he once again punished the Royals for not adequately scouting the talent in their own backyard. In the three-game series, Pujols collected seven hits, homered once, and drove in six.

But baseball soon took a backseat to life. Beloved Cardinals' broadcaster Jack Buck, who had become an institution in the city and won the hearts of millions with his humor and his philanthropy, died June 18. Four days later, the team lost Kile as well. Suddenly baseball didn't seem as important to Pujols or the rest of his teammates. But after the cancellation of the June 22 game in Chicago, the Cardinals decided to take the field the next day—because they concluded it was what Kile would have wanted them to do.

So with hearts aching over the loss of their teammate and friend, Pujols and the Cardinals stepped back onto the field in a Sunday evening game that took on much more meaning than the typical Cubs–Cardinals battles. Emotionally drained, St. Louis couldn't overcome Kerry Wood, and the Cubs cruised to an 8–3 win. Pujols provided about the only highlight for the Redbirds that day, as he stroked a two-run homer off Wood in the eighth inning.

For the rest of the season, Pujols and the Cardinals would wear a black "DK 57" patch on their jersey sleeves, in memorial to Kile, as well as another patch in memory of Buck. As difficult as it may have been to press forward, St. Louis had business to tend to—namely, a pennant race. The Cardinals held a slim one-game lead over Cincinnati when the Reds rolled into Busch Stadium for a three-game weekend series June 28 to 30. In the opener, Pujols had two hits, drove in two runs, and scored twice, as St. Louis edged Cincy 3–2 to increase its division lead to two games. The next day, however, was another story. A costly error by Pujols in left field on a routine fly ball allowed the go-ahead run to score. The Reds would go on to win the game 4–2.

"There's no excuse, man," Pujols said after the game. "I just dropped the ball."

Cincinnati took the next game as well to pull even with the Cardinals in the division. But then, perhaps fueled in part by his mistake, Pujols went on a tear. He cranked three homers in the next four games, all of which were St. Louis wins that nudged the team to a three-game lead. In the first half of the season, Pujols had hit .294 with twenty-one home runs and sixty-six RBIs—a slight drop-off in average from his rookie year, but identical home run and RBI totals—yet failed to make the All-Star team when the fans didn't vote him in, and Arizona manager Bob Brenly didn't pick him as a substitute. It was the only time in the first ten years of his career that Pujols would not be on the All-Star roster.

Pujols downplayed the snub, insisting that the bonus it cost him didn't matter much, and that he preferred the break to spend time with his family. But the slight may have served to inspire Pujols to greater things in the season's second half. In August, he hit .368 with nine homers and thirty-two RBIs. In September, he hit only two home runs, but he drove in nineteen more runs while hitting .348. He hit .436 during one ten-game stretch in late August, with three home runs and ten RBIs.

All the while, Pujols dealt with a variety of nagging injuries in the second half, including a sore groin muscle and a bum shoulder.

He wasn't alone in his ailments. The Cardinals as a whole suffered through injury after injury in 2002, and the pitching staff was especially decimated. La Russa had to use twenty-six pitchers during the season, including fourteen different starters. A trade deadline acquisition of Chuck Finley helped bolster the rotation, and a trade with the Phillies for standout third baseman Scott Rolen gave the Cardinals another big stick in the heart of their lineup. Rolen's arrival, however, meant the departure of Polanco, one of Pujols' best friends on the team, who went to Philadelphia along with Bud Smith and Mike Timlin in the Rolen deal.

As Pujols went down the stretch, so went St. Louis. The Cardinals cruised to a 97–65 record (their best record in seventeen years), winning the division title by a healthy thirteen games.

After a slower start than his rookie year, Pujols put up season totals that didn't quite match 2001, but they came close. He hit .314, with 34 home runs, 127 RBIs, and 118 runs scored. His RBI total was second in the league to Lance Berkman's 128. Pujols also reduced his strikeouts, from 93 to 69. Most significantly, he became the first player in baseball history to start a career with two seasons of hitting greater than .300, with 30 home runs, 100 RBIs, and 100 runs scored.

He also became only the fifth Cardinal ever to post back-to-back thirty-homer seasons (Stan Musial, McGwire, Edmonds, and Ray Lankford were the other four), and was the second Cardinal (in addition to Ray Jablonski) to drive in more than a hundred runs in his first two seasons.

Were it not for Barry Bonds, who put up one of the all-time greatest seasons in baseball history, Pujols would have won his first MVP award. Bonds may have hit 73 home runs in 2001 to break Mark McGwire's single-season record, but his overall stats in 2002 were even more impressive. He hit 46 home runs with 110 RBIs, while leading the league in batting average at .370. Bonds drew an obscene 198 walks, breaking the major league mark of 177 that he set in 2001 (he would break his own record again in 2004, when he walked 232 times). His OBP for the year was .582, his slugging percentage was .799 and his OPS was 1.381. Pujols may have been outstanding in 2002, but he couldn't compete with Bonds' numbers. Bonds was the unanimous pick for the MVP award, and Pujols finished a distant second.

But in early October, Pujols wasn't concerned with his stats, with Bonds' stats, or with the MVP race. All that mattered to him was the Cardinals' rematch with Arizona in the National League Division Series. Little had changed in 2002 for the Diamondbacks, who had held off Bonds and the wild card–winning Giants to capture the National League West. They were still a pitching-rich team, with Randy Johnson and Curt Schilling combining for forty-seven wins during the season. Johnson, at 24–5 with a 2.32 ERA and 334 strikeouts, would win his fourth straight Cy Young Award for his 2002 performance.

St. Louis, however, had some additional weapons in its arsenal that weren't there in 2001—emotion and revenge. When the Cardinals had clinched the National League Central division and the team celebrated on the field, Pujols carried Kile's jersey onto the field on a hanger. As the playoffs loomed, Kile's memory continued to inspire the team. The Cardinals rode into the postseason with a 21–4 record over their last twenty-five games. They were hot, and they were ready.

That became apparent quickly. Though the Diamondbacks held home field advantage thanks to a better record, the Cardinals pounced on Johnson early in game one. Edmonds took the Big Unit deep in the first inning to give St. Louis a 2–0 lead, and with the score tied at two in the fourth inning, Pujols continued his mastery over Johnson. He tripled to deep center field and scored when Rolen hammered a Johnson pitch out of the park. The offensive onslaught continued as the Cardinals raced to a 12–2 win.

Schilling cooled the St. Louis bats in the second game, but Arizona couldn't mount any offense of its own. Behind a solid outing from Finley, the Cardinals eked out a 2–1 win to send the series back to Busch; still, the win came at a cost—with a shoulder injury to Rolen that knocked him out of the series. In game three, with the Diamondbacks leading 2–1 in the bottom of the third, Pujols singled off Miguel Batista to drive in Viña and tie the game. St. Louis would go on to win 6–3 and complete its vengeance, forcing a matchup with San Francisco in the National League Championship Series.

By now, the Cardinals had become the sentimental favorite to represent the National League in the World Series. With everything they had gone through, a World Series berth seemed to be a storybook ending to a tumultuous season. But Bonds and the Giants stood in the way of that happening, and they were not about to go quietly.

Pujols homered in the first game of the series, but it came when the Cardinals were already trailing 7–1. The Giants took the first game in St. Louis 9–6, and Jason Schmidt stymied the St. Louis offense in game two to lead San Francisco to a 4–1 win and a 2–0 advantage in the series, which was headed to San Francisco. The Cardinals rebounded to win the third game, but couldn't find the offense to build on that victory. They lost the next two, thanks in large part to the lack of clutch hitting—the team managed only three hits in thirty-nine at-bats with runners in scoring position in the series. Thus ended the Cardinals' emotionally charged and mentally draining season.

"If Darryl and Jack Buck were here, I don't think they would be disappointed," Pujols said, reflecting on the season. "I think they would be happy how we finished. You need to keep in mind what we went through all season—pitching, injuries. This was real special for everybody. We wanted the World Series, but it didn't happen. That shouldn't make it a failure."

CHAPTER TWELVE

PILGRIMS PROGRESSING

The thing I appreciate about Albert and Deidre is their tenderheartedness toward the Lord. They are growing in the grace and knowledge of what it means that Christ is the Lord of their lives.
—Pastor Phil Hunter, West County Community Church

Four hundred years ago in England, a man sat for twelve years in a cold, stone prison cell for preaching without a license. The man, John Bunyan, made the most of his time by writing a book that has never been out of print since—*The Pilgrim's Progress*.

The main character in the allegorical story is Christian, a man who seeks to escape from the "City of Destruction" and ends up traveling, through trial and travail, to the "Celestial City." Through the allegory, Bunyan teaches the biblical truth that salvation from sin is an immediate gift of God that changes a sinner into a saint. But though the salvation of Christian takes place near the beginning of the story, he still has to walk a long road with trials and temptations that refine him.

The Christian life consists of both an initial act of God and a continuing progression of the pilgrim. A person cannot earn salvation by trying to progress, but neither does a person who has been saved decide to sit down and plateau (or even regress) in the faith.

Accordingly, Albert and Dee Dee Pujols are not perfect, but they are progressing. Todd Perry, CEO of the Pujols Family Foundation, says that God has given them all the notoriety and attention in stages, because if it had all come at once in 2001, they wouldn't have been able to handle it. But it has been a slow progression.

"These guys are espousing faith—Albert, Kurt Warner, you name it—but don't expect perfection from these guys," says St. Louis broadcaster Rick Horton. "I've had plenty of people who come up to me and say, 'There's no way Albert's a Christian. He can't be a Christian. He's too grouchy.' But the Christian message has as much to do with God's grace and mercy in our life and the peace and the joy that we have from being connected with him, not the all-of-a-sudden moral product that emerges."

Though nobody thinks that Pujols lives without mistakes, he is well known for his strong moral character and Christian conviction. "Sometimes baseball players will get kind of bad reputations for certain things. You hear about it in the news," Cards pitcher Kyle McClellan said. "I'm not stepping out on a limb by any means by saying that you'll never hear that about Albert. He's about as straight as they come. He really takes pride in the fact that he does things the right way. He looks at that as a great accomplishment. He's never in the news for the wrong reasons. Every time you hear about him, it's either his greatness on the field or his greatness off the field. He doesn't give anybody an opportunity to bring him down. I think that shows a strong presence of the Lord in his life and that he's headed down the right path."

One foundation of Pujols' growth as a Christian has been his reading and study of the Bible. The Bible feeds the Christian: "Like newborn infants, long for the pure spiritual milk, that by it you may grow up into salvation" (1 Peter 2:2). The Bible guides pilgrims: "Your word is a lamp to my feet and a light to my path" (Psalm 119:105).

When Pujols arrived in St. Louis he began studying the Bible with his pastor, Phil Hunter, and Hunter's three sons. "Pastor Hunter developed a system called 'Who Jesus Christ Is,'" sportswriter Lee Warren wrote, "to teach Christians about the various character qualities of Christ from A to Z. Pujols went through the study with him."

Walt Enoch, the Cardinals' former Baseball Chapel leader, recalls an early example of Pujols' commitment to the Bible: "The year he made it up [to the majors], I remember vividly, he met me as I came in from the parking lot, wanting a copy of *Our Daily Bread* [a Bible study booklet]. At that time we had a Bible study for players and their wives in spring training, and he and his wife came to the Bible study."

Bible study among ballplayers takes place in stadiums through an organization called Baseball Chapel. Grant Williams, former offensive tackle for the St. Louis Rams, serves as the Baseball Chapel leader for the Cardinals. He sits down with the guys at the beginning of the year and asks them what kind of study they want to go through. Williams says that one thing he knows about Pujols is that he doesn't want to read a book *about* the Bible, he just wants to stay in the Bible itself. He says that Pujols insisted, "You can do any book in the Bible that you want, but we need to stay in the Bible."

And Pujols is faithful in attendance. "I'll shoot them a text the day before saying, 'Bible study tomorrow.' It can be so easy for a guy not to come to some," Williams says. "But Albert is always there—every chapel, every Bible study, in the middle of such a long season, on Wednesday afternoons at two o'clock when he could come in at three—he is always there. I think he missed one chapel this year, and he came up and apologized afterward."

Not content with being a warm body, Pujols shares in the discussion and personal reflection. "A lot of times Albert will speak up and give his side of a discussion and his thoughts and his experiences," McClellan says. "People don't understand this man deals with so much that we can't even grasp. People are pulling and tugging at him so many different ways. When he sits there and opens up in the study and talks about how he deals with it and how strong his faith is, and how he relies on that a lot—he and his wife—and a lot of the decisions he makes are very thought out on his part and prayed for a lot."

Another catalyst of Christian growth comes as established believers pour themselves into new Christians through mentorship and accountability. Just as a veteran ballplayer can take a rookie under his wing and teach him from the reservoir of his own experience, so, too, can a mature Christian provide invaluable help and advice to those just beginning in the Christian life.

Such was the case in Pujols' early spiritual pilgrimage. His first pastor, Jeff Adams, says, "When Albert was in his rookie season in St. Louis, Dee

Dee was very encouraged by the fact that there were several believing players that worked with him. They would have Bible studies and pray together when they were on the road."

Pujols related those experiences in an interview with James Dobson: "When Mike Matheny was on our team, he was pretty much the guy that took me under his wing in 2001. As a young believer, I didn't know how tough it was going to be. Matheny was one of the leaders on the team that told me, 'Everything is going to be all right, brother. Just relax and do your thing.'"

The early accountability that Pujols had with other Christians was invaluable. "We used to get together after the game," he said. "It could be one o'clock in the morning and we were still talking about the great things God has done in our life. A bunch of Christians on the team—Mike Matheny, Woody Williams, and J. D. Drew—would still be in the room at two in the morning, even when we had a day game the next day. That's how much pressure there was, and how important it was for you to have that relationship with God."

A Christian is not ashamed of the gospel (Romans 1:16), and will publicly identify with Christ, responding to his words: "So everyone who acknowledges me before men, I also will acknowledge before my Father who is in heaven" (Matthew 10:32). Pujols' Christian faith has been front and center. "In the baseball world, it is hard to keep that a secret," Horton says. "Albert had been thought of as a man of faith right from the get-go. Minor league chapel does such a great job of ministering to guys in their younger, formative years in baseball. So I think the cat was already out of the bag on that."

The Christian life does not shield a person from trials, pressures, or suffering. Identifying with Christ, the Savior who himself bore the suffering of a Roman cross, involves believing his words: "In the world you will have tribulation. But take heart; I have overcome the world" (John 16:33). Albert and Dee Dee have not been immune from tough times. "I wouldn't trade places with him," Perry says. "There would be some wonderful things about being Albert Pujols, but it takes a very, very special person to handle what they have to handle."

But does being a Christian make a difference when the storms of life hit? "Albert has had his struggles. He struggles with a lot of things," Perry says. "If it wasn't for the Lord, he'd be a completely different person, because I think there are certain personality traits in Albert—as in me—that can war against the spiritual side."

The Bible teaches a Christian to "count it all joy" when trials come into one's life because "you know that the testing of your faith produces steadfastness. And let steadfastness have its full effect, that you may be perfect and complete, lacking in nothing" (James 1:2–4). Trials refine Christians, molding them into the likeness of Christ.

That is good for a professional ballplayer (and his wife) to remember as the pressures of living in the public spotlight beat down on them. "He thinks about his game so much that sometimes when he's stressed or frustrated, he walks around with that downcast feeling," Dee Dee told *Sports Illustrated* in 2003—still early in his career. "I always remind him, as long as he's giving his best, what else can he do?"

Former teammate Woody Williams says, "We're all guilty of taking the game of baseball too serious, where it really starts to affect us, but I've seen him grow to where now he's able to enjoy what he is doing, he enjoys his teammates, and enjoys playing. He controls his own emotions."

Echoing that sentiment, McClellan says, "Albert is a strong follower of Christ. I think he can leave at the end of the day and say, 'I might not have succeeded today at the field, but there are other things in life that are more important than baseball.'"

Just like his baseball play, Pujols' Christian walk and leadership are best characterized by passion and consistency. "Sometimes he really gets going, and once something hits him, you can tell he's just passionate about it," McClellan said. "I think he tries to keep quiet, and then something will come up and he just can't help it anymore. Sometimes when we are on the road, the chapel leader for the other team is busy or there's not a lot of time for chapel. But Albert will be chomping at the bit, saying, 'I'll lead it. Let's go. I'll give everybody the Word.'"

Pastor Adams says, "Albert has a faith that appears to be absolutely rock solid, just that basic childlike faith that says, 'This is the way it is, and this is who I am,' and he doesn't budge from that. That's very consistent with the way that he does everything else in life."

Or, as Dee Dee said in an interview, "You know, we're just sold out for God and his plans for our lives."

CHAPTER THIRTEEN

a national treasure

Pujols isn't a jerk; he's just obsessed with hitting . . .
—*Bernie Miklasz,* St. Louis Post-Dispatch *columnist*

Tony La Russa knew he was taking a colossal gamble by putting Pujols in left field against the Florida Marlins early in the 2003 season. *St. Louis Post-Dispatch* columnist Bernie Miklasz said it may have been the biggest gamble of the manager's career. The St. Louis skipper even acknowledged that his job was on the line for doing so.

"If it doesn't work, if something goes wrong, I'll quit," La Russa was quoted as saying. "You won't have to fire me."

But La Russa was desperate. The Cardinals had lost five straight, victimized by a punchless offense that had scored only eleven runs over that stretch. And now they were heading to Miami for a series that would pit them against the intimidating combination of A. J. Burnett, Josh Beckett, and Brad Penny over the next three games. A five-game losing streak could easily become an eight-game losing streak under such conditions, as La Russa knew all too well.

So he was willing to take a risk. The circumstances demanded it, and he had some explicit instructions for Pujols as he patrolled left field April 25: "Don't throw. Whatever you do, don't throw."

That may seem an odd directive from a manager to one of his outfielders, but Pujols was dealing with a sore elbow, specifically an ulnar collateral ligament he had sprained a week earlier. Players who tear the ligament typically require "Tommy John surgery" to reconstruct it (named after the pitcher who first successfully underwent the operation), which can shelve a position player six months or more. Fortunately, Pujols' injury was only a sprain, and the Cardinals' medical staff ordered him not to throw a baseball for three weeks—so the sprain wouldn't worsen into a tear before it healed.

His inability to throw meant that Pujols was relegated to a pinch-hitting role, giving him only one at-bat per game and severely hampering the Cards' offensive attack. St. Louis won the first game with Pujols on the bench, but then the losses started piling up—four in a row before La Russa decided to insert Pujols at first base for an April 24 matchup against Braves southpaw Mike Hampton, against whom Pujols had hit well while regular first baseman Tino Martinez had struggled. Though Pujols came to bat three times in the game, the Cardinals still lost 4–3 to extend their losing streak to five.

Now with the Marlins series looming, La Russa decided to take the chance. He *needed* Pujols in left field because he *needed* the offense he knew Pujols could provide. So he put himself, Pujols' season—and possibly even Pujols' career—on the line. He was willing to do so only because of his deep faith that Pujols would follow his orders devotedly, even in the heat of the moment. Lesser players might succumb to the temptation, and cut loose with a bullet to the infield if they had to make a play. But La Russa knew he could trust Pujols to do the right thing. If someone hit the ball to left field, Pujols was under strict orders to flip the ball lightly either to shortstop Edgar Renteria, who would dash out to retrieve it, or to center fielder Jim Edmonds, who would do the same.

"He can make most plays and we're going to make some adjustments to get the ball into play," La Russa said. "He said to me, 'I can throw,' and I said, 'No, you can't.' The thing that allows me to do it is the fact that he is as smart a player as I have ever managed. I know he'll be smart enough about it."

In the top of the first inning, Burnett struck out leadoff hitter Fernando Viña, and it looked like the St. Louis offensive woes might continue. But then Orlando Palmeiro doubled, bringing Pujols to the plate, since La Russa had bumped him up from his customary cleanup spot to third in the batting order, allowing Pujols perhaps to get an extra at-bat before being removed in the late innings for defensive purposes. Pujols justified La Russa's gamble, driving a 1–0 Burnett pitch over the right-center field fence to give the Cardinals a quick 2–0 lead. They would explode for nine runs that night, snapping the losing skid. After dropping a 5–3 game to the Marlins the next day, St. Louis put together a seven-game winning streak that left the team in a tie for the division lead in early May. And Pujols would stick at third in the batting order for years to come.

First place was where the Cardinals and most baseball pundits expected the team to be at that time. Though the loss to San Francisco in the 2002 NLCS was the "toughest kick in the gut I've ever experienced," according to La Russa, St. Louis seemed poised to make another postseason run in 2003 after the year they had endured in 2002. Yes, there had been questions at the outset. The perpetual question mark, J. D. Drew, had knee surgery in October and wouldn't be ready to start the season. Closer Jason Isringhausen was also coming off shoulder surgery in October and would miss time in the early going. The team had revamped its bullpen. Andy Benes and Chuck Finley were gone from the rotation, with Brett Tomko coming in to claim one of the slots.

But even with the uncertainties, the Cardinals had the advantage of playing in what many considered to be a weak NL Central. Woody Williams and Matt Morris still anchored the rotation. And perhaps most importantly, the middle of the St. Louis lineup had never looked stronger—Edmonds hitting third, Pujols cleaning up, and Scott Rolen batting fifth. Add to the mix the steady, Gold Glove–winning Edgar Renteria at short (who would go on to have a career-best season in 2003, hitting .330 and driving in one hundred), and the Cardinals certainly had a potent lineup.

While lesser hitters need the weeks of spring training to get their timing and rhythm back, Pujols looked like he was ready to go from the beginning. He hit safely in the first fifteen spring games in which he played, posting a batting average of .447 with six home runs and twenty-two RBIs during that stretch. Even the contract negotiations with which he was involved didn't faze him. While talks of a long-term deal simmered, Pujols and the Cardinals agreed to a one-year deal in March worth $900,000, the highest one-year contract ever for a player with fewer than three years of major league service.

"It's good money, $900,000," Pujols said. "But I don't think about the money. I'm thinking about going out to help my team to win. If I stay healthy, I'll help the team and get my numbers. . . . If you put up numbers every year, you're going to be paid what you're worth."

As he had done in his first two seasons, Pujols began putting up those numbers immediately. The Cardinals took the first two games of the year against Milwaukee, with Pujols driving in a run in each game. In the series finale, Pujols broke a scoreless tie in the bottom of the fifth inning by slamming a Matt Kinney pitch for a two-run homer. A run-scoring Pujols double an inning later extended the lead, and the Cardinals held on for a 6–4 win to complete the sweep.

His offensive production was ever present (Pujols hit .382 during the first month of the season), but a string of injuries limited his playing time. He missed a game after being hit on the hand by a Curt Leskanic pitch, and a minor hamstring injury also pestered him before the elbow injury struck and lingered for weeks.

In one of the most thrilling games of the year, on May 23, the Cardinals trailed Pittsburgh 7–5 in the top of the ninth. After Drew reached on a fielder's choice, Pujols singled and scored two batters later on a three-run shot from Rolen that gave St. Louis an 8–7 lead. The Pirates tied the game in the ninth, but the Cardinals responded with two runs in the top of the tenth on an RBI triple from Drew, who then scored on a bunt single from Pujols. The Cardinals held on to win 10–8, in a game in which Pujols went 5-for-6 (the first five-hit game of his career), scored two runs, and drove in two.

His hot hitting continued into June, and he feasted especially on American League pitching in the first interleague games of the year. Against Baltimore, the Orioles held a 6–5 lead in the eighth. Pujols, who was already 3-for-3 in the game, stepped in to face Jorge Julio, the Baltimore closer, with two outs and the bases loaded. Pujols lined a double into the left field corner, clearing the bases and giving the Cards an 8–6 lead that held up.

"Without a doubt, he's remarkable," St. Louis relief pitcher Cal Eldred told the *Post-Dispatch* after the game. "The thing about him is he can look bad on a ball and on the very next pitch, even if it's a good pitch from the pitcher, it's on the sweet spot. And his composure is tremendous. He loves that kind of situation."

Over the twelve interleague games at the beginning of June—against Toronto, Baltimore, Boston, and New York—Pujols hit .438 with three homers and twelve RBIs. His batting average climbed to a league-leading .394 in late June, and his heroics prompted Cardinals broadcaster Mike Shannon to dub him "The Machine," a nickname that has stuck.

While he was doing what Cardinals fans had grown to expect from him on the field, Pujols was also beginning to show the city of St. Louis what he was like off it. He and Andy McCollum of the St. Louis Rams were cochairmen of an annual golf benefit April 28 to raise money for the Down Syndrome Association, with Pujols demonstrating the generosity and care for children with Down syndrome that would only grow in the years to come. At the event, Pujols purchased two Florida vacations, at a total cost of $6,000, in an auction fund-raiser and promptly gave those trips to the families of two kids with Down syndrome.

One of those children was Kathleen Mertz, who had become one of Pujols' friends in recent months. She threw out the first pitch in a 2002 game as part of Buddy Walk Day, and Pujols caught the pitch. As they walked off the field, ten-year-old Kathleen, decked out in her Albert Pujols jersey, asked him to hit a home run for her. He obliged by clubbing a three-run homer in the first inning.

Another characteristic Pujols displayed during the 2003 season was loyalty, and a willingness to stand up publicly for his friends and colleagues in the face of criticism. He quickly came to Sammy Sosa's defense when the Chicago Cubs slugger was discovered using a corked bat in a game. Sosa's explanation was that he accidentally grabbed the wrong bat, and that he used the corked one only to put on a display for the fans during batting practice. Many in the media doubted that, and Sosa took a public relations clobbering for the incident. Pujols however, wasn't one of those piling on.

"He's a great player, a greater hitter and a great man," Pujols said. "I don't know why people can't leave him alone. He made a mistake. . . . Sammy apologized for it. What else is he supposed to do?"

But even with Pujols pounding the baseball in the middle of the St. Louis lineup, the Cardinals couldn't seem to capture any momentum. Playing in a weak division, they stumbled along through much of the season's first half, clinging to a record only a few games above .500. The bullpen was especially problematic, at one point blowing nine of fourteen save opportunities. The team as a whole seemed lethargic, unable to win the close games, and drew the criticism of Miklasz, who blasted the team for being "complacent . . . flat . . . and uninspired."

Still, even with the problems and the sometimes less-than-stellar performance on the field, the Cardinals managed to stay in the thick of the pennant race throughout the first half of the season, and Pujols was one of the major reasons why. After earning National League Player of the Month honors in May, Pujols replicated that feat in June by collecting fifty-one hits during the month, the first time anyone had fifty hits in a month since Philadelphia's Von Hayes did it in August 1984. In late June, Pujols' league-leading average climbed to .394.

His no-nonsense approach to hitting earned him the continued admiration of La Russa, who called Pujols "the best player I've ever managed." That list includes such stars as Mark McGwire, Carlton Fisk, Rickey Henderson, and other Hall of Famers. "It's a helluva compliment because I've been fortunate to manage some great ones," La Russa said in an interview. "But it's an absolute pleasure to manage Albert. How lucky and fortunate I am to have him on my team."

"I went to Tony and asked him if he said that about me, that I was the best he's managed," Pujols said at the time. "And I told him that was a great honor. If anything, it motivates me even more to live up to what he's said about me. I just want to do everything I can to get better."

While La Russa may have been raving and appreciative of Pujols' work ethic, some wondered if Pujols wasn't at times too focused. From Miklasz, in a *Post-Dispatch* column:

> He walks around the clubhouse with a perpetual scowl on his face, he's so locked in mentally. He studies video, tinkers with his swing and takes extra sessions in the batting cage while teammates are relaxing before the game. Pujols' intensity is so strong that he sometimes ruffles other Cardinals, who wonder why he's so aloof. Pujols isn't a jerk; he's just obsessed with hitting and has no time for small talk or horseplay.

Those who know him best would agree with Miklasz's assessment that Pujols isn't a jerk. Yes, he's direct, and yes, he's intent on developing his skills—but not for his own glorification.

"He recognizes that God gave him talent, but boy, he's going to work his butt off to be the very best that he possibly can be," says Jeff Adams, Pujols' pastor at Kansas City Baptist Temple. "He's just a no-nonsense type of guy. You just know that when he says something—'God gave me this talent'—he really means that, as opposed to somebody that may do a Jesus dance when he makes a touchdown. With Albert, it is genuine. He is not going to do anything that is phony. He's just not. And he doesn't have a lot of patience for anybody that does.

"Hence his relationship with the press," Adams continues. "He's not going to be the type of guy who's going to try and butter anybody up. He's going to tell it like it is, and if you don't like it, tough."

His devotion to hitting, however, isn't the only area of his life where Pujols has a dogged determination to succeed.

"Albert doesn't do anything unless he does it 100 percent," Adams says. "So when he plays baseball, he's going to be the best he can be. And he takes that same thing to his faith. When he makes a decision that he's going to be a Jesus follower, he means that. There's no backing up. There's no phoniness involved at all. He takes that same discipline that he has on the field, the same work ethic that causes him to train for eight hours a day, that's the way he lives his life. He puts his family first. He puts God first. And he just means it. It's as simple as that."

Facing San Diego prior to the All-Star break, Pujols singled in the third inning to drive home Bo Hart and give the Cardinals a 3–2 lead. In the fifth, with the Cardinals trailing 6–3, Pujols again stroked a base hit to chase Hart home as part of a four-run inning that would give St. Louis the lead.

San Diego tied the game in the ninth, and in the eleventh inning with Drew on first base and nobody out, Pujols jacked a game-winning, two-run homer off Matt Herges, the first walk-off home run of Pujols' young career. But the Padres, especially catcher Gary Bennett, thought Pujols spent too much time admiring his blast before beginning his trot around the bases. Bennett yelled at Pujols, and his yelping continued the next day when San Diego pitcher Adam Eaton plunked Pujols in the middle of the back in his first plate appearance, ostensibly as retaliation for what the Padres considered to be his showboating the night before.

"He hit the hell out of it and watched it and watched it and watched it," Bennett said in an AP story. "Look, nice going. Just get around the bases. It irritated a lot of us."

Pujols accepted his fate and prepared to take his base. But Bennett wouldn't let it go at that, got up in Pujols' face and began jawing again, causing both benches to empty. Pujols responded by throwing a punch at Bennett before the two were separated and then ejected. A few days later, Pujols was given a two-game suspension from the league for his actions in the brawl.

"I threw the punch. I should have been [ejected]," Pujols said about the incident. "It's something where you react. It's part of the game."

The ejection put an end to a stellar first half for Pujols, in which he hit a league-leading .368 (coming back to earth a bit after his ridiculous June), with twenty-seven homers and eighty-six RBIs. This was Triple Crown territory, a milestone baseball hadn't seen since 1967 when Carl Yastrzemski pulled it off. Pujols' twenty-seven homers were only three behind Barry Bonds, who led the league with thirty, and his eighty-six RBIs were only five behind Preston Wilson's league-leading ninety-one.

The Cardinals entered the break in second place, two games behind Houston. Pujols earned a starting spot on the All-Star team (despite inexplicably lagging in the fan voting until the very end), along with four other Cardinals—Edmonds, Renteria, Rolen, and Williams. He competed in his first Home Run Derby the day before the All-Star Game in Chicago, finishing second behind Garrett Anderson. He tied a derby record with twenty-six homers through the first three rounds of the competition and gave the 48,000 fans at U.S. Cellular Field a thrill by threatening in the second round to break a single-round record. The next day, he collected his first All-Star Game hit, a run-scoring single off Minnesota's Eddie Guardado in a 7–6 National League loss.

The exposure on a national stage in the All-Star festivities, as well as major feature stories by ESPN, *Sports Illustrated*, Fox Sports, and *Sporting News*, meant that Pujols was quickly becoming more appreciated outside of St. Louis. Baseball fans across the country were beginning to notice the exploits of the twenty-three-year-old slugger, and not just the fact that he could hit the tar out of a baseball. They noticed his selflessness and the joy he took in playing the game. They noticed the way he cheered for his teammates and always deflected attention away from himself and onto their contributions. They noticed that Pujols was more than a one-dimensional player who just hit home runs. No, he did it all. Though not fleet of foot, he took the extra base every chance he got, even stealing bases when the opposing pitcher forgot he was on first. Pujols truly seemed to have a sixth sense when it came to playing baseball, and doing the things he needed to do for his team to win.

The added attention—and with it, the added pressure—did little to derail Pujols' offensive production. The July 12 game against San Diego launched a Pujols hitting streak that would reach thirty consecutive games before the Phillies would snap it in late August. During that streak, on July 20, Pujols took the Dodgers' Odalis Pérez deep for his twenty-ninth homer of the season—but more significantly, the one hundredth homer of his career. He became only the fourth player ever (along with Joe DiMaggio, Eddie Mathews, and Ralph Kiner, all Hall of Famers) to reach the 100–home run mark in their third season. At 23 years and 185 days old, he reached the mark at a younger age than all but six players in baseball history.

"It's 100 home runs, so what?" Pujols said, downplaying the feat. "I'm glad I'm one of the youngest, but it's not a big deal. I've got a lot more to reach. . . . I'm playing now to reach 100 more."

More importantly to Pujols, he was also playing to help his team make the playoffs for the fourth straight year. The Cardinals fell to four games behind Houston in late July but began chipping away. By August 24, they had moved into a first-place tie with the Astros—but the surging Cubs had made it a three-team race and trailed by only half a game. Now Chicago was coming to town for a pivotal three-game series that became the subject of the Buzz Bissinger book *Three Nights in August*.

Writes Bissinger about Pujols:

> There was nothing quite like Pujols. Players like that don't come along once in a lifetime; they never come along. Yet Pujols had another quality

that La Russa treasured even more, maybe because he himself had come of age in the game during the 1960s. It was selflessness in this ultimate age of selfishness, a joy in others' accomplishments that exceeded whatever joy Pujols took in his own accomplishments. He liked baseball, all of baseball, didn't condescend to it. He was the first one to leap to the dugout's top step to celebrate someone else's hit. He took a walk when he needed to take a walk. He liked the challenge and surprise of bunting with men on. It made Pujols a new old-fashioned superstar, in the mold of other Cardinals greats such as Red Schoendienst and Stan Musial and Lou Brock. "The numbers and the money take care of themselves," said La Russa of him. "He's just out there playing to win. That's why I admire him."

The Cardinals took two of three from the Cubbies in that series, and continued to seesaw with the Astros over the next several days: tied, up a game, tied, up half a game, down half a game. Against Cincinnati on August 31, Pujols hit two home runs and drove in all five Cardinal runs as St. Louis shut out the Reds to recapture the division lead by a game. All the while, the Cubs continued to lurk in third place, just waiting for a chance to move up.

They got it the first week of September, with the Cardinals heading north to Wrigley for a five-game series because of an earlier rainout. St. Louis clung to its one-game lead over Houston, with the Cubs two and a half games back, when the series started. The Cubs jumped on the Cardinals quickly in the series opener, as Mark Prior held Pujols hitless in a 7–0 Chicago victory. The next day, in a marathon first game of a doubleheader, the Cubs scored two runs in the bottom of the fifteenth inning for another win, with Pujols again wearing the collar at 0-for-5, in addition to dropping a fly ball (thus ruled by the umpire; Pujols argued that he caught the ball and dropped it while transferring it for the throw) and failing to tag second base while on the base paths. *Post-Dispatch* reporter Joe Strauss wrote that the outing may have been Pujols' worst game of the season.

St. Louis rebounded in the nightcap, but the Cubs grabbed the next two to win four-of-five and leapfrog the Cardinals in the division standings. It was a series the Cardinals and Pujols would like to forget. Pujols hit only .211 in the five games, with no home runs and just one RBI, and the series proved to be the deathblow to the Cardinals' playoff hopes. St. Louis lost again the next day to Cincinnati, dropping to two games behind the Astros, and would never get closer than a game and a half the rest of the way. Even winning six of their last seven was not enough, and the Cardinals finished the year in third place, three games behind the division-winning Cubs.

Though the Cardinals had dropped out of the playoff hunt, Pujols was in a neck-and-neck race of his own for the National League batting title. He had led the league in hitting all year, and with a little more than a week left in the season, sported a .364 average. The Colorado Rockies' Todd Helton was second at .353. But then Helton got hot: 3-for-4 against San Diego, 1-for-3 against Arizona, 2-for-3 against Arizona, 1-for-4 against Arizona, 1-for-3 against San Diego. Going into the last game of the season, Helton was 207-for-579 on the year, for an average of .3575.

Pujols, meanwhile, was tailing off a bit. After going 0-for-5 against Arizona September 26 and 0-for-3 the next day, Pujols carried an average of .3584 (210-for-586) into the finale. The batting crown was up for grabs. In his first at-bat against Brandon Webb in the closing game, Pujols struck out, dropping his average to .3577. Helton, against the Padres' Jake Peavy, singled in his first at-bat to give him the momentary batting lead at .3586. Pujols knocked a base hit in his second at-bat, while Helton flied out, allowing Pujols to retake the lead, .3588 to .3580.

A groundout in the third inning nudged Pujols down to .3582, while Helton also grounded out in his third at-bat to fall to .3573. Then Pujols doubled in the seventh inning—batting average up to .3593—and Helton also singled in his fourth plate appearance—batting average up to .3584. When Pujols struck out in his final at-bat of the season, giving him a batting average of .3587, he and his teammates sat in the clubhouse watching the end of the Rockies game, which had begun an hour later. Helton came to bat in the eighth inning. A hit would give him the title, but the Padres walked him intentionally, keeping his average at .3584, just under Pujols' by the narrowest of margins—the closest, in fact, in National League history.

So Pujols won his first batting crown, while hitting 43 homers and driving in 124. The Triple Crown eluded him (he finished tied for fourth in homers and tied for fourth in RBIs), but he led the league with 212 hits,

137 runs, 51 doubles, and 394 total bases. Among his accomplishments during the season:

- His batting average was the highest for a Cardinal since 1937, his runs scored the highest for the team since 1948, his hits the most for the team since 1985, and his doubles the most since 1953.
- He tied Ralph Kiner (who did it from 1946–48) for the most home runs in a player's first three major league seasons (114).
- He and Edmonds became the first Cardinals teammates ever to have thirty-five or more homers in the same season.
- He became the eighth player in major league history to hit fifty doubles and forty homers in a single season.
- He was the third player ever to hit at least thirty home runs in each of his first three seasons, and the first player ever to hit .300 with at least thirty home runs, a hundred RBIs and a hundred runs scored in each his first three years.
- He was the youngest batting champion in National League history (at 23 years, 256 days old).
- He joined Rogers Hornsby as the only other Cardinal to have more than forty homers and more than two hundred hits in the same season.

"Certainly, no player has achieved what Pujols has in the first three years of his major league career," wrote the *Washington Post*'s William Gildea. "None: not Ruth or Cobb, DiMaggio or Williams, Mays or Mantle, Brett or Gwynn. No one before José Alberto Pujols, who is from the Dominican Republic, amassed at least 30 home runs, 100 runs scored, and 100 RBI during each of his first three seasons."

Postseason awards began streaming in. First was the *Sporting News* Player of the Year Award, followed by the Hank Aaron Award (given to the best overall hitter in each league), the Silver Slugger (for top offensive players at each position) and the Players Choice Award. Had the Cardinals made the playoffs, Pujols may have been in line for his first MVP. But for the second straight year, he finished second in MVP voting to Bonds.

"It's amazing these last three years. What I've done is unbelievable," Pujols said late in the season. "I think this year is really special. Even though we probably don't have as good a chance to go to the postseason like the last three years, it's been pretty special."

Pujols didn't yet realize that "special" was just beginning.

CHAPTER FOURTEEN

ALMOST

Every time I go out there, it's to glorify my God.
—Albert Pujols

The Cardinals stood on the bank of baseball's promised land—the World Series—which they hadn't seen since 1987. That kind of a drought in St. Louis, where fans are accustomed to winning, was an eternity. Not since the days of Ozzie Smith, Willie McGee, Terry Pendleton, and Tommy Herr had the Cardinals played in the Fall Classic, but now they were just one win away, with division rival Houston standing in their way.

With the 2004 National League Championship Series tied at three games apiece, the Cardinals would have to go through Roger Clemens if they wanted to taste World Series play. The forty-one-year-old fireballer may have been on the downside of his career, but he was still a formidable opponent. Clemens had won eighteen games for the Astros in 2004, losing only four, with an ERA of 2.98. The performance would earn him his seventh—yes, seventh—Cy Young Award.

The St. Louis hopes rested on the shoulders—and right arm—of Jeff Suppan. A new acquisition for the Cardinals prior to the 2004 season, Suppan was just the kind of hurler that St. Louis pitching coach Dave Duncan loved. Suppan was a workhorse, taking the mound every five days and racking up more than 200 innings for five straight years before arriving in St. Louis. Game seven was a rematch of game three, in which Clemens had gotten the best of Suppan and the Cardinals, 5–2. Now vengeance was Suppan's for the taking.

Unsurprisingly, the game proved to be a pitchers' duel as inning after inning went into the books. Houston scored once in the first and once in the third, but in the middle innings, Suppan had settled in and retired nine straight batters. The Cardinals had pushed across their only run of the game when Tony Womack scored in the third on a suicide squeeze from Suppan. It was now the sixth inning, and Clemens, holding a 2–1 lead, had been dealing, giving up only three hits so far on the night. St. Louis fans couldn't help but notice the sand start to empty from the hourglass.

Desperate for offense, and with Suppan scheduled to lead off in the bottom of the sixth, Tony La Russa went to his bench. Roger Cedeño was his choice to pinch-hit for Suppan, and the speedy Cedeño rewarded his manager's decision by singling to center off Clemens. Edgar Renteria laid down a sacrifice bunt to move Cedeño into scoring position, with Larry Walker coming to the plate. Walker, a late-season addition by the Cardinals, grounded out to Clemens, but Cedeño moved to third on the play.

That brought up Pujols with two outs and an immensely valuable tying run ninety feet away in Cedeño. During the regular season, Pujols had hit .333 with two outs and runners in scoring position. But thus far in their matchups, Clemens had the upper hand on Pujols. The Cardinals slugger had been hitless against the Rocket in game three, and had managed only one hit against him in seven at-bats during the season. But Clemens quickly discovered that when it comes to Pujols, past success is no indication of future performance.

Pujols took the Rocket's first pitch for a called strike. The next pitch evened the count at 1–1, but Pujols fouled off the third pitch to go back in the hole. Hitting Clemens on any count is tough, but hitting Clemens with two strikes is nearly impossible. Over the course of his career, Clemens held batters to a .153 average after he got the second strike. Clemens, indeed, had Pujols set up.

But Pujols had other plans. He smoked Clemens' next pitch down the line in left field for an RBI double, tying the game and giving Cardinals fans reason for optimism. They didn't have to wait long, as Scott Rolen on the next pitch punished Clemens with a two-run homer, giving the Cardinals a 4–2 lead, which was all they needed as they beat Houston 5–2 and earned their first World Series berth in seventeen years.

"In that moment, you just want to get a good pitch to hit," Pujols told the *Post-Dispatch*. "You don't think about how many times you struggled. You know the guy is the best out there. You see the ball and hit it. That's what happened."

The 2004 season was indeed a special one in St. Louis, but before it could get started, the Cardinals had had to deal with the looming contract situation with Pujols, a matter of great concern to the team and its fans. The Cardinals had the rights to Pujols through the 2006 season, but with three years of major league service time, Pujols was eligible for salary arbitration for the first time. That meant if the Cardinals and Pujols couldn't agree on either a one-year contract or a multiyear deal by the date of the arbitration hearing, a panel of arbiters would determine Pujols' salary for 2004.

With the statistics he had amassed during his three seasons, Pujols was about to shatter the record for the amount of money awarded to a first-time arbitration-eligible player. Pujols had earned a base salary of $900,000 in 2003, and an additional $50,000 for making the All-Star team. He submitted a figure of $10.5 million in the arbitration process. The Cardinals countered with $7 million. Based upon the established rules, the arbiters would have to select one or the other, with no middle ground.

The Cardinals, however, didn't relish the thought of taking Pujols to arbitration. They would be forced to stand before the panel of arbiters and argue why Pujols was not worth the $10.5 million he had requested. Such a process can lead to bruised feelings and strained relationships, which the Cardinals wanted to avoid if possible. After all, you're talking about the team's most prized commodity, a player who had just put up three seasons unlike anything baseball had ever seen before. Offending him wouldn't be the wisest course of action, and the Cardinals knew it.

Pujols, meanwhile, appeared to have offended some of the St. Louis fans with comments he made as the contract negotiation process moved forward. While Cardinals fans were hopeful that Pujols would give the team a hometown discount, Pujols quashed such notions.

"This is business. There are no breaks," he told the *Post-Dispatch*. "You try to get what you deserve. That's what I want. I think my numbers speak to that. I don't want to be cocky about it or change my attitude. Like I say, this is business. I've taken care of my business the last three years, so hopefully I get treated respectfully. That's all I ask for."

Such comments did not always play well with the St. Louis faithful, who seemed to forget that the two sides were in the middle of a negotiation, and it's never shrewd business to show your cards before the hand is over. It's also easy to take offense and claim moral superiority when it isn't your salary negotiation being played out publicly.

In Pujols' defense, the Cardinals had profited significantly from his exploits over the past three seasons. They had him at a bargain basement price, and got far more for their money than they ever could have dreamed. Pujols knew his value to the team, and knew his value to other teams should the Cardinals fail to offer him a salary comparable to what he could get elsewhere after the 2006 season, when he would hit free agency.

The Cardinals sidestepped the arbitration process and locked Pujols up for the long haul. They agreed with him, just before the arbitration hearing, on a seven-year, $100 million contract that would keep him in St. Louis through 2010, with a club option for 2011 that would pay him $16 million. The contract was the largest the Cardinals had ever dished out—the largest in baseball history for a player with three years' experience—and Pujols' hard work and determination had paid off immensely. He was now a wealthy man, and that wealth would soon benefit countless others.

"This is what I dreamed about before I started playing baseball," Pujols said at the time. "Everything is happening. Things are working great. This is part of the dream I always had as a little boy—having a great family; great relationships; have a great career, hopefully, and stay healthy."

But Pujols was quick to point out that while the money would be of benefit to his family, it wouldn't change the way he played the game, and that it wasn't his money anyway.

"I'm pretty sure people think, 'What can I do with that money?'" Pujols said. "But it's not my money. It's money that I have borrowed from God. And He has let me use it. Whatever He wants me to do with it, that's what I'm going to do. Right now, it's not about the money. It's about myself, getting ready for the 2004 season and about the team. If you play this game and don't win a championship, it doesn't matter how much money you make."

His contract signed and his finances in order, Pujols could focus on baseball. The Cardinals were looking to rebound from a disappointing season in 2003 in which they missed the playoffs after three straight postseason appearances. The team had gone through a massive shake-up prior to spring training, for starters trading Tino Martinez to Tampa Bay. Martinez's departure would pave the way for Pujols to take over at first base permanently. The first three years with the team Pujols had bounced around between the outfield, third base, and first base, but first base seemed to be the position for which he was best suited, especially with the lingering elbow problems that posed a threat if he had to throw the ball regularly. Playing first base would allow Pujols to settle into a position for good, a position that would limit his need to throw the ball.

General manager Walt Jocketty also pulled the trigger on a blockbuster deal with Atlanta, swapping J. D. Drew for pitcher Jason Marquis, who would join the St. Louis rotation in 2004 and win fifteen games; lefty specialist Ray King; and heralded prospect Adam Wainwright, who would soon develop into one of baseball's elite hurlers. In addition to Suppan, outfielder Reggie Sanders came to the team in free agency and would replace Drew in right field, and for the first time the team was expecting a contribution from starting pitcher Chris Carpenter, who had missed the entire 2003 season because of injury.

Even with all the peripheral changes, however, the Cardinals nucleus was intact for 2004. Pujols, Rolen, and Edmonds—and Renteria, to a lesser extent—would be a juggernaut in the middle of the St. Louis lineup, with Matt Morris and Woody Williams still anchoring the rotation. Pujols was intent upon reducing his strikeouts and increasing his walks in 2004—not that he needed much improvement (he struck out sixty-five times in 2003 and drew seventy-nine walks).

The Cardinals' main competition appeared to be the Cubs, who, after choking away the NLCS in 2003 and blaming it on poor fan Steve Bartman, had improved themselves by trading for Derrek Lee and reacquiring star pitcher Greg Maddux as a free agent. And the Astros with the Killer B's—Lance Berkman, Jeff Bagwell, and Craig Biggio—were always a threat.

After losing three of their first four games, St. Louis bounced back to sweep the Arizona Diamondbacks in Phoenix. In the series finale, Pujols went deep off Randy Johnson in the first inning—his fourth homer of the season, tied for tops in the league—to give the Cards a quick lead. He later drove in a second run on a groundout, and in the seventh inning, again facing Johnson, doubled to drive in So Taguchi.

The Astros came to town and swept St. Louis in the next three-game series, but the Cardinals exacted revenge a few days later with a three-game sweep of Houston at Minute Maid Park. In the opener, Pujols knocked a two-run homer off Wade Miller in the sixth inning to break a 1–1 tie as the Cardinals went on to win 5–3. The final game of the series was a thrilling 2–1 St. Louis win, with Sanders scoring on a squeeze play by rookie Hector Luna. Pujols, who had taken the young Luna under his wing, leaped over the dugout railing and was the first to congratulate him on his game-winning RBI. It was vintage Pujols—though not involved personally in the decisive play, acting as though he were, and expressing genuine happiness for the successes of his teammates. "Rejoice with those who rejoice" is a biblical mandate he takes seriously.

"I was excited for him," Pujols said. "He's looking to us as leaders, as guys he's going to stay close to so they can help him out, because English is his second language. DK [Darryl Kile] put his arm around me when I first came up. I'm putting my arm around Hector and the young guys coming up. That's what it's all about. . . . Anything I can do to help [Luna] out, I'm going to do it. It's about being a teammate. I'm a teammate guy. I want to be a winner."

Despite the early sweep of the Diamondbacks and Houston, the Cardinals continued to flounder early in the season, hovering around .500 and falling to as many as four and a half games behind the division-leading Astros in mid-May. Pujols, though he was getting hits, driving in runs (seventeen RBIs in April and eighteen in May), and ranking among the league leaders in runs scored, wasn't quite the same Pujols. He seemed to be pulling off too many pitches, trying to yank everything to the left side instead of going to the opposite field. After a 1-for-5 outing in an 11–8 loss to Pittsburgh May 26, Pujols' season average was .279, up a bit from the .267 to which he had dropped earlier in the month, but a long way from the standards Pujols had set for himself.

Three games later, Pujols exploded against Houston, going 4-for-5 with two homers and three RBIs in a 10–3 St. Louis win, the third straight victory for the Cardinals, who were now in second place, two and a half games behind Cincinnati. Hitting coach Mitchell Page made a prediction after watching Pujols' performance: "We can get on his back now and go for a ride," Page said.

He proved to be a prophet. Pujols had two more hits and another homer the next day in a 7–1 loss to Houston. In the opener of a four-game series at Pittsburgh, Pujols added another two hits and two RBIs. In game two, he went 5-for-5 (the second five-hit game of his career) with a home run and three RBIs in a St. Louis win. In fact, including the 4-for-5 performance against Houston that launched his offensive onslaught, Pujols hit .581 over an eight-game stretch, with five homers and eleven RBIs, raising his season average to a more typical .325. The Cardinals won seven of those eight games to pull to within a game of first place.

A 12–4 thumping of the Cubs on June 9 moved St. Louis into a first-place tie, and with a 12–7 win over Texas on June 11, the Cardinals moved to nine games over .500 (35–26), their high-water mark at that point, and into sole possession of the division lead. They wouldn't lose it the rest of the season.

The Cardinals won eight of nine to close out the season's first half, and held a seven-game division lead at the All-Star break. Pujols, with a .304 average, twenty-two home runs, and sixty RBIs, again earned a starting spot in the All-Star Game. He went 2-for-3 in the exhibition, with two doubles and two RBIs, but the National League lost its eighth straight game to the American League, 9–4. And though his first-half stats were good, Pujols was just getting started.

His signature game of the season came July 20 against the Cubs at Wrigley. A Pujols double in the first inning off Glendon Rusch scored Tony Womack and gave the Cardinals a quick 1–0 lead. But then St. Louis pitcher Matt Morris fell apart in the second inning. He walked Moisés Alou to lead off the inning and served up a two-run homer to Derrek Lee to give the Cubs a 2–1 lead that was just the beginning. Chicago would get five more hits in the inning, and by the time Cal Eldred came in to relieve Morris, the Cubs had scored seven times.

With the Cubs holding a 7–1 lead, the game appeared to be over—to everyone but Pujols. With one out in the next inning, he hit a solo home run to narrow the lead to five. Hit number two of the day. The Cubs answered in the third with another tally to retake a six-run lead, and the score stayed that way until the sixth when Pujols led off with a line drive single to center. Hit number three. Pujols scored two batters later on a two-run single by Edmonds, part of a four-run inning that pulled the Cards to within two, 8–6.

Pujols led off the seventh inning with a blast off Kyle Farnsworth. Hit number four, and St. Louis now trailed by only a run. But Pujols wasn't finished.

The Cardinals tied the score in the eighth on a Taguchi homer. With the score still tied in the top of the ninth, Cubs manager Dusty Baker turned the game over to his closer LaTroy Hawkins. Hawkins promptly gave up a lead-off single to Renteria, bringing Pujols to the plate. On a 1–0 count, Pujols lifted a Hawkins pitch deep to right-center field. It carried into the netting above the wall for a two-run homer, giving St. Louis a 10–8 lead. Reggie Sanders would later go deep, extending the lead, before Jason Isringhausen nailed down the win in the bottom of the ninth.

Pujols had gone 5-for-5, with three home runs, five RBIs, and four runs scored. It was his first three-homer game. And in typical Pujols fashion, he called Taguchi's shot the biggest homer of the game.

"The best thing about Albert is he's playing to win," La Russa said after the game. "He's playing for a ring for himself, his teammates, and the Cardinals fans. That's what I admire about him most. Nothing else is a close second. The true winning player lets the numbers, the stats, and the money happen. That's what he does."

Pujols hit .374 in July, with nine homers and twenty-two RBIs. The Cardinals, meanwhile, rolled to an incredible 20–5 mark on the month, extending their division lead to ten and a half games. On August 4 against Montreal, Pujols hit his thirtieth home run of the year—making him the first player in major league history to start a career with four straight thirty-homer seasons.

"It's great if I can go out, stay healthy, and do what I can and hopefully I can do that every year," Pujols said. "If I hit 30 next year, I'll be the only guy (to do it in the first five). It's something that I don't think about. I care about the winning."

Winning was what the Cardinals continued to do. In August, St. Louis went 21–7, moving out to a fifteen and a half–game lead in the NL Central, while Pujols continued his torrid hitting. As if the team's offense weren't potent enough, the Cards added Colorado slugger Larry Walker in an August deal with the Rockies for three minor leaguers.

Pujols was again posting MVP-type numbers, battling for the league lead in home runs and RBIs. Of course, Rolen and Edmonds were making their own cases for the award as well. (Rolen would finish the season hitting .314 with 34 homers and 124 RBI, while Edmonds would hit .301 with 42 homers and 111 RBIs. Each won Gold Glove awards.) But while Pujols continued to scorch the ball, in August he acknowledged that he had been playing for several weeks with a left foot injury that caused excruciating pain. The condition, called plantar fasciitis, is a swelling of the ligament connecting the heel bone with the toes. The only effective treatment options for the condition are surgery or rest, neither of which appealed to Pujols late in the season with the Cardinals making a playoff run. So he gutted it out, relying more on the power of God to strengthen and heal him rather than undergoing medical treatment that would have sidelined him for weeks.

"It bothers me, but when I cross that white line, I'm ready to play," Pujols told the *Post-Dispatch*. "The only reason I'm playing is that God has given me the power to play. I don't believe in surgery that's going to heal it. I believe in God—and rest in the off-season, like [God] did with my [elbow]. A surgeon can go 50–50. It's not 100 percent that it's going to heal. I know that God can heal better than surgery. And we've got great trainers in Barry [Weinberg] and Mark O'Neal. They work all day, day in and out, to make sure I'm ready for a seven o'clock game."

The condition, as painful as it was, did little to slow Pujols. In August he hit .351 with twelve home runs and twenty-nine RBIs, including a game against Cincinnati August 16 when he went 3-for-5 with a homer and five RBIs to lead his team to a 10–5 win. It was the fourth straight game in which Pujols went deep, raising his season output to a major league–leading thirty-seven homers. In a 4–0 win against Pittsburgh August 29, Pujols hit his fortieth homer of the year and drove in two, giving him 100 RBIs for the fourth straight year. The only other players to drive in at least 100 runs in their first four years? Al Simmons, Ted Williams, and Joe DiMaggio, all of whom are in the Hall of Fame.

"Forty and 100 is tough to do at this level, but I don't care what kind of numbers I put up or who they compare me to," Pujols said. "I just want to be a winner. When you start thinking about your numbers and what you've done in the big leagues, that's when you start feeling comfortable, and I don't want to do that."

Also in August, the *Post-Dispatch* reported on a project spearheaded by St. Louis catcher Mike Matheny to build a baseball field in Chesterfield, Missouri, for physically and mentally challenged children. Pujols, who had set aside $100,000 to build a baseball field in the Dominican Republic with funds from his participation in the 2003 Home Run Derby, changed course and gave the money to Matheny's project instead. This example of Pujols' generosity, and his care and compassion for disadvantaged children, was just a small foreshadowing of what was to come in the years ahead.

As the season wound down, and as the Cardinals moved out to a lead as large as seventeen and a half games in September, St. Louis had a chance to post the best regular season record in team history. The franchise record for wins was 106, set in 1942 by a team that included Stan Musial, Enos Slaughter, Marty Marion, Terry Moore, and Mort Cooper. Two other teams won 105 games—in 1943 and 1944. Not since 1985 had a Cardinals team won more than 100 games. Through August, the team had amassed a record of 87–44, putting it on pace to win 107 games on the season. The franchise wins record was easily in reach during the season's final week, with the Cardinals sitting at 103–52. But St. Louis stumbled to a 2–5 record, ending the season with a record of 105–57—tying the mark for the second-highest win total in team history.

"[I'd be] hard pressed to find many teams that [the 2004 team] can compare to, ever," Woody Williams says. "The lineup we had, the defense we played, the pitching was good. None of us were really that overpowering, but at the same time, we all knew how to pitch. We had a good bullpen and there weren't a whole lot of holes."

Pujols finished the year hitting .331 with 46 homers (a career-high at that point) and 123 RBIs. His 133 runs scored led the league, as did his 389 total bases. Though his statistics were certainly MVP-worthy, Pujols again lost out on the award to Barry Bonds after the season ended, with Adrián Beltré of the Dodgers finishing second (.334, 48 HR, 121 RBIs) and Pujols placing third. Though Bonds' Giants failed to make the postseason, voters were swayed more by his .609 on-base percentage, .812 slugging percentage and 232 walks than they were by San Francisco's failures around him. Rolen and Edmonds followed Pujols to round out the top five. Pujols also won the third Silver Slugger of his career.

But more important to Pujols than the hardware he would win at season's end was the postseason. The last time the team had won 105 games—in 1944—the Cardinals beat their crosstown rival St. Louis Browns in the World Series. So fans were expecting much from the team as the playoffs ramped up, with the Cardinals set to face the Los Angeles Dodgers, champions of the National League West, in the first round. Thus far in his career, postseason play had been one of Pujols' weaknesses. In thirteen games, he had hit only .213 with two home runs and seven RBIs. He would remedy that quickly.

In the bottom of the first inning of game one of the National League Division Series, Pujols took Odalis Pérez deep to give the Cardinals a 1–0 lead. In the sixth inning, Pujols followed a Larry Walker homer with a single to center. He then scored on a Renteria double, and the inning ended with the Redbirds holding a commanding 6–0 lead. St. Louis took the opener 8–3, and won game two by the same score. Los Angeles rebounded to take game three 4–0, as Jose Lima stymied the St. Louis offense, setting up the fourth game in the best-of-five series and what would prove to be one of the most dramatic moments of Pujols' young career.

With the score tied 2–2 in the fourth inning, Pujols stepped in to face Wilson Alvarez with two outs and two on. Alvarez quickly fell behind 2–0, and appeared to want little to do with the Cardinals slugger. Pujols took the third pitch for a called strike, and then watched ball three go by. Though first base wasn't open, walking Pujols wouldn't have been the end of the world for the Dodgers.

But Alvarez didn't take that course of action. Instead, he fired a fastball on the inner half of the plate that Pujols lifted over the left field fence for a three-run dinger that sank the spirits of the Dodgers and their fans alike. An

RBI single from Pujols in the seventh inning increased the St. Louis lead to 6–2, which proved to be the final.

"So far, I'd say this was the best moment of my career," Pujols said after the game. "We lost Game 3. We were shut down. That doesn't happen very often to us. So we had to respond the way the Cardinals have all season. I was happy to come through. It was the biggest hit for me, so far. Hopefully, there's a lot more where that came from. We can't stop now. This was one step."

For the series, Pujols hit .333 with two home runs and five RBIs. He was just warming up.

The win set up a showdown between the Cardinals and the wildcard Astros, who had finished thirteen games behind the Cardinals in the NL Central but had beaten the Braves in five games in their NLDS matchup. The Astros had bolstered their contingent of Killer B's down the stretch by the trade deadline acquisition of outfielder Carlos Beltrán. They also had Jeff Kent, who didn't fit with the Killer B's description, but who nonetheless was the team's RBI leader in 2004.

With Clemens having pitched in game four of the NLDS and Roy Oswalt going in game five, St. Louis caught a break. The two Houston aces weren't available to start the next series, so the Cardinals opened against Brandon Backe instead. As he did in the NLDS, Pujols made his presence felt early. Beltran had given the Astros a quick 2–0 lead in the first inning of game one with a two-run shot off St. Louis starter Woody Williams, but Pujols answered in the bottom of the inning with a crucial game-tying, two-run, opposite-field blast of his own.

The game was tied again in the sixth, 4–4, when the Cardinals pounced for six runs. Pujols walked in the inning and scored on a three-run double by Edmonds that gave the St. Louis pitchers all the runs they would need, as the Cards took the opener 10–7. In game two, Houston led 3–0 in the fifth when a two-run Larry Walker homer pulled St. Louis to within one. Pujols then walked and scored on a two-run blast from Rolen, giving the Cardinals the lead.

The Astros threatened to regain the lead in the sixth when José Vizcaino and Brad Ausmus led off with consecutive singles. Eric Bruntlett laid down a sacrifice bunt in front of the plate, attempting to move the two runners to second and third. Pujols, charging from first on the play, barehanded the ball and alertly threw to Rolen at third base to force Vizcaino and keep runners at first and second. Kiko Calero was able to pitch out of the jam.

"On Pujols' play, we kind of knew [Houston was bunting]," St. Louis third base coach José Oquendo said. "I wish he would have used his glove because he had plenty of time. But that's Pujols for you. He gets a little excited. He forgets he has that glove on his hand. He wants to catch it with his teeth."

With the game tied at 4 in the seventh, Pujols led off the inning against Dan Miceli by driving a pitch over the left field wall to give St. Louis the lead. When Rolen followed with his own homer to put St. Louis up 6–4, it became the first time ever that Cardinals players had hit back-to-back home runs in the postseason. Jason Isringhausen preserved the lead in the ninth to give St. Louis a 2–0 lead in the series.

Houston won game three behind Clemens (Pujols went 1-for-4), and evened the series by taking game four 6–5, despite a 3-for-4 night from Pujols, including a home run and three RBIs. Houston closer Brad Lidge retired Pujols on a warning track fly ball in the top of the ninth with one out and Larry Walker on first. Backe exacted his revenge in game five, giving up only one hit in eight innings, as the Astros won the game in the bottom of the ninth on a three-run homer by Kent off Isringhausen, giving Houston a 3–2 lead in the series as it headed back to St. Louis.

The Cardinals stood on the brink of elimination as game six opened, and a solo Lance Berkman homer in the top of the first off Matt Morris did little to engender optimism from St. Louis about the game's outcome. But then Pujols struck a mighty blow in the bottom of the inning—a two-run bomb off Pete Munro to give St. Louis the lead and hope to Cardinal Nation.

An RBI double from Bagwell tied the game in the third. Pujols doubled to lead off the fourth and scored on a two-run single by Renteria that put St. Louis back on top, 4–2. The Cardinals still led 4–3 in the ninth, but Bagwell tied the score on an RBI single off Isringhausen that sent the game into extra innings. The score remained tied in the twelfth, when Pujols led off the inning with a walk and scored on a dramatic game-winning Edmonds home run that forced a seventh and deciding game—which the Cardinals won on Rolen's homer off Clemens after Pujols' RBI double had tied it.

"It's just a blessing," Pujols said in *USA Today* about his postseason performance. "Every time I go out there, it's to glorify my God. I don't care about who's watching me. I know there are 52,000 people watching me play. I just want to do my job, not try to do too much."

Pujols earned National League Championship Series MVP honors, hitting .500 (14-for-28) with four homers, nine RBIs, and an NLCS-record twenty-five total bases. That was all fine and good, but Pujols still had unfinished business at hand—a World Series against Boston. The Red Sox had done the impossible in the ALCS, coming back from a 3–0 deficit against the hated New York Yankees to win four straight in one of the greatest postseason series ever.

A rematch of the 1967 World Series, in which the Cardinals beat Boston in seven games, the 2004 World Series had the makings of a classic. Baseball's winningest team, the Cardinals, with a powerful offense and sparkling defense, against the Red Sox, trying to win their first World Series since 1918 and forever put an end to the blasted Curse of the Bambino. Pujols, Rolen, Edmonds, and Walker against Manny Ramirez, David Ortiz, Curt Schilling, and Pedro Martinez.

But what may have looked compelling on paper turned out to be a flop, and a disaster for the Cardinals. Boston took a sloppy, error-filled game one, 11–9. Pujols went 0-for-3. Game two: Boston won 6–2. Pujols went 3-for-4, but the rest of the St. Louis lineup managed only two hits. Game three: another Boston win, 4–1. Pujols, 1-for-4, one of only four St. Louis hits. Game four: 3–0 Red Sox, completing the sweep. Pujols again went 1-for-4, and the Cardinals again collected only four hits.

The fearsome threesome of Pujols, Rolen, and Edmonds—the trio that had provided so much life in the St. Louis offense over the entire season—went a combined 6-for-45 over the four games (an average of .133). Pujols, though he drove in no runs in the series, had five of those six hits. Rolen went hitless in fifteen at-bats, while Edmonds knocked just one hit in fifteen at-bats. Credit the Boston pitching staff for doing a number on the Cardinals' best bats. Credit the Red Sox for timely hitting. The fact remains that the Cardinals proved unthreatening in the 2004 World Series because they got no production at all from the ones who had provided it all season long.

"That's the way it goes; that's part of the game," Pujols said in the *New York Times*. "If you look at Manny Ramirez, he didn't get any RBIs the last series. I don't think they pitched so tough. We just hit some balls good and they made some good plays. It's over, what can you do? You can't say you want that pitch back, because it's over."

Disappointed at the outcome of the World Series, Pujols would spend the off-season preparing for a project that would make a lasting difference in people's lives. As significant as his accomplishments on the baseball field were, Pujols, along with his wife Deidre, was about to do something far greater.

CHAPTER FIFTEEN

YOU SHALL RAISE UP THE FOUNDATIONS

Deidre and I have always felt that this was God's calling on our lives, and that His plan for our lives went far beyond what I could do in baseball.
—Albert Pujols, May 5, 2005

On the fifth day of the fifth month of 2005, the man who wore number five on his St. Louis Cardinals jersey stood on a podium alongside his wife to announce the launch of the Pujols Family Foundation. "I want to hit a grand slam on the field," Pujols said, "but this is my grand slam that I want to hit this year."

The initial recipients of the foundation's support were the Down Syndrome Association of Greater St. Louis and the *Orfanato Niños de Cristo* orphanage in the Dominican Republic.

Dee Dee, displaying a generous smile, said, "Going into our fifth year here in the big leagues, we felt like it was time we owned something that would be able to be ours and that we could share with everyone on this continent and all across the world. Hopefully, it will get that big one day."

Todd Perry, CEO of the foundation, remembers well the process that went into its establishment. "Albert had just signed his new contract [seven years, $100 million], and they were being pulled in so many different directions," he says. "Every organization, every charity, every ministry—everybody wanted a piece of Albert. And that's on the private sector side of things."

The Pujolses became frustrated with the media's apparent lack of desire to write about Albert's faith. Sportswriters had marching orders to cover the on-field exploits, but ended up leaving Pujols' Christianity on the bench.

"Every reporter wanted to throw a microphone in Albert's face and talk about home runs and RBIs," Perry says. "If he wanted to talk about Isabella, or something that was going on his life or his faith, it wound up on the cutting room floor. They didn't want to go there. So Albert became very withdrawn and reclusive. He thought the public really just wanted to see one side of him."

Meanwhile, Dee Dee was beginning to put a public voice to her convictions. "Dee Dee was all about being an advocate for Down syndrome, talking about the things that she cared about, talking about their faith and their relationship with the Lord," Perry says. "The people that were hearing it were responding to the message. But it was still difficult for Albert and Dee Dee to get their voice out. Because of the huge baseball story, there was a lid on the rest of the story of their life."

Perry says that though the Pujolses were writing checks in support of various causes, they wanted to have more focus and direction. Perry knew there was a better way to go about it.

"That was the main thing that kick-started the idea in the back of my head," he says. "I thought they should put together some type of charitable trust or foundation so that the things they stood for and what they believed in would become public knowledge. Then they could say, 'These are the things we will support with 100 percent of our time and our effort and our heart.'"

Perry drafted a proposal in the spring of 2004, but kept missing the right opportunity to present it to them. At the 2004 Christian Family Day at the ballpark, Perry carried the proposal with him to a luncheon where the Pujolses were to be. Dee Dee came in, but there was no Albert.

Perry remembers that as Dee Dee rose to speak, she became very vulnerable and said, "I want you to pray for us and especially Albert."

"Dee Dee started talking about how Albert was becoming kind of reclusive," Perry recalls. "The things that they cared about—their voice and their faith—were being shouted down by all the noise about him being a baseball player. She said that Albert was losing motivation to talk about things that were important to him because it was almost as if nobody was hearing him."

As Perry listened to her plea for prayer, he thought of the proposal tucked away in his briefcase and thought, "Dee Dee, I've got it right here." He approached her and said, "I've got what you've been praying for."

A week later, Dee Dee came by Perry's office and sat down to listen to his ideas. "For half an hour, I just walked her through the proposal," Perry said. "If you know Dee Dee, for her to sit anywhere for half an hour and not say anything—that was the first miracle that happened. As I finished, she looked up and said, 'This is what we've been praying for.'"

In reflecting on the harmony of how things came together, Perry says, "God's timing is perfect. He's got me over here working on something, even while he has the Pujolses over there doing their things, and we really had no idea what's going on in each other's hearts. But when we came together, it fit perfectly."

Though this initial meeting went well, some drama unfolded in the decision-making process, especially in Perry's life. Dee Dee took the proposal to Albert to talk and pray it over, but it would be several weeks of silence before Perry had any further contact.

Although Perry enjoyed a successful career in marketing, his company informed him of a proposed move that would take Perry and his family right out of St. Louis. Perry recounts, "Somewhere in the midst of all this, my boss took me to lunch and asked, 'How do you feel about living in Kansas?'"

As the executive team moved to Kansas, Perry took a severance package and remained in St. Louis.

"I felt like I was led to stay here," Perry says, "and I felt like this was something we could do together. But there was no movement on it, so I turned up the heat a bit by saying, 'I'm going to be out of a job. Let's make this happen.'

"I had to make sure this wasn't about me, or that this wasn't about my working in Major League Baseball—a George Costanza thing," he says. "That was the time when I honestly got to the point where I prayed, 'God, you build it or kill it. I am completely resolved about the outcome.' Once I really got to the point where I prayed that and meant it, that is when things started turning."

Pujols invited Perry to his house to talk, and had many questions to ask. "You could tell that he had thought about the potholes and the things we hadn't really buttoned up," Perry says.

A few days later, Dee Dee called and said, "Let's do it."

"That was an awesome day," Perry says. "You knew God had a plan, and now you are part of it, and it's bigger than you."

Though Perry had no experience running a nonprofit, he quickly assembled a team of advisors, attorneys, and accountants. The original thought was to launch the foundation on Opening Day of the 2005 season—always a momentous time of celebration and fanfare in St. Louis. But with 2005 set to be the last year the team would play in old Busch Stadium, the launch would get lost in the shuffle of the other events from the day.

So they pushed the date back a few weeks, only to have that date bumped too. Finally, they worked out a day that stuck—the first Thursday of May—05/05/05.

"I promise you, I had no idea until I got to the ballpark," Perry says, "Even now, when I talk about it, this overwhelming peace of God's timing comes over me, that from the foundation of the earth, this was meant to be—on this date and at this time. It absolutely boggles my mind."

The Pujols Family Foundation (PFF) mission statement reads: "To live and share our commitment to *faith*, *family* and *others*." This threefold mission builds on the teaching of Jesus who, when asked, "Teacher, which is the great commandment in the Law?" answered:"You shall love the Lord your God with all your heart and with all your soul and with all your mind. This is the great and first commandment. And a second is like it: You shall love your neighbor as yourself" (Matthew 22:36–39).

The Pujolses live out the first command—love the Lord your God—by walking in relationship with Jesus Christ their Lord. They state, "Our faith in Jesus Christ is the central point of our individual lives, our marriage, family and Foundation. Take Jesus Christ and faith in Him out of the equation and all those other things would not exist."

They live out the second command—love your neighbor—through the work and mission of the foundation. But who are the neighbors of the Pujolses?

With a world full of hurting people in need of love and compassion, the Pujolses rightly understand that one family cannot heal all hurts. Perry says, "We wish the best for the rest of the charities, but we can't be everything to everyone."

Though the Pujolses cannot meet the needs of everyone, they *can* reach out and touch the lives of people who, through God's providence, are already intertwined with their own. "When everything is stripped away," Perry says, "these are the causes that Albert and Deidre are most passionate about, for obvious reasons." Hence, the official purpose of PFF states: "The Pujols Family Foundation, an IRS 501(c)(3) organization benefiting people with (a) Down syndrome (b) disabilities and/or life threatening illnesses as well as (c) children and families living in impoverished conditions in the Dominican Republic." PFF's mission to people with disabilities and Down syndrome, flowing from the love and care the Pujolses have for their own daughter Isabella, is described in chapter 19, while chapter 23 tells the story of PFF's work in Albert's native homeland, the Dominican Republic.

Financial support for PFF comes from several sources. First, Albert and Dee Dee provide sizable amounts of annual funds directly. Second, individual donors contribute online or with a check in the mail. Upon the death of a loved one, many St. Louis-area families have directed donations be sent to PFF, "in lieu of flowers."

And kids pitch in with enthusiasm too. Four youngsters in the St. Louis suburbs sold lemonade and raised $107. Leah Hammann, a young lady who has Down syndrome, holds a special birthday party for herself, asking her friends to skip buying her a present and instead to make a donation to PFF. "Each year she gives up her birthday presents so that we might expand our programs," Perry says. "That's what I call a very special person!"

The foundation also throws memorable fund-raising events like golf tournaments and Christmas banquets. These events bring out a crowd of supporters and a lineup of celebrities and sports legends like Stan Musial, Lou Brock, Orlando Cepeda, and Meadowlark Lemon.

Donated items are sold through both silent and live auctions, and grand displays of generosity are common. At the 2009 "O Night Divine" Christmas banquet, Chicago White Sox ace pitcher Mark Buehrle cast the winning bid of $10,000 for a La Russa–donated "Manage the Cardinals for a Day in Spring Training" event, only to turn around and give it away to a mother and daughter who are friends of the Pujolses. At the 2006 event, Albert bid on and won a Rolex watch, before reaching over and giving it away to his friend Rene Knott, sports director for local NBC affiliate KSDK and the guest auctioneer at the event.

Even larger numbers of everyday people support the work of PFF through means other than financial—prayer, e-mails, letters. At times, so much correspondence comes in that it is difficult to keep up with it all. But that is a good problem to have when you are running a nonprofit organization. Perry says, "I've really been amazed at the public's perception, the public's understanding, of what we're trying to do."

Pujols' life path looks to include a trip to baseball's Hall of Fame. Therefore, barring injuries, he is only halfway through his career as a professional athlete. But what then? How will Pujols' retirement from baseball affect the work that he and Dee Dee do through PFF?

Jan Mueller, a St. Louis–area doctor who traveled on medical-mission trips with PFF, recalls one afternoon in the Dominican Republic: "There was a guy talking to Albert, interviewing him about the work we were doing. I was treating the kids but was close enough to hear what they were saying. The man asked Albert a question and Albert looked up and he said, 'What people don't understand is that this work is what I've been put on earth to do, and when baseball's gone and I'm not famous, I'm still going to be doing this work because this is what God's called me to do.'"

By all accounts, it appears that Albert and Dee Dee have a long-term perspective to their PFF investments, living out the words of Jesus: "Do not lay up for yourselves treasures on earth, where moth and rust destroy and where thieves break in and steal, but lay up for yourselves treasures in heaven, where neither moth nor rust destroys and where thieves do not break in and steal. For where your treasure is, there your heart will be also" (Matthew 6:19–21).

CHAPTER SIXTEEN

MVP

It's a great feeling. But you still need to be humble.
You can't let this award take you too high.
—Albert Pujols, November 16, 2005

The atmosphere on the Houston Astros' flight to St. Louis after game five of the 2005 National League Championship Series was less than jovial, and the team needed the levity that catcher Brad Ausmus would soon provide. After all, the Astros didn't even expect to be on that plane. They didn't want to be on that plane, as they'd thought they had the series won in Houston. But instead of celebrating a trip to the World Series, they were on their way to St. Louis to play the Cardinals yet again. Pujols had seen to that the day before, in quite possibly the most memorable plate appearance of his career.

The Astros had led the Cardinals 3–1 in the NLCS, and in game five carried a 4–2 lead into the top of the ninth inning with their stud closer, Brad Lidge, on the mound. Lidge had been deadly in 2005, racking up forty-two saves with a stingy 2.29 ERA. And sure enough, he was proving to be unhittable in the ninth. He fanned John Rodriguez. He fanned John Mabry.

Two outs, nobody on. The Astros had every reason to think that the game and the series were theirs.

But then David Eckstein poked a two-strike single to left and Jim Edmonds walked, bringing Pujols—the go-ahead run—to the plate. The Houston fans, 43,470 strong, were on their feet, ready for Lidge to retire the slugging first baseman and end the series right then and there. St. Louis fans were praying for a miracle. The 2005 season was the last for Busch Stadium, which had been home to the Cardinals since 1966, and Cardinal Nation wanted nothing more than for Pujols to send his team back home for one last celebration at the old ballpark.

Lidge wound up and delivered to Pujols. A slider, swing, and a miss. Lidge ahead in the count, and looking strong. On his second pitch, however, Pujols looked stronger. He crushed a second Lidge slider up in the zone, blasting it into orbit. Viewers watching the game on TV could clearly see Houston pitcher Andy Pettitte in the Houston dugout mouthing the words, "Oh my gosh." The towering shot bounced off the railroad tracks high above the wall in left field as Minute Maid Park fell silent, stunned at the monstrous blow that Pujols had just delivered. Lidge hung his head behind the mound as Pujols rounded the bases. Pujols crossed home plate, pointing heavenward as is his custom after going deep. The Cardinals led 5–4, and would shut down the Astros in the bottom of the ninth to send the NLCS back to St. Louis for at least one more game at Busch.

The next day, as the Astros traveled to St. Louis, Ausmus decided to have some fun at Lidge's expense. He coaxed the pilot into making an announcement once the plane had taken off.

"If you'll look out the windows on the left side of the plane, you'll notice that Albert Pujols home run ball," the pilot joked.

The home run off Lidge was the signature swing for Pujols during the 2005 season, which began with lingering questions about the health and stability of Pujols' left foot. After suffering through much of the 2004 campaign with the painful plantar fasciitis condition, Pujols had at first expected to undergo surgery late in 2004 to help alleviate his suffering. The procedure would have left him in a cast for about six weeks, giving him ample time to recover ahead of spring training. But Pujols instead chose a noninvasive option, using high-frequency sonar as treatment.

The procedure helped at first, but after a few weeks, the pain gradually returned, forcing Pujols to undergo a second procedure that left him improved and ready for the start of spring training. Still, the condition left St. Louis fans at least a little concerned about how he would hold up over another full season.

"If it comes to that point again—that I'm going through the pain that I went through last year—I don't think I'll be able to do it," Pujols told the *Post-Dispatch*. "I don't want to go through that pain. I went through that pain once, and I don't think I can do it again. It's not good for my body."

While Pujols' foot may have been one of the questions for the team as it prepared for a new season, the middle of the St. Louis lineup wasn't. Pujols, Rolen, Edmonds, and now Larry Walker were back for 2005 after leading the Cardinals to 105 wins in 2004, but the supporting cast around them had changed considerably. Edgar Renteria, Mike Matheny, Tony Womack, and Woody Williams had all departed via free agency. Newcomers included David Eckstein at shortstop, Mark Grudzielanek at second base, rookie Yadier Molina at catcher, and Mark Mulder moving into the rotation after being acquired from Oakland in exchange for Dan Haren.

Pujols' time in spring training was spent doing more than just focusing on his own preparation for the upcoming season. His mentoring of younger players in the Cardinals system, especially young Latin American players, some of whom didn't speak much English, continued to develop.

"I think the main thing is I lived that," Pujols told the *Post-Dispatch*. "I was there [in the Dominican Republic] once and I know what it takes. I know what it is and how tough it is to come here knowing no English. Anything they need I'll try to make it available to them. If I don't have it, I'll try to get it. You don't need to give money to these kids. You just need to encourage them to keep working hard and take advantage of the opportunities they get."

Pujols has a reputation for nurturing the inexperienced Latin players on the team, even providing them with equipment, and that reputation began early in his career. It's not something that his contract requires of him, or something he does because he thinks it's expected of him. He does it because his heart motivates him to do so.

"I want to help those kids out," Pujols said. "I love the game. You play for little kids and hopefully to make a good name for yourself. It's not about getting credit."

Pujols and the Cardinals got off to a winning start in 2005, with Pujols collecting two hits in the season-opening win against Houston. After going 3–4 in their first seven games, the Cardinals headed to Milwaukee for a three-game set against the Brewers April 15 through 17. Pujols homered off Ben Sheets in the fourth inning of the first game, his second home run of the season, to break a scoreless tie in a 3–0 St. Louis win. His next time to the plate, Pujols struck out for the first time since spring training began—a string of 101 straight plate appearances without whiffing.

He homered again the next day to help the Cardinals to a 5–3 victory that would move them into first place by half a game. They would stay in that position the rest of the season, cruising to the National League Central title for the second straight year and the third time in the last four seasons. The Cardinals led the division by eleven and a half games at the All-Star break and by as many as sixteen games in the second half. The season was, in every way, a blowout for St. Louis.

In April, Pujols added another entry to his ever-expanding résumé—his photo on a Wheaties box, an honor that would come again in 2010.

"It's like winning an MVP award," Pujols said. "It's exciting. It's awesome. There are a lot of great players out there that Wheaties could have picked, and they chose me. It's an honor. It's a great day."

Pujols may have considered his appearance on Wheaties akin to winning a Most Valuable Player award, but that was one honor that had eluded him so far in his young career. In 2005, he was intent on changing that. Facing the Braves on April 29, Pujols took Tim Hudson deep in the fifth inning with a two-run pop that broke a 4–4 tie. The homer proved the game winner, and the hit extended a Pujols hitting streak to ten games. Overall in April, Pujols hit safely in twenty of the team's twenty-two games en route to a .322 batting average at the end of the month, to go along with six home runs and nineteen RBIs.

Pujols continued his mastery of Los Angeles Dodgers pitcher Odalis Pérez (he was 6-for-12 against Pérez previously) in a May 9 game during which he jacked two home runs—a solo shot in the first and a three-run bomb in the fifth—and drove in all four St. Louis runs in a 4–2 win that moved the

Cardinals to nine games over .500 and a five-game lead in the division. The two hits improved Pujols' season batting average to .341.

The next day, Rolen collided with Dodgers first baseman Hee Seop Choi and injured his shoulder. Though the injury at first wasn't considered to be serious, Rolen went on the disabled list and ended up missing more than a month. As much as he was carrying the Cardinals offensively, Pujols would have to do even more with Rolen sidelined. He proved to be up for the task.

Later that month, facing Pittsburgh and trailing 1–0 in the sixth inning, with Walker on first and Molina on third, Pujols stepped in to face Pirates hurler Dave Williams, who had fanned Pujols in two previous at-bats that afternoon. A similar fate appeared to be in store for the Cardinals first baseman when Williams jumped ahead in the count 0–2. Pujols stayed alive by fouling off a couple of pitches, then lined a double to the left field wall that scored both Walker and Molina. St. Louis went on to win the game 4–2, and the two RBIs moved Pujols into a tie for the league lead with thirty-nine.

"It doesn't matter what happened before," Walker told the *Post-Dispatch*. "His name is Albert Pujols. That speaks volumes right there. You can strike him out twice, get him 0–2 but he still has that one strike to beat you."

The clutch at-bat by Pujols didn't come without a cost. The final foul ball that Pujols smoked into the stands beyond third base struck two-year-old Bryson King in the forehead. An ambulance arrived and carted Bryson to St. Louis Children's Hospital, where he was treated for a fractured skull and released a couple of days later. But before he went home, Bryson got a visit from Pujols, who came bearing a box of baseball treasures—two game-used batting gloves, a pair of his cleats, an autographed bat, autographed hat, autographed balls, and autographed baseball card.

In a May 30 game against Colorado, the Rockies led 3–1 in the seventh inning. Eckstein drew a two-out walk and Roger Cedeño singled ahead of Pujols, who nailed a Jay Witasick pitch over the left-field wall for a three-run homer (his thirteenth of the season), giving St. Louis a lead that would hold up. Pujols' bat heated up even more in June, when he hit .370 and began a seventeen-game hitting streak. The Cardinals went 11–6 during the duration of that streak and increased their division lead to twelve and a half games.

Pujols was hitting .337 with twenty-two homers and sixty-nine RBIs at the All-Star break in mid-July. The Cubs' Derrek Lee was having a career year and won the fan balloting at first base, but La Russa named Pujols to the team as the starting DH—marking the fourth position at which Pujols would play in an All-Star Game. In Detroit's Comerica Park, Pujols had one hit in two at-bats in the 2005 midsummer classic.

The first game after the break was more of the same for the Cardinals and Pujols as they faced the rival Astros. With the game tied 2–2 in the top of the thirteenth inning, Houston's Mike Lamb stroked an RBI single off Ray King to give Houston a 3–2 lead. Pujols responded in the bottom of the inning with a game-winning, two-run homer.

In late July, the Cardinals headed west for a six-game road trip against the Padres and Dodgers. The opener against San Diego brought a matchup against former St. Louis pitcher Woody Williams—one that Pujols had been anticipating since the previous year when he'd asked Williams how he would pitch against him if Williams left St. Louis for another team.

"I told him I was going to pound him inside," Williams says. "He looked at me and smiled, and I said, 'I'm not joking.' The first time I faced him I threw one right down the middle and he popped it up. Then the next time I tried to pitch him inside and he hit one about 440 feet to left-center at Petco, which is almost unheard of."

When Pujols slammed his thirtieth homer of the season August 5 off John Smoltz, he became the first player in major league history to hit at least thirty home runs in each of his first five seasons. When he tripled in So Taguchi on August 31, he became only the fourth player (Ted Williams, Joe DiMaggio, and Al Simmons being the others) to have at least one hundred RBIs in each of his first five seasons.

Those were the bright spots in an otherwise forgettable month for Pujols. With the Cardinals plagued by injuries to some key players down the stretch—including Rolen, Walker, and Sanders—and with Edmonds having a less-than-stellar season, Pujols felt compelled to expand his strike zone and do more to carry the team himself. He frequently swung at pitches he normally would have taken, in an effort to be the run-producing machine the team expected him to be. As a result, his stats in August suffered. Though not abysmal, his .287 average on the month was a bit off the norm that Pujols had established for himself.

His average rebounded a bit in September, and when he hit his fortieth homer of the season (a grand slam off Cincinnati's Matt Belisle), he became the third youngest player in the game's history to hit 200 homers—at 25 years, 257 days old. Only Mel Ott (25 years, 144 days) and Eddie Mathews (25 years, 242 days) achieved the feat at a younger age. Pujols also became only the second player in Cardinals history to belt forty home runs while stealing fifteen bases in a season—Rogers Hornsby, the great Rajah, was the first to accomplish that when he hit forty-two homers and swiped seventeen bases in 1922.

Pujols finished the season hitting .330 (second in the league to Lee's .335) with forty-one home runs and 117 RBIs, plus a surprising sixteen stolen bases. His 129 runs scored led the league, and Pujols was the leading contender for his first MVP award, with Atlanta's Andruw Jones and the Cubs' Lee also strong candidates. Lee, with forty-six homers and 107 RBIs, had been a threat to win the Triple Crown until late in the year. Jones, meanwhile, led the league with fifty-one homers and 128 RBIs, and many voters seemed content to overlook his mediocre .263 batting average and his horrible .207 batting average with runners in scoring position.

But before that announcement came, the Cardinals had the playoffs before them. The team, with a 100–62 record on the year, rolled to the division crown by an eleven-game margin over the Astros, whose 89–73 mark was good for the wild card. While Houston would face Atlanta in the division series, the Cardinals were pitted against the Padres, champions of the NL West. The National League West had proved to be baseball's worst division in 2005, and the Padres were able to win it despite a lackluster 82–80 record.

The Cardinals certainly appeared to have the advantage on paper, and that edge was quickly apparent on the field as well. They pummeled Jake Peavy for eight runs in a series opening win (Pujols went 1-for-3 with two runs scored), and took a 2–0 series lead after a 6–2 win in game two (Pujols went 2-for-3 with an RBI and one run scored). Woody Williams faced his former St. Louis teammates in game three, and was reminded of the difficulty in pitching to Pujols.

In the top of the first inning, with Eckstein on first and one out, Williams intended to pitch around Pujols. Williams had gone 3–0 on him and tossed his fourth pitch eight inches outside. Pujols reached out and drilled it into the gap in right-center field for a run-scoring double.

"I wasn't even trying to pitch to the guy, and he's standing on second base," Williams says.

The Cardinals torched Williams for five runs in less than two innings en route to a 7–4 win and a sweep of the Padres. With the Astros disposing of the Braves in four games, the National League Championship Series would be a rematch of the 2004 version featuring the two division rivals. Beltran and Kent were gone from the Astros, but the Killer B's of Bagwell, Biggio, and Berkman were still around, as were the rotation anchors of Clemens, Oswalt, and Pettitte.

St. Louis pounced on Pettitte early in game one, scoring twice in the first inning and adding another run in the second. Pujols singled in Eckstein in the fifth to give the Cardinals a 5–0 lead in a game they would win 5–3.

In the second game, with Houston leading 2–0 in the sixth, Pujols led off the inning with a solo shot off Oswalt to cut the lead in half. But that would be the only run St. Louis would score. The Astros evened the series as it headed to Houston for the next three games.

Pujols collected two hits off Clemens in game three, but Lidge retired Eckstein in the ninth with the tying run on base to preserve a 4–3 win for Houston. Pujols broke a scoreless tie in game four with a sacrifice fly that scored Eckstein in the fourth inning, but Jason Lane homered the next inning to knot the game 1–1. With the Astros holding a 2–1 lead in the ninth, Pujols led off with a single off Lidge that raised his series batting average to .478. When Walker followed with a single that moved Pujols to third base, the Cardinals were poised to tie the game—or better. But Sanders chopped one to third base and Houston's Morgan Ensberg fired home to nail Pujols, who was trying to score on the play. John Mabry then grounded into a game-ending double play that left the Cardinals facing a 3–1 deficit in the series.

But Pujols wouldn't let the Cardinals despair. "Can we pull off a miracle?" Pujols asked after game four. "Of course we can. We just need to win one game. If we can do that, if we can just get past tomorrow, it puts all the pressure on them."

The probability of that looked slim, especially after Berkman did his part in the seventh inning of game five. With the Cardinals leading 2–1, Berkman banged a three-run homer off Chris Carpenter that electrified the hometown fans. The Astros could taste the World Series—their first World Series ever.

Clubhouse attendants had begun hanging plastic to protect the players' lockers from the champagne that would cascade down in the postgame celebration. Houston fans buzzed with anticipation, ready to explode in delirious excitement once their team had shut down the Cardinals for two more innings.

Everything was going according to script for Houston until the ninth, when, with two outs, Lidge gave up the single to Eckstein and the walk to Edmonds, setting up the showdown with Pujols, who was hitless on the night. Pujols was praying to have a chance at the plate.

"Just give me the strength, Lord, to get one at-bat and hopefully I can come through for my teammates," he said.

Pujols' prayers were answered, as he blasted his dramatic home run to send the series back to St. Louis. "When I hit it, it was like, 'Wow. I don't believe I did that,'" he said after the game. "It's the best hit I've had in my career. Hopefully, I'll get many more in this series and some more in the World Series. You're facing the best closer in the game. It doesn't get any better than that."

As elated as the Cardinals were with their unlikely win, they still had a challenging task to face. Yes, Pujols had given Busch Stadium at least one more game before the old ballpark would be demolished. Oswalt was intent on making sure that one game was all it would be. The starting pitcher for the Astros in game six, Oswalt was nearly untouchable. The magic that the Cardinals had tapped in game five was nowhere to be found again. Pujols went 0-for-4, and the entire lineup managed only four hits as Houston would not be denied its first World Series berth. The lights went out at Busch Stadium that night for the last time.

"It's tough to lose," Pujols said. "Baseball is something you live and breathe. And because this is it for the stadium, it's sad. We wish we could have played one more World Series here."

Consolation came about a month later, when on November 15 the announcement came that the Baseball Writers' Association of America had voted Pujols the National League's Most Valuable Player. Pujols' 378 points and eighteen first-place votes surpassed Andruw Jones' 351 points and thirteen first-place votes. After four seasons of finishing in the top five, 2005 was the year for Pujols to claim baseball's most coveted individual honor. Bernie Miklasz of the *St. Louis Post-Dispatch* described the scene:

> Last season, Deidre Pujols surprised her husband with the gift of a new car to celebrate the Cardinals' 2004 National League pennant. On Tuesday, after he received the overdue honor of his first NL Most Valuable Player Award, Albert Pujols wondered what Deidre had in store for him this time. Actually, Deidre was holding the most precious gift as she sat to the side, watching Albert accept the MVP honor: It was their newborn daughter, Sophia, who wore a "Daddy's Girl" shirt as she nestled in her mother's arms. "This is it," Deidre said with a warm smile. "She is Albert's present." Little Sophia was born Nov. 5. Her father wears No. 5. And, of course, Pujols finally won the MVP in his fifth big-league season. "We obviously like the number 5 in our family," Deidre said.

The announcement came on the most fitting of days, noted the *Belleville News Democrat*'s Joe Ostermeier—the Catholic feast day of St. Albert the Great.

"I slept two hours last night," Pujols said the day of the announcement. "I couldn't wait for this moment. When I got that call, it felt almost like that home run I hit against Brad Lidge. Everyone was calling saying how much I deserved that. It's a great feeling. But you still need to be humble. You can't let this award take you too high."

As pleased as Pujols and the Cardinals were with his first MVP, the award provided only a small dulling of the pain inflicted by the Astros in their upset win over St. Louis in the NLCS. The Cardinals had put together two of the best seasons in franchise history in 2004 and 2005, with no championship to show for it. And for Pujols, that was the barometer of his success in baseball. "The thing I want to appreciate at the end of my career is a championship ring," Pujols had said during the 2005 season. He'd have to wait for 2006 to try it again.

CHAPTER SEVENTEEN

YOU WILL BE MY WITNESSES

Baseball is simply my platform to elevate Jesus Christ, my Lord and Savior.
—*Albert Pujols*

Jordan Henderson was a sixteen-year-old who brimmed with baseball ability and college aspirations. But in July of 2007, the teen from Tennessee died in a car wreck. His parents, Doris and Ken Frizzell, grieved and wept as any parent would do in the face of such loss.

In making funeral preparations for Jordan, a folded and worn piece of paper was pulled from his wallet. It was a "My Story" feature about Albert Pujols, clipped from *Sharing the Victory*, a magazine produced by the Fellowship of Christian Athletes. In just a few paragraphs, Pujols explains why his relationship with God is "more important than anything I could ever do in baseball." He appeals to readers to "accept Him as your Lord and Savior, and you will have eternal life and peace here on Earth."

The local paper, the *Daily News Journal*, reported that a thousand copies of the Pujols piece were distributed at Henderson's funeral. Word about the story got around, and Todd Perry made a few phone calls. Doris and Ken were brought to a Cardinals game and showered with love by Albert and Dee Dee.

The following year, the entire team for which Jordan had played was brought to Busch Stadium for a special day on the field, touring the clubhouse, and watching the game from the owner's suite. The *Daily News Journal* story said that the team "joined Pujols, the Frizzells and Riverdale parent Greg Hart outside the Cardinals locker room for a prayer."

"Make sure that you stand up for Christ," Pujols said that night. "If you look at the whole picture, hopefully some of these kids take [Jordan's life] as an example. Our lives are so short."

As followers of Christ, Albert and Dee Dee seek to obey him in the commissioning that he spoke to his disciples before ascending into heaven:

> All authority in heaven and earth has been given to me. Go therefore and make disciples of all nations, baptizing them in the name of the Father and of the Son and of the Holy Spirit, teaching them to observe all that I have commanded you. And behold, I am with you always, to the end of the age. (Matthew 28:18–20)

And again:

> You will be my witnesses in Jerusalem and in all Judea and Samaria, and to the end of the earth. (Acts 1:8)

Jesus' command is straightforward and simple—share the good news of Christ with everyone. Or, as it was once well said, "Evangelism is just one beggar telling another beggar where to find bread."

Every Christian is to be a witness for Christ. When Albert and Dee Dee share Christ, they are not doing something reserved only for the so-called celebrities of the faith. However, it is also true that Pujols' baseball prowess supplies him with the incredible opportunity to "find bread" with huge numbers of people. Telling others about Jesus is a stewardship and responsibility embraced by the Pujolses.

Even mainstream journalists stop and take note of the centrality of Christianity in Pujols' life. In a candid article titled, "Pujols is a faith-based mystery," Yahoo.com sports columnist Jeff Passan wrote about the relationship between Pujols' faith and his talent:

As conditioned as we are to hear the word God out of an athlete's mouth and immediately tune it out, knowing well the hypocritical piety perpetuated by so many, what if there really is something to Pujols' devotion? What if it weren't so much faith vs. science but something more symbiotic: faith driving science? Without God, Pujols might be like a Bentley without a key. Belief in God ignites something inside of Pujols, something that motivates him to train, to draw out whatever resides inside of him, no matter whether inborn or developed. He traces all those hours in the cage and all that natural ability to the breadth of his belief.

The Pujolses use the word *platform* to explain their understanding of why God gave Pujols such phenomenal baseball talent. Pujols said, "God has given me the ability to succeed in the game of baseball. But baseball is not the end; baseball is the means by which my wife, Dee Dee, and I glorify God. Baseball is simply my platform to elevate Jesus Christ, my Lord and Savior."

The Pujolses express passion and joy when they speak about Christ. Their faith animates them.

"It is a wonderful paradox that the more of Christ's love you share with others," Todd Perry said, "the more you are blessed in return."

And they share a simple message of Christ's love that can be understood by anyone willing to listen. "He's very vocal and very simple. If anybody has talked to Albert at all, he probably told them that they need Jesus," said Grant Williams, Baseball Chapel leader for the Cardinals. "At the end of the day, Albert is right when he says that Jesus is the answer. You know where he is coming from."

Pujols talks in plain language: "How do I know that I will spend eternity with God in heaven? It goes back to the original discussion—faith. The Bible says, 'For it is by grace you have been saved, through faith—and this not from yourselves, it is the gift of God—not by works, so that no one can boast.' It is my faith in Jesus Christ's work in my life that grants me eternal life with God. Nothing more, nothing less."

Opportunities for Albert and Dee Dee to share their faith come through both big events with large crowds gathered to hear a sports star and through personal encounters with friends, family, and teammates.

On a Saturday night in January 2010, Pujols stood before 500 men and boys and spoke about being satisfied in Jesus Christ. "As a Christian, I am called to live a holy life," Pujols said. "My standard for living is set by God, not by the world. I am responsible for growing and sharing the gospel."

Manly Night, a semiannual event sponsored by Pujols' own West County Community Church in St. Louis, served up heaping portions of barbeque to fill the stomachs of the men. Then Christian men—different ones each time, but with Pujols as the constant every winter—gave their spiritual testimony.

The 2010 event fell on Pujols' thirtieth birthday. "I can't think of a greater place to celebrate my 30th birthday than with you guys, sharing my heart and lifting up the kingdom of Jesus," he said.

Only a few days before Manly Night, former Cardinals slugger Mark McGwire, confessed to steroid use during his playing career. In the midst of the ensuing media storm, McGwire raved about Pujols to Bob Costas: "He is, by far, one of the most terrific human beings—and when it's all said and done, he will be probably the greatest baseball player to ever play this game."

People throw high praise at Pujols on a regular basis, but this sort of thing poses a spiritual threat to Christian athletes. Pujols told the Manly Night crowd, "In baseball, every night there are thousands of people telling me how great I am. That can go to my head really quickly if I don't keep my spirit in check."

Reading Philippians 2:3, Pujols told the men, "One way for me to stay satisfied in Jesus is for me to stay humble. Humility is getting on your knees and staying in God's will. What he wants from me, not what the world wants."

"Many men come to hear Albert," says Pastor Phil Hunter, "but what works in their hearts is when they hear professional men just like them talk of how Christ has changed their life and made them the godly men they've always wanted to be. After that, I ask everyone to get on their knees, and I invite men to trust Christ."

One of the best-organized and attended evangelistic opportunities for the Pujolses came with Christian Family Day at Busch Stadium, an annual event for nineteen years.

The idea was simple. Months in advance, organizers chose a day game and worked with the team's box office to reserve a large number of tickets. Christian music groups and ballplayers committed to taking part in the post-game festivities, providing music and testimonies.

Churches made large group purchases of tickets and invited friends to come along to the game. Some of the funds went to provide free tickets to underprivileged kids. Judy Boen, founder and director of the event, saw more than 40,000 kids come to the park for this game over the years. Prior to the game, volunteers stood at the turnstiles and handed out specially made "testimony cards"—baseball cards of the Cardinals' Christian players, including their testimonies.

Dee Dee has served as honorary chairwoman of the event. When Pujols won the Roberto Clemente Award in 2008, Major League Baseball awarded him $50,000 for a charity of his choice; he split the money between his own foundation and Christian Family Day.

"Albert and Deidre Pujols have become such great supporters of Christian Family Day," Boen says. "Both Albert and Dee Dee support us with their time, money, and prayers."

Boen remembers well the 2001 event. "The first year, Albert came out onto the field and waved. Dee Dee was sitting in the stands," she says. "But afterward, Dee Dee told Albert 'There will be no more of that. We are going to be involved. This is an incredible event. You're not going to go out there and wave. You're going to tell them how you have Jesus in your life.'"

Pujols gave his testimony the very next year.

"He was a relatively new Christian at that point. So we had to build him up," Boen says. Before he went on the field, Pujols realized that he was supposed to have a "life verse" to share from the Bible. He asked Boen for help. "I gave him Philippians 4:13, 'I can do all things through Christ who strengthens me,' Boen says. "Albert said, 'Hey, that's a good one.' So he went out there and told them that was his verse. And it *has* become his verse now."

Pujols looked forward to Christian Family Day. "This is an opportunity to share my testimony with those people who really need to know the Lord. That's my job as a believer," he said in a news story by Tim Townsend, religion reporter for the *St. Louis Post-Dispatch*.

Many people have encouraged and prayed for the Pujolses to be bold in sharing their faith—Phil Hunter (pastor of West County Community Church), Perry, evangelist Tony Nolan, and Boen all come to mind. But an evangelist and author named Mark Cahill helped Pujols see and begin to take advantage of the unique opportunity he has to share his faith, one-on-one, with other baseball players.

Former Cardinals pitcher Mike Maroth recounts hearing how Cahill told Pujols to ask people about God when they're on first base. "Mark told him, 'You have that time when you're playing first base and you get these runners down there—ask them questions.' And Albert did," Maroth says.

In an interview with *Charisma* magazine, Pujols said that when an opposing player would get to first base, he would ask them, "What do you think is going to happen to you when you die?" or "If you died today, where do you think you're going to go?"

Maroth says, "Here you're playing a game at the highest level, you've got a guy at first, and to know that some of those conversations go on like that, that's pretty cool. With Yadier Molina behind the plate, nobody's stealing. They're there for a little while."

And Pujols showed tenacity in his witness. "There were some that would say their family was the most important thing in their life or money or baseball and I'd say, 'You're wrong.' Then I would grab one of Mark's [Cahill] books and send it to them and if I had the time before batting practice, I'd try to spend some time with them and try to witness to them," Pujols said.

"One funny thing about Albert is, he is reserved and quiet," Grant Williams says. "But when he starts talking, he will go on and go on. He's the Energizer bunny."

Pujols' boldness in his witness has had an effect on other Christian players.

"You'd be surprised how many people I witnessed to at first base," Pujols told *Charisma*. "Some of them were Christians, and I encouraged them to do the same thing at their position or in the dugout with their teammates."

Williams says, "Being one of the star players in the game and being that clear and visible about his faith, the beauty of Albert is that he really makes it a safe environment for any young guy. Whereas if there's not clear Christian leadership in the clubhouse on a team, and you're a rookie young guy coming in, it would be really easy to hide your faith. But when you come in and the leaders are just rock solid, it is such a great environment."

Pujols has given particular attention to other Latin players. "I've seen him share himself with minor league players, especially Latin players," says Walt Enoch, longtime Baseball Chapel leader for the Cardinals, "many of them who hardly knew a word of English. With his stature in the organization, he shows himself as the servant that he is."

In an August 2006 radio interview with Pujols, James Dobson commented, "One of your greatest thrills is to lead your fellow baseball players to the Lord."

Pujols responded, "Definitely—that was better than anything—home runs or anything. There's nothing that I can compare that to." He told Dobson about an opportunity he had to witness to a teammate; he spent about a year and a half asking and answering questions. "I just let the Lord work on him," Pujols said. During a series in San Francisco, the teammate approached Pujols and said he was ready to commit his life to Christ. "I thanked God that he had opened his heart and his eyes," Pujols said. "He's my youngest brother in Christ, and I love him so much."

Pujols continued, telling Dobson about another teammate he had counseled. The teammate had approached Pujols and said he wanted to change his life. Pujols told him that following Christ wouldn't be easy, that there would be hard times, but that he should keep his eyes on the Lord in both the good times and the bad. "He's always going to be there for you and He's never going to put you in a situation that you won't be able to handle," Pujols told the young player. "He gave his heart to the Lord, and it's just been great—two teammates."

A few months after the interview with Dobson, the Cardinals went on to win the World Series. This was Pujols' first championship and the first for the Cardinals since 1982. After working so hard to achieve this goal, certainly Pujols would say that the championship was the greatest event of his life, or at least 2006.

But Perry knew the truth: "Albert said that his personal highlight of 2006 was when he led his teammate and friend to Christ on a flight back from San Francisco. Albert confesses 'nothing even comes close' to the excitement of sharing his faith and leading a lost friend to the Lord."

Sometimes Christ is shared through a microphone while standing in front of ten thousand fans. At other times he is shared in a word quietly spoken to a teammate or friend. And, sometimes Christ is even shared when a folded magazine clipping is discovered in the pocket of a beloved young man who died all too young.

In the end, Albert and Dee Dee believe that to whom much has been given, much will be expected (see Luke 12:48). Flowing from a heart of gratitude to the Lord for what he has done, they want to point others to Jesus Christ.

"Every time I step on the field it's to glorify him," Pujols said in his testimony at the ballpark on Christian Family Day. "No matter if I'm going 5–5 that day or if I'm 0–4. No matter if we win the game or we lose the game, I still glorify him. I look up at the sky every time I get a base hit and every time I cross the plate to remind myself it's not about Albert Pujols. It's about the Lord Jesus Christ."

CHAPTER EIGHTEEN

THAT'S A WINNER

If you don't get a ring, you're not a winner.
—Albert Pujols

Fans in St. Louis were fed up with the uninspired, lackluster play from their hometown team late in the 2006 season. The bullpen stunk and was blowing leads faster than the government spends tax dollars. The offense wasn't hitting in the clutch. Overall, the team showed low intensity, little drive, and no fire as the season wound down.

As recently as September 20, Cardinal Nation had every reason to be hopeful, as the Redbirds had waltzed from a tie in the standings less than a month earlier to a comfortable seven-game lead with twelve games remaining. But 2006 had proven to be a season of streaks for St. Louis, and another untimely one was about to begin.

After a 1–0 loss to Milwaukee September 20, the Cardinals went to Houston for a four-game series holding a seven and a half–game lead over the Reds and a seven-game lead over the Astros. Houston swept the Cards and slashed their division lead to three and a half games.

Back at Busch against San Diego and clinging to life, the Cardinals dropped their next two games as well, extending their losing streak to seven as their division lead shriveled to a mere one and a half games. Though Pujols had hit well over those seven games (.320, in fact), nobody ahead of him was getting on base (he had only two RBIs over that stretch), and nobody behind him was driving him in (he scored only twice, despite being on base fourteen times).

The St. Louis faithful, at least the older ones, knew about a collapse like this, but in 1964, the Cardinals were on the other side of it. That year, the Phillies held a six and a half–game lead over St. Louis with only twelve games left to play, but a ten-game losing streak allowed the Cardinals, who won nine of their last eleven, to zoom past them and into the World Series. Now, the 2006 Cardinals were doing their best to give that Philadelphia team some company in the Chokers' Hall of Fame.

Things didn't look so hot in the series finale with the Padres, as San Diego held a 2–1 lead in the eighth inning. But So Taguchi drew a leadoff walk off Scott Linebrink, who gave another free pass to Aaron Miles two batters later to bring Chris Duncan to the plate. Pujols was on deck. The throngs in Cardinal Nation held their collective breaths, and pleaded with their right fielder. Don't ground into a double play, Chris. Whatever you do, don't ground into a double play.

Duncan obliged, striking out on a full count. Never had baseball fans been so pleased with a strikeout by their own player—because now the Cardinal fans knew their best chance to win the game was standing at home plate. Pujols had always been clutch, but in 2006 he had redefined the word, hitting .435 with two outs and runners in scoring position, and driving in game-winning runs regularly all season long.

San Diego manager Bruce Bochy brought in righty relief specialist Cla Meredith to face him. Right-handers were batting only .103 against the side-winding Meredith, who held a 0.72 ERA at the time. But Bochy overlooked the fact that Pujols is no ordinary right-hander. And with a base open—even if it were third base—other managers would have been perfectly willing to hand Pujols an intentional pass and take their chances with utility player Scott Spiezio hitting behind him. Bochy, however, chose to go after Pujols.

That proved to be a costly mistake. Pujols, on a 1–0 count, nailed a three-run homer into Big Mac Land in left field to put St. Louis on top, and the bullpen, which had been shaky in recent days, preserved the lead in the ninth. With one mighty swing, Pujols had ended the demoralizing losing streak and salvaged the season that had been quickly slipping away.

St. Louis couldn't build on the win immediately, falling 9–4 to Milwaukee the next day as the division lead dwindled to only half a game with three left to play, all against the Brewers. The Cardinals responded with a 10–5 drubbing of Milwaukee on September 29, a game in which Pujols cranked another three-run blast, his forty-eighth homer of the year. Houston's loss to Atlanta that day left the Cardinals with a lead of one and a half games, and a St. Louis win the next day maintained that lead. When Houston lost to Atlanta October 1, the Cardinals clinched the division that had almost slithered away.

They may have limped into the playoffs, but they were there. And Pujols and his teammates were ready to put their near disastrous collapse behind them and concentrate on what lay before them.

Prior to the season's start, what lay before Pujols was a season of many firsts, starting with a new experience that excited him: a chance to play for his native Dominican Republic in the inaugural World Baseball Classic. "This is a great opportunity to represent your country," Pujols said in the *Post-Dispatch*. "If I can honor my country every time, I'm going to do it. Don't get me wrong: I love the United States. This place gave me the opportunity to develop myself, to play the game and to live better. But to represent my country, to me, that is a big deal." Pujols hit .286 in the competition, with one home run and three RBIs in seven games, with the Dominican Republic losing to Cuba in the semifinals.

Even by Pujolsian standards, 2006 proved to be a banner year for the St. Louis first baseman. He exploded for a major league record fourteen home runs in April. On Opening Day in Philadelphia, Pujols knocked two homers and four RBIs in a 13–5 thrashing of the Phillies. The Cardinals returned to St. Louis after a six-game road trip to start the season, and Pujols christened the new Busch Stadium with a third-inning home run, making him the first Cardinal to homer in the new ballpark.

Facing Cincinnati on April 16, Pujols put together one of the highlight games of his career. He walked and scored in the first to give St. Louis a 2–1 lead. In the fifth, after the Reds had retaken the lead, he belted a two-run homer off Bronson Arroyo to tie the game. Scott Rolen followed the Pujols shot with one of his own to put the Cardinals in front 5–4.

Two innings later, Pujols went deep again to add to the St. Louis lead. But the Reds fought back, scoring three runs in the eighth and snatching the lead again, 7–6. The Cardinals were down to their last chance in the ninth inning with Pujols up and Jason Marquis on at first. On a 1–2 pitch from Reds closer David Weathers, Pujols blasted his third homer of the game to give St. Louis a thrilling 8–7 win. Rick Hummel of the *Post-Dispatch*, citing the Elias Sports Bureau, reported that Pujols' final home run was the first time in major league history for a player to turn a deficit into a walk-off win with his third homer of the game.

That game was part of a fifteen-game stretch in which Pujols hit .396 with ten home runs and twenty-two RBIs to lead the Cardinals to a 12–3 mark and a tie for the division lead at the end of April. Also during that span, Pujols collected his one-thousandth career hit when he homered against the Cubs in a 9–3 win.

While he was putting together his outstanding April, Pujols managed a couple of times to irritate at least a few baseball fans. First, he stood up for his teammates Juan Encarnación, signed as a free agent in the off-season, and Jason Isringhausen, both of whom struggled at times in the early going and drew the ire of some St. Louis fans. Pujols wouldn't tolerate it. "For the fans in St. Louis to be booing Encarnación, I don't think that was right," Pujols told the *Post-Dispatch*. "I didn't say anything the other day because I respect our fans. You're booing him right now, but when he gets his approach, everybody's going to love him. I got really mad at our fans the other day."

Some criticized Pujols for his stance. Bernie Miklasz of the *Post-Dispatch* defended him, arguing that Pujols was doing what leaders do. "They sense a teammate needs a boost, they stand up on his behalf, offer support and try to raise the spirit of a demoralized friend," Miklasz wrote. "If you want Pujols to be what he is—a great leader—fine. But that leadership isn't a part-time job. Leadership skills aren't applied only in positive situations."

The second episode centered on the showy Pittsburgh hurler Oliver Pérez, who likes to dance a little jig on the mound when he does something that pleases him. In an April 18 game, Pérez got Pujols out on a grounder to the pitcher and did a little showboating, which didn't sit well with Pujols. "I went to the video room and told my guy Chad (Blair), 'I'm going to hit the next ball and I'm going to hit it a long way,'" Pujols said later.

He was as good as his word, taking Pérez deep in his next at-bat. After hitting the ball, Pujols flipped the bat high into the air before he began his trot around the bases. The display earned Pujols a rebuke from Rolen, who told him not to stoop to Pérez's level. And Pujols admitted his mistake, saying he looked stupid getting caught up in the moment. In the same column, Miklasz once again jumped to Pujols' defense, praising him for his competitiveness and drive that makes him the best player in the game. "It's difficult for Pujols to turn it off," Miklasz wrote. "And when a high-strung pitcher like Pérez gets fired up on the mound when he gets Pujols out, then Pujols will be just as cranked up when he wins the next battle against that pitcher."

And win the next battle he did. When the Pirates came to St. Louis a few days later and Pérez took the hill again, Pujols hit a solo homer in the first (after which he laid down his bat and sprinted around the bases) and an RBI double in the fifth to lead the Cardinals to a 7–2 victory.

His exemplary April, in which he hit .346 with fourteen homers and thirty-two RBIs, began earning Pujols more and more exposure, and by now he was widely considered to be the best player in the game. Nate Silver of Baseball Prospectus, in an ESPN article, ranked Pujols as the game's most valuable player by far. "Pujols has done to the Best Player in Baseball debate what he did to Lidge's slider," Silver wrote. "Eighteen months ago, there was a healthy argument going between A-Rod and Barry Bonds, with Pujols just hanging around taking his cuts in the on-deck circle. Now, Pujols has passed them both, and it isn't even close."

Pujols' hitting barrage continued in May. From May 5 to 21, in which Pujols played in fourteen games, he hammered seven more homers and drove in twenty-one. The Cardinals went 12–3 over that stretch (Pujols sat out one game).

But then Pujols experienced another first—a maddening one. He made his first trip to the disabled list after straining an oblique muscle in a game against the Cubs. At the time of his injury June 3, he was hitting .308 while leading the majors with twenty-five home runs and sixty-five RBIs. The muscle strain cost him fifteen games, but his teammates picked up the slack in his absence and still held a four-game cushion in the division when

Pujols returned to the lineup June 22, despite having lost their last two games. However, Pujols' return, instead of providing a spark to the team, had, for whatever reason, the opposite effect—the Cardinals proceeded to lose six additional games in a row for an eight-game losing streak, and at one point had dropped ten of eleven to fall back to a first-place tie with the Reds. The slump could hardly be attributed to Pujols, whose missed time did little to chill his torrid bat. In the seventeen games from his return to the lineup until the All-Star break, Pujols hit at a .338 clip.

After Pujols' fourth-straight All-Star Game appearance (he went 0-for-3), the Cardinals got hot. In keeping with their streaky season, they won seven straight to retake a four-game lead, then at the end of July lost eight in a row, again, to give back much of that ground. A three-game sweep by the Mets in August left them in another tie, but fortunately for the Cardinals, nobody else in the NL Central seemed interested in winning, either. So St. Louis managed to move out to a seven-game lead in September despite a mediocre 80–70 record.

Though they came close to choking that lead away, they held on to the division crown, fueled throughout the season by Pujols' .331 batting average and career-highs of forty-nine home runs, 137 RBIs and a .671 slugging percentage. He became the first player in the game's history to hit .300 with thirty homers, one hundred RBIs and one hundred runs scored in each of his first six seasons. He also won his first Gold Glove for his defense at first base, a testament to Pujols' commitment to improve himself in every facet of the game. Early in his career, Pujols was often described as an offensive force who would never win a Gold Glove, but his dedication to playing better defense proved those prognostications wrong.

Pujols and Philadelphia first baseman Ryan Howard were the two obvious frontrunners for the MVP award. Howard, playing in his first full season with the Phillies, busted fifty-eight homers and drove in 149 runs to lead the league in both categories, but he also struck out 181 times (Pujols whiffed only fifty times) and the Phillies failed to make the playoffs. Howard also had a strong lineup around him, with Chase Utley hitting .309 with thirty-two homers and 102 RBIs, Pat Burrell hitting twenty-nine homers and driving in ninety, and Jimmy Rollins adding twenty-five home runs, eighty-three RBIs and thirty-six stolen bases. Pujols, meanwhile, was a one-man wrecking crew. Rolen was second on the team with twenty-two homers and ninety-five RBIs, and nobody else drove in more than eighty runs.

Pujols had the edge on Howard in other ways as well. With runners in scoring position, Pujols hit .397 to Howard's .256. With two outs and runners in scoring position, Pujols hit .435 to Howard's .247. Pujols had been Mr. Clutch all season long on offense, while playing the best defense at first base in the league. Howard, meanwhile, was average at best defensively.

Still, when the votes came in, Howard collected 388 points to Pujols' 347, making Pujols the runner-up for the award for the third time. Pujols touched off a minor controversy following the announcement, when at a news conference in the Dominican Republic he appeared to take issue with the voting. "I see it this way: Someone who doesn't take his team to the playoffs doesn't deserve to win the MVP," he said in Spanish, as reported by various media outlets. The headlines portrayed Pujols as a whiner, miffed that Howard got the award and he didn't. But Tom Finkel of the *Riverfront Times* in St. Louis checked the Dominican Republic newspapers that reported on the press conference and discovered a more nuanced approach. Some of the quotes from those papers included: "I was a little hurt because I think I deserved the award, considering I had better numbers than Howard, but these things happen" and "A player who doesn't help his team make the playoffs isn't the MVP. That's what I think, but, sadly, I don't vote."

Upset about the way his remarks had been portrayed, Pujols quickly apologized to Howard in an interview with *USA Today*: "I feel so bad because I love Ryan Howard," Pujols said. "I never said he didn't deserve the MVP. He is deserving of that award. He earned it. That's why he got it. I'm not trying to defend myself; I just want to tell him that I'm sorry for all of this because he earned the MVP. The last thing I want to do is spoil this for him."

All of that was still in the future, though, as the Cardinals prepared for the postseason—a postseason from which nobody in their right mind expected much of St. Louis. At 83–78, the Cardinals had the worst record of all division champions. Not since the 1990 Reds had a team lost as many as eight games in a row during the season and won the World Series. The 2006 Cardinals had two eight-game losing streaks. And not since 1981, when the Dodgers went 63–47 in a strike-shortened year, had a team won the World Series with fewer regular-season wins than the Cardinals had in 2006. The

Red Sox won the World Series in 1918 with only seventy-five wins, but that season was cut short due to World War I. So, if the Cardinals somehow managed to win it all, they would sport the worst regular-season record (in a full-length season) for a team ever to win the World Series.

But before any of that became an issue, the Cardinals had to get there. The Division Series brought a rematch with the Padres, and Pujols set the tone by smacking a two-run homer off Jake Peavy in the opener to break a scoreless tie. That homer proved to be the game-winner, as St. Louis won 5–1. The Cardinals took the series in four games (Pujols hit .333), setting up a battle with the New York Mets in the League Championship Series. The Mets were the National League's best team in 2006, led by Carlos Beltrán, the Cardinals' 2004 NLCS nemesis, who led the Mets with forty-one homers and tied David Wright with the team lead in RBIs at 116. Carlos Delgado was a force in the middle of the lineup as well.

Tom Glavine, who won fifteen games for the Mets in 2006, held the Cardinals to four hits in a 2–0 shutout in game one. Pujols went 0-for-3 with a walk, got doubled off first base, and made comments after the game that sparked a furor in the press, especially in the New York media. "He wasn't good," Pujols said about Glavine. "He wasn't good at all. I think we hit the ball hard, we didn't get some breaks." Pujols also seemed frustrated with reporters who asked about his baserunning mistake.

The New York papers ripped Pujols for his "boorishness." "The real shame of it is seeing such a great player refuse to acknowledge fellow greatness, especially from someone as classy as Glavine," wrote John Harper of the *New York Daily News*. "Pujols is too good for that." The *New York Times*' Murray Chass, meanwhile, took to insulting Pujols as "Dopey." "Pujols, considered by many to be the best player in the major leagues, earned his role by—whether he meant it or not—disrespecting Tom Glavine," Chass wrote.

The firestorm didn't die down, especially when game five was postponed by rain, and Bryan Burwell of the *Post-Dispatch* wrote a scathing column about the way Pujols had been conducting himself:

> For some odd reason, Pujols has once again turned the NLCS into a joyless pursuit of excellence rather than an extraordinary opportunity to display his singular greatness, and I just don't get it.

> He comes to the ballpark every day and treats people with a needless surly demeanor.
>
> Instead of seizing on the chance to step onto baseball's big postseason stage and impress the nation's baseball press with his athletic brilliance, he instead has made quite the impression in the worst kind of way.
>
> "Get out of my freakin' locker—you people are a pain in the [butt], you know that?" he snarled last week inside the crowded Shea Stadium visitors' clubhouse after Game 1 was rained out.
>
> The greatest hitter in baseball is turning into a mirror image of the man who so gruffly held that title before him. Pujols is turning into Barry Bonds, and believe me, this is not a compliment.

The words stung Pujols, who admitted to Burwell that Deidre had read him the entire column over breakfast. Pujols said one of the reasons for his behavior was because of the recent death of his uncle, Antonio Joaquín dos Santos, a man who had been like a father to Pujols. "I still close my eyes and can't believe he's no longer here," Pujols told Burwell in a conversation during batting practice prior to game five. "I still see his face. I still think of him as being alive."

Burwell told Pujols he wasn't sure if that insight changed his opinion about the way Pujols had been acting—because Burwell said he had seen "this moody chip on his shoulder" for longer than just a week. "I told him that whenever I see this side of him rise up, it always surprises me because I know another Albert Pujols—the guy I was talking to right then, a likable man with a wit and intellect and a deep respect for the game he loves to play," Burwell wrote. At the end of their conversation, Pujols smiled at Burwell and told him that his uncle's death reminded him of something: "Life's too short. I do need to enjoy this thing."

His relationship with the media has been one criticism leveled at Pujols over the years, especially by reporters. They have their way of doing things, and Pujols has his way of doing things—and sometimes those practices conflict. Some of that criticism may have merit, as Burwell's apparently did, evidenced by Pujols' efforts to explain himself. Others, like Kevin Slaten, formerly of KFNS radio in St. Louis, who called Pujols a fraud for his comments about Glavine, cross the line. According to a story reported in the

Post-Dispatch, Slaten slammed Pujols for professing to be a Christian, but yet doing things (like being ungracious in defeat) that contradict his faith.

But people like Slaten who make such statements don't understand Christianity. Christians like Pujols aren't perfect, and never claim to be. They're going to mess up, especially when they live in the spotlight, in which so many of their actions and statements will be reported (and interpreted) to the world by the media. That's a difficult task for anyone, and nobody living under such scrutiny will succeed 100 percent of the time.

"Who of us wants to have the tape played back of every time we got on an elevator, and every time we talked to a waiter or waitress?" asks Cardinals broadcaster Rick Horton. "I think Albert has great respect for people, and I think it can be misunderstood, because there's times when he'll walk right past you and not say hello to you. And that's what people don't like. That's the side that gets him in more hot water than anything else, the sense of, 'Boy, Albert just doesn't seem to be friendly to me today.' Yeah, Albert's at work. You ever been working on a project at work and you don't feel like smiling to a stranger? Gee whiz. I think that's the fishbowl he's in, and I think by and large he handles it very well."

After the controversy following game one, the Cardinals' bats awoke in game two. Pujols, who had been playing with a sore hamstring, snapped an 0-for-11 slide with two hits in a 9–6 St. Louis win. Two more Pujols hits followed in the next game, another St. Louis win, before the Mets evened the series 2–2. In game five, with the Cardinals facing Glavine again, Pujols took the southpaw deep as St. Louis won 4–2.

New York rebounded to take game six, setting up a seventh and decisive game in New York that proved to be a classic. The Cardinals' Jeff Suppan and the Mets' Oliver Pérez (acquired from Pittsburgh during the season) each pitched brilliantly. With the game tied 1–1 in the sixth and Jim Edmonds on at first, Rolen slammed a Pérez pitch deep to left field that looked to be a game-changing home run. But Mets left fielder Endy Chávez reached over the fence to make a dazzling catch and rob Rolen, then doubled off Edmonds at first.

The score remained tied in the top of the ninth, when an unlikely hero emerged for St. Louis. After Rolen singled with one out, Cardinals catcher Yadier Molina—one of Pujols' best friends—who had hit only .216 on the year, hammered the first pitch he saw from Aaron Heilman for a two-run homer that gave St. Louis a 3–1 lead. The Mets threatened in the ninth, with José Valentín and Chávez each stroking singles off rookie closer Adam Wainwright, who struck out Cliff Floyd and got José Reyes on a lineout to center. A walk to Paul Lo Duca loaded the bases with two outs for Beltrán, who had destroyed St. Louis pitching in the 2004 NLCS. Wainwright unleashed a knee-buckling curve on an 0–2 count that froze Beltrán as it broke over the plate for a called strike, propelling the Cardinals into their second World Series in three years.

Their foe was a Detroit Tigers team that had engineered one of the greatest turnarounds in baseball history. The 2005 Tigers had finished fourth in the American League Central, twenty games under .500, which was still a considerable improvement from the 2003 team that went 43–119. The franchise hadn't seen a winning season since 1993, but the 2006 Tigers (95–67) raced to a ten-game lead in the division as late as August 7 before squandering it. They dropped the last five games of the season to lose the division to Minnesota by a game and settled for the American League Wild Card.

Led by a young pitching staff that featured twenty-three-year-olds Justin Verlander, whose seventeen wins tied Kenny Rogers to lead the team, and Jeremy Bonderman, who won fourteen games, the Tigers also sported a balanced offensive attack that included Magglio Ordonez (.298, 24 homers, 104 RBIs), Carlos Guillén (.320, 18 homers, 85 RBIs), Craig Monroe (.255, 28 homers, 92 RBIs), Brandon Inge (.253, 27 homers, 83 RBIs), and Iván Rodriguez (.300, 13 homers, 69 RBIs). Detroit had defeated the Yankees in four games in the American League Division Series and then swept Oakland in the ALCS to earn the team's first World Series berth since 1984. The contest with St. Louis was a rematch of the 1968 World Series, when Bob Gibson set a World Series record in game one by striking out seventeen batters. Despite Gibson's presence for St. Louis, Detroit stormed back from a 3–1 deficit to win the series in seven, with Mickey Lolich outperforming Gibson, the greatest of St. Louis pitchers, in the deciding game.

With the rookie Verlander taking the ball in game one, Tony La Russa countered with his own rookie in Anthony Reyes. Detroit jumped on Reyes in the bottom of the first to take a 1–0 lead, but Rolen homered in the second to tie the game, and Duncan doubled in Molina in the third to give St.

Louis the lead. Pujols followed with a two-run shot off Verlander to put the Cardinals ahead by three, and scored the first of three St. Louis runs in the sixth after a leadoff walk. Reyes pitched eight innings and gave up only two runs on four hits in the 7–2 win. The veteran Rogers shut down St. Louis in the second game, allowing only two hits, as Detroit tied the series. Unlike the NLCS, and perhaps learning from the experience, Pujols praised Rogers. "He pitched a good game," Pujols said. "He kept the ball down. We hit some balls hard, but they were right at people."

Pujols hit only .200 in the World Series, though he did walk five times. And though the two runs he drove in during game one were his only RBIs of the series, his very presence in the lineup changed the way the Detroit pitchers worked, and his leadership in the clubhouse provided an important spark to the rest of his team. The Cardinals won game three at Busch behind eight shutout innings from team ace Chris Carpenter, and took game four when David Eckstein doubled in the game-winning run in the eighth inning. Shoddy defense plagued Detroit throughout the series.

One win away from Pujols' first World Series championship, the Cardinals finished business at home. Jeff Weaver turned in a strong start in game five, and a two-run single by Rolen in the seventh put the Cardinals in front 4–2. Wainwright, with two men on base in the ninth, shut the door by fanning Brandon Inge to give the Cardinals their first World Series title since 1982 and their tenth overall, tops in the National League. Pujols celebrated with his teammates in a throng around Wainwright in the middle of the Busch Stadium infield, as fireworks boomed and fans erupted in a jubilant frenzy.

Albert Pujols was a World Series champ. Throughout his career, as he was amassing outstanding statistics, Pujols insisted that personal achievements mattered little. Records, awards, All-Star appearances, stardom, and fame—all of it paled next to a World Series ring. And now he had achieved what had been his goal from the outset.

"I said when I won the MVP, if I can tear that thing into 25 pieces and give everybody a piece, that's great," Pujols said. "It's something you work hard for. But the World Series is what you play for. It doesn't matter what kind of numbers you put up, or how much money you make. If you don't get a ring, you're not a winner."

CHAPTER NINETEEN

FEARFULLY AND WONDERFULLY MADE

This is what it is all about. Just seeing these young men having so much fun with their fathers. That is why we started this foundation in the first place—to bless people, strengthen families, and honor God. We are covering all the bases tonight!
—Albert Pujols, at PFF's Hitters and Splitters

Tim Sitek was as excited as you'd expect any three-year-old to be about seeing Fredbird, the burly red St. Louis Cardinals mascot. Fredbird stole the attention at the 2009 Pujols Family Foundation's prom for teenagers and young adults with Down syndrome.

"Fredbird!" Tim exclaimed, pointing toward the dance floor.

When asked, "Who do you like more, Fredbird or Albert Pujols?" Tim shot back with a grin, "Both!"

Though Tim's jubilant and boisterous responses would remind you of the response coming from an innocent three-year old, Tim was not three. He was twenty-three. He has Down syndrome. And he was one of the special guests invited by the Pujols Family Foundation to get all dressed up for the formal event at the Crowne Plaza Hotel in Clayton, Missouri.

It's one of the year's signature events sponsored by the foundation. Albert and Deidre's daughter Isabella has Down syndrome, and they wanted to use their resources to make a difference in the lives of others with the same condition—like Tim.

As the young people arrived at the hotel—many of them in limos—they walked into the lobby on a red carpet. A group of volunteers cheered each guest as they entered. Some came with dates. Some came with their parents. Some wore Cardinals hats with their tuxedos. Some gave high fives to the greeters. And some began dancing before they even got in the door.

They had reason to be overjoyed. Todd Perry, executive director of the Pujols Family Foundation, says the prom gives young people with Down syndrome a chance to interact with their peers and celebrate who they are—Down syndrome and all.

As the party moved to the seventh-floor ballroom, the music blared, but the four hundred in attendance didn't mind. The Pujolses were there, but despite Albert's status as the best baseball player in the world, Fredbird was by far the more popular attraction. The special guests got busy dancing, and the parents who brought them sat back and watched their children with satisfied smiles.

"This is heaven-sent," said Ron Hoskin of St. Louis, the father of Shawn, twenty-four. Ever since Shawn got an invitation in the mail from the Pujols Family Foundation, the prom was an everyday topic of conversation.

Shawn got a shoe shine, a haircut, and a bow tie. Ron chauffeured him to the prom in the family Cadillac, used only on special occasions. Then Shawn abandoned his dad in favor of the dance floor, but Ron didn't mind a bit.

"It's a treat for me as well," he said.

From its inception, the Pujols Family Foundation sought to be an agent of great joy and good in the lives of families and children who live with Down syndrome. As its mission statement explains, the foundation was designed to "promote awareness, provide hope and meet tangible needs," and "provide extraordinary experiences for children with disabilities and life threatening illnesses."

"Through the PFF, we want to showcase their abilities," Perry says. "I think a lot of times when you see a person with Down syndrome your eye immediately goes to those physical telltale signs that say, 'I have a disability,' or you think about what they can't do."

Prior to the Pujolses' arrival in St. Louis, the advocacy and support for those with Down syndrome fell entirely on the shoulders of the Down Syndrome Association of Greater St. Louis (DSAGSL). And just as Pujols forever changed the fortunes of the St. Louis Cardinals, in like fashion he and Dee Dee had a permanent impact on the support of the St. Louis Down syndrome community. For instance, when the Pujolses came to town, the DSAGSL was an answering machine in a mother's home. Now the organization has an office and a director.

Thousands of families affected by Down syndrome have found support all because God gifted the Pujolses with Isabella, and with the gift came a lifetime mission of service and joy. Albert and Dee Dee have to look no farther than Isabella to be reminded of the impact that a loving home can have on *any* child, and this is certainly true for a child with Down syndrome. But Dee Dee also believes that the impact goes both ways, and that Isabella is a gift from God to their family and the world. "God is using Bella's life in such a major way to impact people around the world who have anything to do with Down syndrome," Dee Dee said. "Nobody could have set that up, nobody could've planned that—that was God."

Unfortunately, not everyone perceives the blessing of having a child with Down syndrome. Their population is a shrinking one, because ours is a society obsessed with perfection and devoid of a healthy appreciation for the beauty of all human life. According to the *New York Times*, "About 90 percent of pregnant women who are given a Down syndrome diagnosis have chosen to have an abortion."

In "A letter from Deidre Pujols" in 2006 that cast her vision for the foundation's work that year, Dee Dee wrote: "God has put something in my spirit this year that I feel led to speak about. I recently found out some alarming statistics on births that are terminated because women are told their baby will be born with Down syndrome. Wow! What a blow that is for me to hear."

Truly, our culture is deprived of the honesty, the loyalty, the unbridled joy, and the unconditional love that so often characterize those with Down syndrome, those who despite their shortcomings bear the distinct image and imprint of their Creator.

"The fact that 92 percent of women who are told that their unborn child carries the high risk of Down syndrome choose to abort the baby should shock us all," theologian Albert Mohler writes. "What does that say about our devaluation of human life and human dignity? This can only mean that these women see a child with Down syndrome as not worth having—and the baby as a life not worth living."

George Will, Pulitzer Prize–winning columnist and baseball aficionado, has written that when his son Jon, born with Down syndrome, was a day old, the hospital geneticist asked Will and his wife whether they "intended to take him home." Will responded by saying that "taking a baby home seemed like the thing to do."

In what may be the most poignant paragraph in all his work, Will writes:

> Because Down syndrome is determined at conception and leaves its imprint in every cell of the person's body, it raises what philosophers call ontological questions. It seems mistaken to say that Jon is less than he would be without Down syndrome. When a child suffers a mentally limiting injury after birth we wonder sadly about what might have been. But a Down person's life never had any other trajectory. Jon was Jon from conception on. He has seen a brother two years younger surpass him in size, get a driver's license and leave for college, and although Jon would be forgiven for shaking his fist at the universe, he has been equable. I believe his serenity is grounded in his sense that he is a complete Jon and that is that.

Jon Will, although perhaps a fan of Albert Pujols, too, is first and foremost a sports fan of teams within the Beltway—the Orioles, Redskins, and Nationals. "Jon experiences life's three elemental enjoyments—loving, being loved and ESPN," his father writes. "For Jon, as for most normal American males, the rest of life is details."

As a part of her ministry that flows from her own experiences with her daughter Isabella, Dee Dee provides honest reflection on the difficulties she knows that mothers of children with Down syndrome will face. Not all children with Down syndrome are born to comfortable families that can afford help and know where to go for it. She also believes that some things could be easier with a change in the cultural attitudes of our day. She tells mothers that just living and getting the kids out there is the only way to help the world become more accepting of differences and disabilities. She tells them that being a parent of children with disabilities is about living and not hiding—even when it isn't easy.

PFF has served as a bridge, via Bethany Christian Adoption agency, between the birth mother of a baby born with Down syndrome and a couple who adopted the child. James 1:27 says, "Religion that is pure and undefiled before God, the Father, is this: to visit orphans and widows in their affliction." Certainly the adoption of a child with Down syndrome communicates in a tangible way that all children, regardless of disabilities, are created in the image of God and have a right to life and love.

Dee Dee concluded her letter: "My goal for the year is to kick it up a notch. I am going to really push awareness this year to allow men and women to not feel pressured into making a most regretful decision. I say get informed, knowledge is power!"

Fun. Creative. Memory-making. These are just a few words used to describe the packed schedule of events that PFF sponsors each year for the joy and enrichment of the Down syndrome community. Jen Cooper, PFF program manager, and CEO Perry bring an amazing amount of energy and organizational abilities to the task, benefitting the most people for each dollar contributed to PFF. "With only two full-time staff members, realistically we should not be able to do what we do, and we realize that," Cooper said in a foundation newsletter. "But we know it's not us. We know that the Lord has blessed us, not only financially but with time and great volunteers and great partners and great sponsors."

Here are a few of the events from past years.

LOSE THE TRAINING WHEELS

Learning to ride a bike is an important rite of passage for a child, providing the opportunity for a lifetime of fun and exercise. Though they may need extra help on the front end, children with Down syndrome can learn to ride a bike too. The PFF underwrites a weeklong bike-riding clinic called Lose the Training Wheels. Using progressive-learning bikes and the sweat of many volunteers who run alongside them, the happily terrified kids acquire new skills. More than thirty-five children a year learn to ride, and are sent home with a donated safety helmet and a gift certificate for their own bike.

HIGH TEA

At the High Tea event, more than 250 mothers and daughters join together for an afternoon of being pampered like a princess. Dee Dee and Isabella have hosted the event atop the Chase Park Plaza in St. Louis.

"They had so much girly stuff to do," said one participant. Activities included cookie decorating, purse and necklace creation, makeup sessions, portrait taking, and girl-to-girl chatting.

Linda Orso, mother of Lydia, said, "I just remember how as a new parent, I never thought in my wildest dreams that this would be something that we would get to do together."

Karen Kramer, mother of Emily, said, "My favorite part was Dee Dee reading from Psalm 139:

> *For you formed my inward parts;*
> *you knitted me together in my mother's womb.*
> *I praise you, for I am fearfully and wonderfully made.*

That was really meaningful to me and I think about that all the time. I left the tea recharged and ready to face the adventures of a new school year."

HUMMERS

"Anybody want to ride through muddy fields in a Hummer?" Ask that question to a group of kids and you're likely to incite a mob reaction of delight. More than 250 kids and young adults with Down syndrome got a chance to do just that thanks to warm spring rains, PFF, the St. Louis Corvette club, and the local dealership, Lynch Hummer.

Ten Hummers at a time took off with their wide-eyed crews, roaring and rolling down into the muck of mud, trees, and two-foot ruts along the Missouri River levee. After the speed and slosh ended, everyone ate their fill of food and enjoyed the chance to rekindle friendships.

BATTER UP

Another program with a clever title, Batter Up provides an opportunity for young adults with Down syndrome to learn culinary skills and nutrition. Sponsored by PFF and Dierbergs supermarkets, parents team up with their son or daughter to create a meal from scratch.

Decreased metabolism is one of the effects of Down syndrome, so learning the basics of nutrition is a great benefit. "We are all confronted with needing to make better food choices for our health," Jen Cooper said. "To be successful, it's not about being on a diet but making better choices every day."

Through Batter Up, the students learn skills that build self-sufficiency—one tasty bite at a time.

HITTERS AND SPLITTERS

In 1958, St. Louis native Yogi Berra partnered with his Yankee teammate Phil Rizzuto to open a bowling alley in New Jersey. Yogi quipped, "I'm bowling 300 but hitting .220." Baseball and bowling are both leisure-time activities enjoyed by millions.

When you put 120 families on forty lanes of pins and then turn Albert Pujols loose as the host, special times are sure to follow. Hitters and Splitters is a PFF event that now happens twice a year, once for the guys and once for the girls. Pizza and ice cream fill the belly before everyone grabs a pair of those two-tone bowling shoes and a ball.

Albert and Dee Dee walk through the fun, one lane at a time, spending time talking to everyone and posing for photographs. Even though this event has often fallen on the same day as a Cardinals game, Pujols has shown up afterward, taking great delight in the joy given to others.

"It was obvious to anyone who attended that Albert Pujols, as great a ball player as he is, is an even greater humanitarian," said one father, Eric Mosely. "Many of us figured that if Pujols made an entrance, it would be quickly in and out, while we bowled. We couldn't have been more wrong. Deidre and Albert took their time in greeting everyone who wanted to see them."

Other special guests have included Charlie, a one hundred–pound sulcata turtle who delights children at PFF events, courtesy of Petropolis, a local pet care center. Also, St. Louis resident Mickey Carroll, one of the last surviving Munchkins from *The Wizard of Oz*, regularly attended PFF events before passing away in 2009.

"This is what it is all about," Pujols said. "Just seeing these young men having so much fun with their fathers. That is why we started this foundation in the first place—to bless people, strengthen families, and honor God. We are covering all the bases tonight!"

ALBERT'S ALL-STARS

What could be more natural for Albert Pujols than to lead the way in sponsoring a baseball game played by young adults with Down syndrome? PFF organizes an annual game between the Bulldogs, a local twelve-and-under baseball team, and Albert's All-Stars.

The only game modifications are that the Bulldogs can't get a walk, and the All-Stars can only strike out after three missed swings. "We told our players that the All-Stars understand everything, it just takes a little longer to process," said Bulldogs coach Jim Zimmerman. "We've got to try our best or they'll know we're not and we don't want to offend them. Our guys know to give it 100."

With former Cardinals' pitchers Andy Benes and Al "the Mad Hungarian" Hrabosky pitching, competition between the teams is fierce.

"That's what a day like today is all about, where you can see these kids that are coming out and they are playing baseball and they are playing good baseball," Perry said. "That's the thing that we want the community to walk away with. We're not here to fix them. We're here to celebrate them. And that's really our mission at the PFF."

Hrabosky said, "To see how athletic the All-Stars are is really remarkable." Cardinals' manager Tony La Russa agreed, "These players do it exactly right. They're very intense and they're having a great time."

Each year the game is close, coming down to just a run or two difference between the teams. Pujols gives instruction, pitches, coaches, encourages—anything needed by the players. And the event is a highlight of the year for the players. "You have these dads come up to you and say, 'He's been looking forward to this for the last six weeks and he couldn't even sleep last night he was so excited,'" Perry said. "I hear those types of stories over and over."

Tony La Russa has been around the major leagues long enough to see greatness displayed in many ways—pitching, hitting, field, managing. But when it comes to Pujols' service to people with Down syndrome, La Russa said, "As great as he is on the field, he's greater off the field. He and his wife Dee Dee are committed to the community. They're sincere about their wish to help these kids."

Perry, who has seen Pujols' affections pour forth time and time again, said, "There is a light that goes on inside of Albert when he's around these kids. There's no other way to put that. He beams. He exudes love."

Kevin Garrett, Area Developer for Cold Stone Creamery, donates his time and ice cream products at numerous PFF events throughout the year. As such, he has first-hand experience working aside the Pujolses, and can testify to their genuine love for the children and families who attend their functions. "It is a great blessing to be allowed the opportunity to participate in events with the Pujols family," said Garrett. "The moment the Pujolses enter the room, the kids see them as celebrities, but Albert and Deidre want nothing more than to serve each person in attendance. This family has a talent that goes much deeper than the talents displayed on the baseball field."

CHAPTER TWENTY

SOMETIMES, IT'S PRETTY TOUGH

There's no crying in baseball. And the Cardinals have had to remind themselves of that many times this season.
—Bernie Miklasz, St. Louis Post-Dispatch *columnist, September 2, 2007*

"He never saw it coming," doesn't describe what happened to Cardinals outfielder Juan Encarnación on the hot August night of baseball in 2007.

He *saw* the baseball coming. He just couldn't duck fast enough to avoid the hit.

As Encarnación stood in the on-deck circle, teammate Aaron Miles foul tipped a pitch, sending the ball screaming and streaming backward until it hit the flesh and bone of Encarnación's face, exploding his orbital bone.

"I can't forget the sound," said shortstop David Eckstein.

Encarnación collapsed to the ground, while players and medics rushed to help. The immediate good news was that he was still alive. The bad news, though not fully known till later, was that he would never play in another major league game. His career was over.

The Cards would go on to defeat the Reds that night, making Tony La Russa the winningest manager in franchise history with 1,042 wins. Any other night, such an achievement would have been the lasting memory of the game—worthy of postgame celebration. Instead, players quietly left the stadium and headed to the hospital where their fallen teammate lay in pain.

Pujols stayed with Encarnación until three o'clock the next morning. "Just pray for him," Pujols said. "It's tough. It's something you don't want to happen to anybody. It's just the toughest situation, and all you want is for him to be better."

Though only two games out of first place the night of the accident, the Cardinals would go 13–18 the rest of the season, finishing third in the division.

In many ways, Encarnación's tragedy serves to illustrate the shock and surprise of the many trials experienced by Pujols and the Cardinals during the 2007 season. In fact, if they had received advance warning of the troubles coming their way—on the field and off—they might have opted to skip 2007 altogether.

January was the exception. Fifteen thousand fans paid top dollar and braved cold St. Louis weather to schmooze with their team at an annual fund-raiser, Cardinals Care Winter Warm-Up. The 2006 championship win still dominated fans' thoughts, especially with the presence of the World Series trophy.

The trophy had made a tour of towns and cities throughout the Midwest. Fans who hadn't even been born at the time of the last Cardinals championship (1982) lined up with their parents and grandparents to get their picture taken with the shiny, mini-flagged trophy. Life in Cardinal Nation was good.

Preparing to enter his eleventh season as manager of the Cards, La Russa acknowledged the sense of relief and accomplishment brought by winning the World Series. He said, "There was an empty feeling about getting beat before you win. The ones [World Series] we lost brought different feelings. You're still able to feel good, but you don't feel great. This year you feel absolutely full. We got it."

Winning the World Series brought an invitation to visit with President George W. Bush at the White House. Bush, a former owner of the Texas Rangers, said, "You build a fan base by being a good citizen and winning games, and the Cardinals know how to do both." Bush recalled listening to the Cardinals on the radio as a young boy growing up in Texas. He said, "It made me a baseball fan, and a Stan Musial fan."

Two thousand miles away, far from the flash of cameras and presidential handshaking, Albert and Dee Dee worked alongside a medical and dental team ministering to children in the Dominican Republic, a trip sponsored by PFF. Even an invitation to the White House couldn't keep Pujols from this trip, just one event in a very busy off-season. He and Dee Dee raised money for the Crisis Pregnancy Center and Save a Life of Mobile, Alabama. Pujols also hosted a baseball clinic for kids in Kansas City, Missouri.

In February, Pujols completed a yearlong process for becoming an official citizen of the United States. In his typical pursuit of excellence, he achieved a perfect score on the written and oral exams. US District Court Judge Richard E. Webber swore Pujols in as a citizen, and by the end of the week he arrived in Jupiter, Florida, for spring training.

Spring training marked the beginning of the difficult days of 2007, though it didn't start out looking so bleak. La Russa and third baseman Scott Rolen, estranged since the last season's playoffs, shook hands and appeared to mend their relationship.

The projected 2007 team payroll came in at $95 million, with most of the position players returning from the championship team of the previous year. Even so, baseball experts predicted the Cards would not even win their division. Milwaukee and Chicago were both on an upward move, with young talent emerging and the teams' signings of star free agents.

Spring training did nothing to quiet the critics. Among NL teams, the Cards ranked near the bottom in batting average and runs scored, and Pujols' bat was just as flat as the rest of the team. He would hit only one home run in Florida.

But concern for lackluster hitting took a backseat on the evening of March 22 as La Russa was arrested on suspicion of driving under the influence of alcohol. A Jupiter, Florida, police officer found him asleep behind the wheel of his running vehicle while at a green light.

The arrest was a great embarrassment to La Russa, and he quickly apologized to "anyone who is close to me, members of the Cardinals organization, and our fans." Unfortunately, La Russa's DUI was only the first of two alcohol-related events in the life of the 2007 team.

Pujols, influenced by childhood memories of dragging his drunken father home after ball games, has never consumed alcohol. Regarding alcohol, he said, "I think something is either good or bad for you. I've never thought it was good for me."

Nevertheless, Pujols responded to La Russa's situation with tough love, saying, "He cares about everybody. I love him to death. He's been like a father to me. Tony's going to have to deal with it. He's probably going to hear about it the rest of his life. It's a shame because it's probably the only mistake he's made like that."

Speaking of mistakes, Cardinals pitcher Adam Wainwright nearly made one early in 2007, and almost ran afoul of Pujols in the process, in a humorous exchange that shows another example of Pujols' generosity. Wainwright had closed out the 2006 World Series but was slotted for the rotation in 2007. And although he had performed well the year before, memories of minor league ball were still fresh in his mind.

One day he walked into the clubhouse, and Opie Otterstad, a famous painter of athletes and sports scenes, was there with several of his paintings spread out over a table. One painting was of Wainwright after he had struck out Brandon Inge for the final out in the 2006 World Series. Wainwright's arms were in the air and the whole team was running toward him.

"Man, that's an awesome picture," Wainwright said.

"You ought to think about buying it," Otterstad replied.

"I'd love to," Wainwright said. "How much is it?"

"Five thousand dollars."

Five thousand dollars for a painting? Wainwright thought. *You've got to be kidding me. I'm not paying $5,000 for a bass boat, much less for a stinking painting.*

Wainwright politely declined to make the purchase, but Pujols was standing behind him listening to the conversation.

"Hey, give him that painting," Pujols told Otterstad. "I'll buy it for him."

Wainwright objected. "No, Albert. Thank you, but no. You can't."

But Pujols overrode Wainwright's veto. "You're going to let me buy that painting for you," Pujols told him, "or you're going to Triple-A."

Wainwright relented, and allowed Pujols to make the purchase.

"He commands that kind of respect," Wainwright said. "He could probably go into Tony La Russa's office—even though I'd closed the World Series out the year before—and tell him to send me to Triple-A, and I'd probably go."

With spring training coming to an end, the Cards headed north to St. Louis. Were they ready? *Post-Dispatch* columnist Jeff Gordon quipped, "Despite the negativity, the Cards still intend to play the 162-game schedule to see what happens."

Fans didn't have to wait long to see what happened, as the New York Mets came to town for a season-opening rematch of the 2006 NLCS. Three days later the Mets left town with three victories, outscoring the Cardinals 20–2.

The Cards didn't just lose the series, though. They also lost ace pitcher Chris Carpenter. After his Opening Day start, Carpenter woke with tenderness in his arm, eventually requiring two surgeries and laborious rehabilitation. Carp's next major league game wouldn't come until July 2008.

Pujols hit only .150 through ten games and .250 through the end of April, mirroring the .248 average for the team. He said, "We're going to get frustrated in September, not right now. We're just a couple of hits away, a couple of wins away from probably turning it around. Sometimes, it's pretty tough, but we can't think about it. . . . I know we're better than that."

Pujols still managed to crank five home runs in the opening month, including number 256 for his career on April 28. This homer put Pujols ahead of Ken Boyer on the Cardinals' all-time home run leader list, trailing only Stan Musial's 475.

On that same day, Josh Hancock pitched the sixth, seventh, and eighth innings for the Cards. Little did anyone know that this would be his last time on the mound.

As St. Louisans drank their Sunday morning coffee, local news began to break the story that Hancock had died early that morning in an automobile accident. Recalling the sudden death of Darryl Kile in 2002, the organization again faced the reality of losing a teammate in mid season.

The details of the accident did not make things easier. When Hancock crashed his SUV into the back of a tow truck blocking the left lane of the interstate, his blood-alcohol limit measured twice the legal limit.

Team chairman Bill DeWitt said, "I wish the report had reflected more favorably on Josh's decisions that night, but they are what they are."

In memory of Hancock, many Cardinals wore a patch on their uniform, stitched with his uniform number 32. Pujols thought about the serious problem of drunk driving, particularly at the end of a ballgame where thousands of soused fans leave the stadium in mass. He said, "Believe me, if I had been around [Hancock], he wouldn't have gotten that key. We would have gotten into a fight."

The Cards struggled to get hot. By the end of May they already had three losing streaks of four games or more. By the middle of May, Pujols' average held steady at a low .250 mark. La Russa came to his defense, explaining, "He's not making enough contact to be hitting his normal .320, .330. But he's made enough contact to hit .270. I think he's getting frustrated. You've just got to deal with it. It's not going to help him. But it's human nature. For all these guys—if you go up there two or three times with men in scoring position, instead of, 'This is my only chance to do it . . .' it's an unreal pressure that's affecting a lot of these guys."

Pujols maintained an optimistic spirit, focusing on the fact that, over the course of a long baseball season, statistics often come back around: "You can write that I'm lost. Some people might say that. But that's not how I really feel. It's a long year. I'm pretty sure that things will look better at the end of the season. I'm not swinging my best right now. But what are you going to do? You work hard. That's what I've done my whole career."

Pujols proved to be prophetic with those words. By the end of May he bumped his average to .296 on the strength of two ten-game hitting streaks.

In the first week of June, La Russa celebrated his one-thousandth win as manager of the Cards and Pujols began to exert stronger clubhouse leadership: "I told the guys, 'Don't worry about what Milwaukee is doing. Don't worry about Houston, Chicago or whoever is in our division. Worry about ourselves and what we need to do to win.' If we keep winning, they're going to lose some games, too. We're going to lose some games, but if we keep winning, we can win this division."

Heading into the midseason All-Star break, the Cardinals found themselves sitting on a 40–45 record, good for third place in the division and seven and a half games behind Milwaukee. *Post-Dispatch* writer Brian Burwell analyzed the first half and concluded, "It could have been a lot worse."

Their *run production* couldn't have been much worse. The Cardinals had scored only 368 runs while giving up 432, the second-worst team run differential in the National League. Would Pujols lead them back to winning ways?

He certainly couldn't help a team win if the manager left him on the bench, and that very thing happened during the 2007 All-Star Game. Adding insult to injury, the NL manager that year was none other than La Russa, since he was the NL manager in the 2006 World Series.

The Brewers' Prince Fielder won the All-Star voting for first basemen, and Chicago's Derrek Lee was the "player's choice" as backup. But, the All-Star manager also gets to choose additional players, and La Russa picked Pujols.

Pujols was elated to be on the team, his sixth All-Star Game in seven years. "I look at it as an honor," he said. "It's a reward that at the end of your career you can look back at, and say, 'Wow.'"

But, as the final out of the game was made, Pujols was the only NL position player left on the bench—a fact that is both easily explained and also unfathomable. La Russa knew that if the game went into extra innings, he would need a player versatile enough to play whatever position was required—and Pujols had experience all over the field. So La Russa chose to save him for the tenth inning and beyond.

But the tenth inning never came. The NL rallied to bring the score close, 5–4. Then the team loaded the bases, providing a perfect opportunity for Pujolsian heroics. Instead, Aaron Rowand batted for the second time and flied out to end the game.

Pujols' bench-sitting did not go unnoticed. Not by fans. Not by the media.

The initial back-and-forth comments made to the media by La Russa and Pujols only added an element of frenzy to the story. When reporters asked Pujols about his lack of play, he responded, "Go ask the manager. He's the one you should ask." Reporters noted his "genial mood" and laughter, even as he said, "Maybe he was saving me for next year's All-Star Game."

Upon further review, La Russa said that he should have batted Pujols instead of Rowand, "just for the drama of the All-Star Game." He said, "It's one of the marquee events. It would have been great theater. People would have been talking about it forever."

In the end, Pujols cleared up the idea that there was tension: "People want to start World War III with me and Tony, and I think they are picking the wrong person, because I have got so much respect for Tony and he has so much respect for me. This is a relationship we built seven years ago with him being my manager, and it isn't ruined because I didn't get into the game."

Still, what an at-bat that *could* have been.

As the second half began, Cards fans wondered when Pujols' home run drought would end. Twenty-two games spanning nearly a month had come and gone without a Pujols blast—the longest homerless stretch of his career. Pujols said, "Do I want to hit a home run so that I can end this streak? Of course I want to. But it's not like I'm coming in here and I'm saying, 'Oh man, I need to hit one out. What can I do?'"

With an average well over .300, Pujols was hitting well, he just wasn't hitting the long ball. He said, "When the home runs come, they come in bunches. You could hit five in one week and then you hit three, and all of a sudden you have 25 home runs and you've made up for the time when you didn't get one."

Pujols was right. He hit four homers in three games against the Phillies, and earned the NL Player of the Week award. Was his swing back? He demurred, "I don't feel good yet. I'll let you know when I feel good. You'll notice right away."

July rolled into August, and the Cards maintained third place in the division. La Russa pulled out one of his old tricks, batting the pitcher eighth. "It's a good strategy to use," La Russa said. "It's not like we're burning up the league offensively."

On August 7, as the world watched Barry Bonds move past Hank Aaron for the career home run record, baseball commentators and fans asked—"What active player might one day surpass even Bonds?" The names Alex Rodriguez and Albert Pujols were mentioned again and again.

Pujols' elbow continued to be a source of concern, prompting La Russa to force Pujols—"I don't want a day off"—to sit out a game. Pujols looked at the upcoming schedule of games and saw that the Cards still might pull off a division win. "The next 14 games will determine if we are going to have a chance to be in the postseason chase," he said, "or if we're going to be done."

The team began to surge. On August 10 the Cardinals were six and a half games out of first place, but went on to win eight of their next ten, including a three-game sweep of division-leading Milwaukee. "We never give up," Pujols said. "That's not how you play Cardinals baseball."

Though playing through persistent pain, Pujols homered in five consecutive games at the end of August, including his thirtieth of the season. This continued his extension of the MLB record for the most seasons with thirty home runs to start a career. Sportswriters began to take note of Pujols as an MVP candidate, a remarkable turnaround since his cold-hitting days of April.

The Cards entered the last day of August only two games out of first place, scratching almost all the way back from the ten and a half–game deficit they faced June 30.

But everything unraveled in September. Encarnación got hit. Rolen had season-ending surgery (shoulder) on the eleventh. Chris Duncan followed Rolen under the knife (hernia) on the twentieth. Eckstein was forced to sit the bench with an aggravated back. With nagging injuries hounding him, Jim Edmonds was a day-to-day question mark as to whether he would play or not. The team began to resemble a hospital ward.

From September 7–18, St. Louis lost nine games in a row and twelve out of thirteen. On September 21, a loss to the Astros vanquished any possibility for the Cards to make it to the postseason—they would not be defending their 2006 World Series championship.

The only remaining question was whether Pujols would continue his string of career-opening one hundred–RBI seasons. He did so with only five games remaining in the season (finishing with 103), and hobbled into the off-season.

Unfortunately, even the off-season provided a trial of its own for Pujols—in the form of a report released in December.

CHAPTER TWENTY-ONE

THE STEROIDS CHAPTER

A good name is to be chosen rather than great riches.
—Proverbs 22:1

"What do you think about Albert Pujols, knowing that he took performance-enhancing drugs?" This was the question posed by a local news reporter who approached people entering Pujols' Pujols 5 restaurant in December 2007.

Hours earlier in far-off New York City, a news affiliate and then a blog both picked up a story about the Mitchell Report, a paper being released by Senator George Mitchell that would expose the extent of steroid use within Major League Baseball. The report had not yet been released, but a fast-circulating e-mail contained a list of players who would be identified in the Mitchell Report as verified users of performance-enhancing drugs (PED).

According to sources deemed credible, Pujols' name was on the list. Certain members of the media pounced and, without even waiting for the official report to be released later that day, began to report as fact the guilt of Pujols and others.

Meanwhile, Pujols sat with his son A. J. in the living room of their St. Louis home, listening to the breaking news being reported about him.

Though the false reporting was quickly retracted, somehow it didn't seem right that Pujols didn't get the benefit of the doubt, even from his own hometown news media. Busting baseball's biggest star would be such an important news story that it could permanently establish a reporter's career. But the truth often gets in the way of a good story.

The first problem for Pujols is that players accused of PED abuse cannot prove their innocence. They can *claim* innocence, but only guilt can be proven. Unless players have provided blood and urine samples on a rigid schedule for the entirety of their athletic career going back into their early teen years, they cannot prove they have never used forbidden substances.

A second problem for Pujols is his incredible baseball ability. "Anytime anybody puts up some eye-popping numbers, there are going to be questions," Bob Costas said. "Even if that person has not been connected in any direct way to performance enhancing drugs."

Nearly everyone agrees PEDs are wrong, regardless of whether or not they actually boost a particular athlete's ability. Even so, a Google search for "Pujols and steroids" returns more than a million results, whereas the same type of search for a low-impact player turns up only a few.

The guilt-by-greatness argument says, "The greater your stats, the greater our unbelief." In Joe Posnanski's 2009 *Sports Illustrated* profile of Pujols, he wrote, "People marvel at how much louder and fuller the ball sounds coming off his bat than off the bat of anyone else. That sound used to make heroes. Now, it only cements his guilt in the minds of the most cynical in the great American jury. This is the uncompromising math of 2009: The more Albert Pujols hits, the less those cynics will believe him."

And Posnanski's piece brings out a third factor, a cultural problem working against Pujols—the whole concept of hero is up for grabs. Knocking heroes off pedestals is a spectator sport. "That's part of being on top—somebody always wants you off of there," Cardinals broadcaster Rick Horton says. "Whether it's because of envy, jealousy, whatever it is, they'll start to try to chip away at you and find out what's wrong with you."

Further, we now have lower expectations for the moral character of our heroes than in years gone by, perhaps as a reaction to being let down so many times in the past. We've told our heroes they don't need to come riding in on a white horse, to be faithful to their spouses, to tell the truth, or, in the case of athletes, to reject the use of PEDs. Having told them it is so, they act accordingly.

Enter Pujols, the anomaly.

"We're living in this dark cloud," Pujols said, "but that doesn't mean that everybody in this game is dirty."

The cynic responds, "Whatever."

A fourth point of difficulty for Pujols has been his willingness to speak a word of defense for Barry Bonds. For example, in 2009 Costas asked Pujols, "On your present pace you would hit 57–58 homeruns. That's within reach of Roger Maris' 61. But you were quoted as saying you still believe the record is 73. That seems a little bit like a contradiction because we are all pretty well sure that Barry Bonds, as great as a player as he was, was involved with performance enhancing drugs. So isn't the authentic record 61?"

Pujols gave a response typical of what he has said about Bonds over the years: "I don't think so. Have you proven that he did something wrong? I don't think anyone has proof, so until you have proof I think he still holds the record. I have a lot of respect for Barry Bonds. He's a great player. Somebody that I admire. I want to play like him—the way he approaches the game and plays the game hard."

Some take Pujols' reluctance as a sign of personal guilt, unwilling to condemn in others what he himself has done. However, Bonds has never admitted to using PEDs, and Pujols does not think that anyone has proven otherwise.

By way of contrast, in January 2010, Mark McGwire admitted to his use of PEDs. Pujols' gracious response to McGwire still maintained that PEDs were wrong. He said, "I'm really proud of Mark for coming out and admitting what he did wrong in the past. He's going to be judged by a higher guy, and that's Jesus Christ—not by you, not by me, not by anybody that is around him. It is going to be by Jesus Christ. I'm not going to be the one to throw that rock at him."

A fifth problem for Pujols is that he finds himself in a no-win situation when it comes to defending himself against false accusations. Pujols said, "If I accuse you [of] something that you haven't done, how are you going to react?"

When he remains silent, some say, "He must be guilty, or he would respond." But when he does speak out against rumors, others say, "Why is he getting so defensive? He must be guilty."

Finally, Pujols acknowledges the problem that even history may not vindicate him. A future generation of fans may be *more* inclined, not less, to doubt the purity of his career. "Let's say I retire 15 years from now," Pujols said. "They're going to say, 'Well, he probably did it back then. He just didn't get caught.' I know that's what they're going to say. And you know what, man? It is sad, but at the same time, it doesn't matter. I know who I am. I don't care." As Dee Dee said, "People just have to make up their own minds."

However, just because Pujols cannot prove his innocence doesn't mean that you, the fan-who-wants-to-believe, must succumb to cynicism and doubt. You want to believe that Pujols is the real deal, but you also don't want to get duped by a doper. So, follow Dee Dee's advice and make up your mind about Pujols. And, to help you along in that process, here are twenty reasons you should believe him.

1. **No smoking gun**

   PEDs don't grow in the backyard; acquiring PEDs involves a paper trail. For an athlete to get his hands on these substances involves actions that, if caught, send more than one person to prison. Athletes are not pharmacists—they need "enablers" to help them along. So, where is the smoking gun? If Pujols *is* guilty, he is doing a great job of hiding people and paper. Is this an argument from silence? You bet, and the silence is deafening.

2. **No cookies?**

   Pujols has a longstanding reputation for being a health nut. "He was so disciplined," recalled Portia Stanke, Pujols' high school tutor, in *People* magazine. "He'd never have a cookie or candy. He'd say, 'This is not good for me.' He did not like to be in places where people smoked because he was concerned about his intake of smoke."

   Take a look at the long list of bad, really bad, side effects from taking PEDs. A lot of "not good for me" stuff happens to a PED user. Is it credible to argue that Pujols passed up Tootsie Rolls and

Oreos out of concern for his health, but then chose to inject himself with hormones?

3. Bienvenido

Though Pujols maintains the honor and respect due to his father, he also speaks candidly about the burden he bore on account of his father's substance abuse with alcohol. As a direct result, Pujols doesn't drink alcohol at all. Without trying to lay down a law for others, Pujols has said that drinking was something that would not be good for him. He set himself a high bar—a liberty curtailing standard—he believes will help him live at a high level of moral and physical excellence. For Pujols, playing a career's worth of baseball in a stadium named Busch is fine, but coming home to a cold brew is another matter altogether. He doesn't want to be a slave to a substance. Does steroid use seem consistent with an alcohol abstainer?

4. Dominican Republic dirt

In February 2010, National Public Radio reported that Major League Baseball had named former executive Sandy Alderson to lead efforts to reform operations in the Dominican Republic. A hotbed of talent, Dominican baseball is also known for performance-enhancing drug use, the signing of underage players, and the skimming of players' pay.

Over the years, some have argued the "guilt by country of origin" attack against Pujols. They hold that Pujols is automatically suspect for PEDs (and a phony birth date) because of his Dominican Republic roots.

There's no denying the reality of baseball-related corruption in the Dominican Republic. When an MLB signing bonus is more money than a hundred DR men earn in a given year, there's immense pressure to be younger, bigger, and better than is actually the case.

But when Pujols left the Dominican Republic with Bienviedo, he was sixteen, an age confirmed by birth certificate documentation necessary for Pujols to become a US citizen in 2007. At this point, the PED argument becomes absurd, given the economic realities of Pujols' family in the Dominican Republic. Pujols is quick to deny that they were impoverished, since they always had at least one meal per day. But when US friends travel to the island with Pujols and he points out the type of dwelling in which he grew up, the friends think the same thing—"Albert grew up in a shack!"

How would a family who "almost always" had one meal per day and lived at the edge of poverty find the resources to supply Albert with PEDs? They couldn't.

Then someone might argue that Pujols was part of the MLB-sponsored system of recruiting and training very young boys, described by Joe Strauss of the *Post-Dispatch*:

"To find prospects, Major League Baseball teams routinely fly across the Caribbean to reach a country where the average per capita income barely exceeds $6,000 and the natural resource is frequently a boy who finds an agent before he receives a nourishing diet. . . . The system allows 16-year-olds to sign with teams and then move into one of the academies that dot the island nation. The younger and more gifted the player, the more marketable he becomes."

Put into such an environment, a teenage Pujols could have been influenced to use PEDs, discreetly supplied to him by those with something to gain in his success. It's a good theory except for one small fact—Pujols never entered that system. He was not part of a baseball academy. He was not some secret weapon of talent hidden within a team's system of development, receiving packages of PEDs from unscrupulous agents. Instead, he quietly immigrated to Kansas City, Missouri, and eventually became the four hundred second pick in the MLB draft. Nobody was tooling and training and juicing this kid.

The next several reasons find their grounding in Pujols' Christianity as expressed by his own words. As the reader, you may not share Pujols' theological convictions, but that doesn't change the fact that these are his framework for understanding himself and the world. These are the genuine and sincere religious convictions of the man, and should be taken into account, even if not shared.

5. "I gave my life to the Lord" and "I fear God"

We've covered Pujols' Christian faith in other chapters, but it bears repeating that he believes himself to be under marching orders from the living Jesus Christ, the Lord. "I believe in the Lord Jesus

Christ," Pujols said. "When I gave my life to the Lord, I made that commitment to follow God."

Pujols says that he prefers to live his life controlled by God and not by his flesh. "It would be easy to go out and do whatever I want, but those things only satisfy the flesh for a moment," he said. "Jesus satisfies my soul forever."

The Christian believes that because of the work of Christ on the cross, the righteous judgment of God against his or her sin has been diverted and poured out on Jesus instead. Even so, a Christian still maintains a "fear of the Lord," such as was written into the Psalm, "the Lord takes pleasure in those who fear him, in those who hope in his steadfast love" (147:11).

When asked whether he had taken PEDs, Pujols simply said, "I fear God too much to do any stupid thing like that."

6. "I forgive them"

Put yourself in Pujols' shoes, and imagine that the allegations of PED use are true. Nobody knows it but you, Albert Pujols. Think about how you would respond to people accusing you of being doped. You would feign being upset, but deep down you wouldn't truly be upset, for you'd know that they were actually writing the truth about you.

Now imagine that someone asks you, "How do you respond to those people who make the accusations against you?" You could pretend being mad. Or you could say something like, "Oh, I don't let it bother me."

But how does the real-life Pujols answer the question about his response to his accusers? He said, "You know what, I forgive those people that talk about it [accusations of PED use] just the same way Jesus Christ forgives me for my sins."

So take your pick—if the PED accusations are true, then his reply is an over-the-top display of hubris, hypocrisy, and blasphemy. But if the PED accusations are false, then Pujols' reply is a display of obedience to Jesus' command, "But I say to you, Love your enemies and pray for those who persecute you" (Matthew 5:44), or the words of the apostle Paul, "as the Lord has forgiven you, so you also must forgive" (Colossians 3:13).

7. "God gave me this talent"

Again, pretend for a moment you are Pujols. You are asked, "Albert, how do you account for your great skills. Did you dope?"

You could provide a quick and verifiable response by answering, "No 'roids, bro', just good old fashioned hard work and dedication." In fact, the real Pujols *does* say such things about his work ethic. But he never leaves it at that. Instead, he constantly throws God into the mix by giving God the credit for his baseball skill. And when we use the word *constantly*, that is no exaggeration—this is his testimony time and again.

If Pujols knows that he used PEDs, why doesn't he just stick with his work ethic excuse for his great skills, and not tack on blasphemy? We would argue that Pujols' words are indicative of a Christian who is full of gratitude for God's endowment of athletic talent—as well as a whole host of other blessings.

8. The glory of God

On a similar note, Pujols and Dee Dee believe God gave him great abilities to grant them a platform for "giving God glory." Though this is a phrase worthy of much discussion, the basic idea is that a Christian should live his or her life in such a manner that God receives praise and honor on account of the person's life. "Let your light so shine before men," says the gospel of Matthew, "that they may see your good works and glorify your Father in heaven" (5:16).

"My focus is on God," Pujols said. "To bring God down by doing something stupid in this game . . . it would be better to walk out of this game and not do anything stupid."

But PEDs ruin all that. There is no glory to God coming from athletic accolades achieved by cheating.

9. Integrity in all, or integrity in none

Integrity implies a wholeness, a soundness that pervades all areas. A dishonest person is going to have a hard time with the truth in all areas of life, not just one. An adulterer, for example, has already fudged on telling the truth in other areas of his or her life.

"Albert is a man very concerned about purity," Horton says. "He's very concerned about appearances. If you're Albert, you've got people trying to knock you down all the time."

In 2006, Chris Mihlfeld, Pujols' friend and personal trainer, said, "I've known Albert since he was 18 years old. Albert won't even drink his protein shakes anymore because he's scared they're contaminated. That's been part of his training for the last five or six years, and all of a sudden he won't even do that. He's tired of it. I'm tired of it. I'm tired of people putting this kid down. He's a great kid. Let him be great. He's clean."

Pujols' friends testify of his refusal to even get into an elevator alone with a woman, because of his desire to live "above reproach." He desires to be free from both the reality and the perception of scandalous behavior. This pursuit of Christian integrity is the very thing that keeps Pujols far from PEDs—a beyond reproach pursuit of integrity.

10. Christian accountability

Pujols surrounds himself with men who keep him accountable to live according to his Christian convictions. These are not yes-men, enamored by moon-shot home runs but unable to speak a firm word to a future Hall of Famer. No, these men have a manly and muscular relationship of Christian accountability with Pujols. By allowing themselves to be identified as a spiritual mentor to him, they have put their own reputations on the line. They know it, and Pujols knows it. If he were to make a mockery by deceiving the world, then Pujols would first be making a mockery of these men. But if that were the case, then one has to wonder why he would build these layers of accountability into his life in the first place.

11. "I'll test every day"

During the early part of the 2006 season, Pujols told reporters, "They can test me every day if they want. I don't care." This was in reference to the MLB-mandated tougher standards for testing players. Players like Pujols were under the microscope to see whether there would be a statistical falloff. Instead, Pujols began the season by setting a record for the most homers ever hit in the month of April. His consistency didn't go unnoticed, and that's when Pujols capitalized on the public's interest in the career-legitimizing nature of PED testing. "Now that they do the testing, and I put up these numbers, it's good," Pujols said. "It's good to prove that because I work hard for it. I don't need any type of things like that."

12. "I'll give back the money"

Here is another example of a Pujols quote that, if he has secretly used PEDs, is completely pointless and unnecessary to make: "Everything that I earn in this game through the Cardinals," Pujols said, "if I test positive when you come and test me, I'll give it back to the Cardinals."

Although the Players Association (the union that represents the players) would not actually allow a player to give back his salary, this does not diminish the potency of Pujols' statement. He equates PED use with the defrauding of fans who spend their hard-earned dollars to see a competition between gifted athletes who are all competing on a level playing field—hard work, dedication, and talent. Pujols' words are a statement of leadership within baseball. They are a reminder to owners, players, managers, and fans that the monetary and entertainment value of the game has always been—and must always be—connected to the integrity of the game. You can't have one without the other.

13. "Follow me around"

Pujols also explains his great achievements by pointing out his work ethic. Of course, others have said the same thing, only to later admit to PED use. But Pujols has communicated a transparency with his work ethic statements, telling the media to come along as witnesses. "I challenged whoever who wants to find out—come and work out with me for three and a half months. I'll pay your hotel. Follow me all around . . . to see my hard work." This sounds like a man who has no fear of getting caught. As such, he is either crazy or clean.

14. Hard work explains the swing, the physique, and the baseball smarts

The secret for all Pujols' great hitting lies in his famous swing. Sportswriters call it perfect. What accounts for this?

"He works harder. If he's struggling at the plate, which happens about once every blue moon, he's out on the field and he's taking extra batting practice," Cardinals pitcher Kyle McClellan said. "He's hitting more in the cage. He's doing more than normal, which is already a lot, to try to get back into that feel and that groove."

"He's one of those guys that leads by example," Mike Maroth said. "His work ethic is top tier—unbelievable. He's constantly working."

What about Pujols' physique? What accounts for his muscular development?

"I grew up in the Dominican Republic, but I never lifted weights there," Pujols told *Muscle and Fitness* magazine. "I didn't do anything crazy until I started working with Chris Mihlfeld in 1998, when I was 18."

Mihlfeld agreed: "He was around 205 pounds, long, lanky, but a little soft around the middle with some baby fat. He had good natural strength in his hands and forearms, but he didn't have any weight-training experience at all."

How does a guy go from baby fat to buff, and what is this talk about doing something crazy? Is this the smoking gun? Relax. Pujols isn't talking about steroids. He is talking about showing up at the gym six days a week, all winter long, every off-season.

"From my first year that we lifted together to right now, I can see the difference in my body," Pujols told the magazine in 2007. "I can see my body changing every year. That's the result of the work we do. I train really hard. There aren't too many baseball players out there who can say they train as hard as me. If you see me in November, December or January, you'd be scared."

Mihlfeld added, "We took small steps. He wasn't very strong with the weights at first, but in the last three years, we've really started to go heavy. In the beginning, he was doing dumbbell bench presses with 35s and 40s. Now, he's throwing around 100s like cupcakes."

Six days a week for years doesn't sound like a sudden burst of steroid-enabled muscle development. No, that just sounds like hard work and discipline and consistency. The *Muscle and Fitness* article outlines the workout Pujols and Mihlfeld go through, and suffice it to say, Pujols lifts more weights in a day than most of us do in a year.

Pujols said, "We're always going heavy with legs, and Chris does everything with me, rep for rep. We get after it. He cusses at me if he needs to."

Another component of the work ethic explanation of greatness is Pujols' commitment to be a student of the game, to ask questions of veterans, and to always be watching and learning more about the game. This fact is corroborated by his managers, coaches, trainers, and teammates from the major, minor, college, and high school leagues. Rip Rowan, the Cardinals' longtime clubhouse manager, told *Muscle and Fitness* magazine, "He watches video on his swing after every single at-bat."

"On any given day, he's at the ballpark at two or three o'clock in the afternoon, and that lasts until eleven or twelve," former Cardinals Baseball Chapel leader Walt Enoch says. "He's in the film room. He is the ultimate professional. He devotes the energy and effort."

Mihlfeld told *Muscle and Fitness*, "I believe in work. All I know is work. It's all old-school. You want to get better at fielding ground balls? You better go field 500, 600 ground balls. And Albert works as hard as anybody."

15. Honoring those who raised you

Pujols has a strong sense of honoring his family, those who invested their lives in him. As he considered the effect his taking PEDs would have on his family, he told *USA Today*, "They would be embarrassed, disappointed, because it would be stupid. That's not the way I grew up. Papa would give me a whoopin'. I can't make you believe what I stand for. I can only tell you my story."

16. Dee Dee and the kids

Another aspect of Pujols' character is his commitment to lead his family by word and deed. "I made that commitment to follow God, in my family and to be a godly man at home," Pujols said.

"He's very careful to honor his family," Perry said. "He's very careful to honor his wife and his name."

Or, as Dee Dee put it, "If he ever got involved in that [steroid] stuff, I would be the first one to kill him."

17. The fans

Pujols wants to be a real hero to the fans, and he knows that hero status is earned through the equation of talent + time + integrity.

"To our fans and to the millions of people that watch me and look at me as a hero," Pujols said, "God is my hero, and I want them to look at God as their hero."

Dee Dee told Posnanski, "He really cares . . . He wants to be a hero to people."

Pujols often gets asked why he takes the game so seriously, and part of his answer relates to the fans sitting in the stands. "This is my job," he said. "I get paid a lot of money to play this game, and I know the people expect a lot from me, and the only way that I can do that is taking it serious. This is my job. If you're sitting in the office and you're in control of two hundred employees and you don't set an example for those employees, do you think they are going to respect you? You need to set the right example—teach them the right way and how to do it—to be a leader."

That does not sound like someone who takes syringe-shortcuts in life. Pujols is an old-school, blue-collar, eye-of-the-tiger type of champion, playing for the respect and admiration of the fans.

"He cares what every little kid thinks about him," Mihlfeld told the *Kansas City Star*. "He cares if some kid picks up a magazine, and they start talking about steroids. He cares that little kids will always link that to him. He's sick of it. He hates it."

18. His respect for the history of the game

It is a well-established fact that Pujols respects the game and respects those who have gone before him. He understands that nobody is bigger than the game, and each generation of players must build on the foundation of heroism, courage, and integrity, found in the lives of men like Jackie Robinson, Lou Gehrig, Roberto Clemente, and Stan "the Man" Musial.

Fans call Pujols "*El Hombre*," but Pujols thinks the nickname shows disrespect to Musial. "I don't want to be called that," Pujols said. "There is one man that gets that respect, and that's Stan Musial. He's the Man. He's the Man in St. Louis. And I know 'El Hombre' means 'The Man' in Spanish. But Stan is The Man. You can call me whatever else you want, but just don't call me El Hombre."

Just like Musial, Pujols desires to live up to the heroic ideals of the fan. Musial gave up smoking, even in private, to be a positive role model to the kids. Pujols seeks to do no less. Red Schoendienst, Cardinals great and a contemporary of Musial, said, "Of course, Stan and Albert are a lot alike. The great ones are all a lot alike. They both love to hit. And they both are good people on and off the field. That matters."

19. Consistent stats

Pujols' career is like Garrison Keillor's fictional Lake Wobegon, where "all the children are above average." Each year has been outstanding, except for the ones that were super-outstanding.

There has not been any sudden spike in his skills, indicating the beginning point of PED use. Nor has there been any sudden falloff in his skills, indicating the ending point of PED use. From his rookie season on, consistency has been the defining hallmark of Pujols' career. Hence another nickname given to him: The Machine.

20. Whoever walks in integrity walks securely

Speculation had long been swirling about the details in the Mitchell Report, and the day had finally arrived for the report's release. Everyone knew the report would name names—those who had been identified by baseball insiders as steroid users. But few knew exactly which names would be included.

Sports reporters were frantic to break the story and inform their readers which players were named in the report. Todd Perry was sitting in his office at the Pujols Family Foundation that morning when the phone began ringing. A FOX Sports reporter was the first to call to inform him that Pujols' name was in the Mitchell Report.

Perry sat in stunned silence. As the PFF executive director, he had worked closely with Albert and Deidre Pujols, and knew Albert to be a model of virtue and integrity.

Something's not right, Perry thought.

He quickly called Deidre, relayed the news to her and asked to speak to Pujols. He wasn't available, Deidre said, so she'd have him return the call. Perry's concern was growing about how an erroneous report would affect Pujols' reputation. By now, reports were spreading that Pujols was included in the report. Some St. Louis media were reporting it as fact.

A few minutes later, Perry's phone rang again. Frantic, he answered. It was Pujols.

"Albert, you've been identified in the Mitchell Report," a harried Perry told him.

In sharp contrast to everyone else, Pujols was not stressed out, or frazzled, or out of control.

"No, I haven't," Pujols told Perry.

"The media's reporting it," Perry replied. "Your name is on that list."

Again, calmly and matter-of-factly, Pujols responded.

"Listen, Todd, there's no way I'm on that list," Pujols told him. "I know what I've done. I know I'm clean. Trust me, I'm not on that list."

Sure enough, Pujols was right. The Mitchell Report hadn't named him. The media reports were inaccurate. Though dozens of other players had been outed as users of performance-enhancing drugs, Albert Pujols was not one of them. He was clean.

Pujols' calm demeanor in the midst of the Mitchell Report media storm illustrates the truth of Proverbs 10:9, "Whoever walks in integrity walks securely, but he who makes his ways crooked will be found out."

At the end of the day, Dee Dee is right when she says, "People just have to make up their own minds." Because there is no way for Pujols to prove his innocence, fans just have to decide whether they trust him, listening to his words and watching his deeds.

Speaking to Posnanski, Pujols laid it all out on the table for us to see: "You know how I want people to remember me? I don't want to be remembered as the best baseball player ever. I want to be remembered as a great guy who loved the Lord, loved to serve the community and who gave back. That's the guy I want to be remembered as when I'm done wearing the uniform. That's from the bottom of my heart."

We believe Albert.

CHAPTER TWENTY-TWO

THE MACHINE

Way to go, St. Louis, for hiring this guy.

—Ken Harrison, San Diego Padres fan, letter to the editor in the St. Louis Post-Dispatch

A hitter's instinct, once bat makes contact with ball in a game situation, is to run to first. It's as natural as breathing, ingrained in a ballplayer from the moment he steps into the batter's box for the first time as a child. Swing the bat, hit the ball, run to first. Swing the bat, hit the ball, run to first. But on a May night in 2008, Albert Pujols' instincts told him to do something else.

The San Diego Padres held a 2–0 lead on St. Louis in the third inning at Petco Park on May 21. The Cardinals, however, were threatening. With one out, Skip Schumaker singled, and then Aaron Miles did the same, bringing Pujols to the plate as the go-ahead run. On an 0–2 pitch, the six-foot-ten Chris Young hurled an 83 mph slider to Pujols, who shot it back up the middle like sniper fire.

Young had no time to react. The ball smashed into the lanky Young's face before caroming away, and Pujols was torn. He knew he was supposed to run to first, but this time, he didn't want to. Not after what had just happened. Not with a man's life in the balance. Not with Young lying in a crumpled mass at the mound. Oh, Pujols did his duty and made it safely to first without a play as silence fell upon the San Diego crowd. But then he quickly turned and started walking slowly toward the mound to check on Young. By this time, Padres trainers were on the scene attending to the fallen pitcher as blood gushed from his face. Pujols was visibly distressed over the turn of events. San Diego first baseman Adrian Gonzalez came alongside him, put his arm around Pujols, and turned him away from the gruesome sight. Then Gonzalez bowed and prayed with his fellow first baseman.

With his bat, Pujols had knocked half of the Padres' battery out of the game and onto the disabled list. Two batters later—this time with his baserunning—he'd do the same thing to the other half of the battery, catcher Josh Bard. After play resumed following Young's exit from the game, Ryan Ludwick grounded out with the bases loaded, but Schumaker scored on the play, and Pujols and Miles moved up to second and third. Troy Glaus then singled to right, and with Pujols heading home, Bard attempted to block the plate. Pujols slid into Bard—hard, but clean—and rolled the catcher's ankle as he crossed home safely. Bard would also leave the game and land on the disabled list. In the same inning Pujols had managed to take out both the Padres' pitcher and catcher through no fault of his own.

Though the Cardinals went on to win 11–3, Pujols went hitless the rest of the night. After the game, he talked about how much the line drive off Young—whom Pujols called "a great guy, a great athlete and a great competitor"—had bothered him.

"He was bleeding all over the place," Pujols said. "I would have rather hit into a double play. . . . Hopefully, God laid hands on him. It could have been worse. It could have been right in the eye or somewhere else. He's in my prayers. It's a pretty tough night. After that I couldn't concentrate in my other at-bats."

Young walked off the field himself and went to the hospital where he was treated for a broken nose. After the game, Pujols called the San Diego clubhouse and left his phone number for Young. A remorseful Pujols didn't sleep much that night out of concern for what he had accidentally done. He and Young talked the next day, and Young assured him that he was going to be okay.

"Just a class act," Young told the *San Diego Union Tribune* in praising Pujols for his sportsmanship. "He felt really bad for myself and Bardo. We all play this game. None of us likes to see anyone get injured. . . . Albert certainly felt bad, but I told him it was out of his control. It was certainly nothing he did. Just a freak thing that happened."

Pujols' actions throughout the ordeal didn't go unnoticed by San Diego fans, either. In a letter to the *Post-Dispatch*, Ken Harrison of Cardiff by the Sea, California, wrote, "In all my years as a San Diego Padre fan, I have never seen a player act with more class and sportsmanship than Albert Pujols did last Wednesday night. The way Pujols behaved when he accidentally took out two of our best players, his obvious anguish at breaking our pitcher Chris Young's nose with his driving hit, and breaking the 'good ol' boy' ranks to console one of our players, shows not only his qualities as a sportsman, but as a human being as well. Way to go, St. Louis, for hiring this guy."

Pujols' assault upon the Padres that night may have been inadvertent, but the way he continued to demolish the league's pitching throughout the 2008 season was certainly deliberate. He did it surrounded by a team of youngsters that looked vastly different from what the Cardinals lineup had been in recent years. After the 2007 season, St. Louis traded both Jim Edmonds and Scott Rolen—two-thirds of the fearsome threesome that had teamed with Pujols for six years to form one of the most potent 3-4-5 combinations in baseball. Edmonds went to the Padres for prospect David Freese, and Rolen, whose rocky relationship with Tony La Russa had reached a tipping point, was shipped to Toronto for third baseman Troy Glaus. David Eckstein, who had spent three years at shortstop in St. Louis, had also left via free agency. The departures were painful for Pujols, but they weren't debilitating to the team.

"We're getting ready for the season with the guys that we have," he said during spring training. "You miss the relationships with guys I've played with almost my entire career. You hate to see them leave. You have great memories. But you can't just lock yourself away. People are going to forget about it. You can't just come in and say, 'We miss Rolen. We miss Edmonds. We miss Eckstein.' Yeah, we do. But when you take the field, you can't look at that because then you're just beating yourself."

The annual "Pujols elbow watch" began afresh in spring training, with the team concerned over the status of Pujols' right elbow, which had been a longtime problem. Pujols almost decided to have surgery in the off season, which would have sidelined him for several months, but ultimately chose a path of rest instead of the surgical option.

As questions over the status of Pujols' elbow lingered in the early days of the spring, another problem loomed for La Russa, who for the first time since Pujols' debut in 2001 had to worry about finding protection for him—someone who could wield a strong enough stick behind Pujols in the lineup to keep teams from pitching around him. Edmonds and Rolen had held that role for years, but now the new-look Cardinals were depending upon offensive production from a host of inexperienced players like Rick Ankiel, Skip Schumaker, Chris Duncan, and Ryan Ludwick. The team was also without the services of pitching ace Chris Carpenter for most of the season, and few were expecting a team so unproven to be much of a factor in the National League Central. But in the early days of the season, the Cardinals seemed to be a force. They dropped the season opener to Colorado before winning five straight to grab a share of the division lead. Pujols had no home runs and only one RBI through the first eight games, but busted out April 9 against Houston, going 3-for-4 with two homers and three RBIs in a 6–4 win.

Houston pitcher Brandon Backe may have had something to do with that. Prior to the game, Backe verbally accosted Pujols for a play from the previous night, when Pujols toppled Houston catcher J. R. Towles on a hard slide at the plate, rather than sliding around him. Pujols acknowledged that he was out of line on the play, and apologized in a call to Towles after the game. Case closed between the two involved in the play. But that didn't satisfy Backe, who griped to Pujols during batting practice the next day before Houston manager Cecil Cooper and other Astros players intervened and pulled Backe off the field. In the end, Backe's yelping served only to rouse Pujols (who had only two hits in his previous four games) from a light slumber.

"The last thing he needs is some extra edge," Schumaker said about Pujols after the Backe incident.

Two days later, Pujols homered again and drove in four in an 8–2 pasting of the Giants, and followed up that performance the next week, also against the Giants, with his fourth home run of the season and another four RBIs in an 11–1 win.

Pujols ended April with an uncharacteristically low five home runs, but with a .365 batting average and twenty RBIs, in addition to getting on base in all twenty-nine games in the month. One reason for the decline in his power output was the way opposing teams were pitching around him. He drew thirty walks in April, the most walks for Pujols in a single month over his entire career. And though the hodgepodge of players hitting behind Pujols—sometimes Ludwick, sometimes Glaus or Ankiel—weren't tearing it up, the Cardinals were still finding ways to win, and were tied with the Cubs for first in the division at month's end.

On May 5, Pujols won the game for the Cardinals against Colorado not with his bat, but with his baserunning. With the score tied 5–5 in the top of the ninth, Pujols doubled with one out and took off for third on a Brian Fuentes pitch to Ankiel. When Ankiel grounded out to second, Pujols didn't stop running when he saw second baseman Jonathan Herrera throw to first to get Ankiel. Pujols rounded the base and darted home to beat Todd Helton's throw to the plate, giving the Cardinals a 6–5 lead that the St. Louis bullpen would preserve to put the team in first place by two and a half games.

"You need to take that chance," Pujols said after the game. "You need to be aggressive playing the game, and that's what I did. . . . I am not a fast runner. But I take advantage of every situation when I'm on the bases."

"Albert has a knack and a sense about him, knowing when he can take the next base," his former teammate Woody Williams says. "We always used to say he ran the bases like a little leaguer. In little league, you run until you get put out. And for whatever reason, even when he was supposed to be out, he was never out. He just had that sense about him where he could make things happen."

Though his aggression may have won that game, it cost the Cardinals a few days later against Milwaukee when Pujols was picked off once, and got thrown out trying to go from first to third on a base hit by Duncan (though his bravado did allow Adam Kennedy to score). In the sixth inning, the Brewers doubled Pujols off second on a line drive from Glaus.

"I play the game the same way all the time," Pujols said. "I play aggressively. I play to win. Sometimes it works. Sometimes they make a play."

When Pujols collected two hits against Pittsburgh on May 15, it marked the forty-second straight game he had been on base from the start of the season. The streak ended the next day when Tampa Bay kept Pujols off the base paths, but the 2008 streak far surpassed the one from 2005, when he reached base in the first thirty-three games of the season for a new team record. His longest on-base streak at any point in a season was in 2001, when he reached base in forty-eight straight games.

"You can't do that without having a consistent tough mental attitude," La Russa said. "It's about not taking an at-bat off, not taking an inning off, not taking a game off."

Pujols continued to pound opposing pitching, hitting .369 through May, but a strained left calf reduced him to pinch-hitting duty for a June 5 doubleheader against Washington (he hit a pinch-hit homer to lead off the seventh in the first game, won by St. Louis 4–1). Pujols aggravated the injury in a June 10 game against Cincinnati. He had smacked a two-run homer in the third inning, but in the seventh, after grounding to first, screamed out, in pain and collapsed when he took his first step out of the batter's box. The strain landed Pujols on the disabled list, and the team expected him to be out of action for about three weeks.

If that weren't bad enough for the Cardinals, Adam Wainwright, their number one pitcher, went on the DL the same day as Pujols with a sprained finger on his pitching hand. Wainwright was 9–4 with a 3.14 ERA when he was shelved and missed more than two months with the injury. Pujols bounced back sooner than expected, returning to the lineup June 26 (a game in which he went 4-for-4) after missing thirteen games, during which time the Cardinals went 6–7 and fell to four and half games behind the Cubs.

With a chance to cut into the Cubs' division lead, the Cardinals welcomed Chicago into Busch for a three-game series over the Fourth of July weekend. Pujols provided the only fireworks for St. Louis in the opener, belting his three-hundreth career homer in the eighth inning of a 2–1 loss. Only four people in baseball history reached the three hundred–homer milestone at a younger age—Alex Rodriguez, Jimmie Foxx, Ken Griffey Jr., and Andruw Jones.

"Just a home run, man," Pujols said after the game. "Hopefully if I can stay healthy I can have a lot more in my career. Three hundred home runs, obviously, it's a great honor to be named with some of the great players in the game. . . . If we had won the game it would have been a little more special."

The Cardinals split the final two games of the series, and when the All-Star break rolled around a week later (with Pujols starting at DH in the All-Star Game and collecting two hits in a 4–3 National League loss), the team remained four and a half games behind Chicago.

In the third game after the break, with the Cardinals trailing the Padres 5–0, Pujols' three-run double in the fifth was the highlight of a four-run inning. After César Izturis had scored in the sixth to tie the game, Pujols singled in Brendan Ryan to drive in what would prove to be the game-winning run. A 9–5 win the next day gave the Cardinals five straight wins and moved them to within two games of the Cubs. But then the Brewers swept a four-game series with St. Louis, and the Cards dropped the opener of a three-game series with the Mets.

Facing the possibility of a six-game losing streak, in the second game with the Mets, St. Louis pounced for four runs in the top of the first, with Pujols singling and scoring. He smacked his second hit in the second, and singled in the sixth for his third hit, driving in two runs to give the Cardinals a 6–5 lead. With the score tied at 8 in the twelfth, Pujols stroked his fourth base hit of the night. He capped his performance in the fourteenth inning when, with two outs and Schumaker on at first (Schumaker had six hits in the game), Pujols drove an Aaron Heilman pitch over the left-center field fence for a game-winning homer, his nineteenth of the season and his first since hitting his three-hundreth career homer. Pujols and Schumaker became the first Cardinals teammates since 1930 to have five hits each in a game.

The win left the Cardinals three games back of the Cubs. It was the closest they'd get the rest of the season. Chicago sported a balanced offensive attack, with five players—Alfonso Soriano, Aramis Ramirez, Geovany Soto, Derrek Lee, and Mark DeRosa—who would finish the season with twenty or more homers and hitting between .280 and .307. The Cubs closed out July with a five-game winning streak, then posted an impressive 20–8 record in August to run away with the division. But at the end of July, the wild card remained a possibility for the Cardinals, as they began play in August tied with Milwaukee for the wild card lead. And Pujols was just getting warmed up.

In a 9–6 win over the Dodgers August 6, Pujols went 4-for-4 with a grand slam, raising his average to .352 on the season. He banged out three hits, including two solo home runs, in a 9–3 win over Cincinnati August 16, the Cardinals' fourth straight victory. The problem for St. Louis, however, was that the Brewers were even hotter. Milwaukee won ten of twelve in the first part of August, including eight in a row at one point. By August 13, the Brewers had pulled out to a four-game lead in the wild card race.

Pujols continued to do everything he could to keep the Cardinals' playoff hopes alive. Over an eight-game stretch from August 15 to 24, he hit at a .563 clip, with four home runs and twelve RBIs. By now, Pujols was in a race of his own for the National League batting title. He had spent most of the season chasing Atlanta's Chipper Jones, but after raising his average to .364 at the end of August, overtook Jones for the batting lead. "Us mere mortals go through slumps," Jones told Bernie Miklasz of the *Post-Dispatch*. "Albert doesn't."

Late August brought an important two-game series against the Brewers, who held a three and a half–game lead in the wild card standings. A sweep would put St. Louis in the thick of the race with a month of baseball left to play. With no games left against Milwaukee the rest of the season, this was the Cardinals' best chance to make up ground quickly.

Ben Sheets quickly killed those hopes, scattering five hits and pitching six shutout innings as the Brewers destroyed the Cardinals 12–0 in the opener. The outcome in the second game didn't look promising, either, as Milwaukee held a 3–1 lead in the seventh. But then the Cardinals began to threaten, with Molina leading off the inning with a hit and Josh Phelps singling off Carlos Villanueva two batters later. Felipe López struck out, and with two outs, Izturis reached on a bunt single to load the bases for Joe Mather. When Villanueva got Mather to pop out to the catcher to end the inning, he looked into the St. Louis dugout and flexed his muscles, then pointed into the dugout and started screaming. Pujols, who was in the on-deck circle, didn't appreciate the showy gesture from Villanueva and yelled something at the pitcher, who responded by cursing Pujols in Spanish. St. Louis coach José Oquendo had to restrain Pujols as Villanueva exited the field.

"I don't care when a player does whatever he wants," Pujols said after the game. "But when a player starts pointing into the dugout like he was doing and saying the things he was saying, a guy who respects the game like myself doesn't appreciate it. I had to let him know."

Villanueva obviously hadn't learned anything from the Backe incident earlier in the season about the foolishness of inciting Pujols in the heat of competition. With the Cardinals still trailing 3–1 in the eighth, Pujols lined a double to center to lead off the inning and came around to score in a four-run inning that gave St. Louis the win, and kept them within striking distance in the playoff chase.

"I guess he did us a favor," Pujols said about Villanueva. "He woke up a sleeping giant, obviously."

Unfortunately for Cardinal Nation, the sleeping giant went right back to bed. The Cardinals dropped their next four games to fall into third place in the wild card race, six and a half games back. They would cut that deficit to three and a half games September 9 after winning three straight, with Pujols homering in all three. On September 7, at Buddy Walk Day to raise awareness of Down syndrome, Pujols took Marlins pitcher Josh Johnson deep in the first inning. The homer marked the sixth time in eight Buddy Walk days that Pujols left the yard.

"He's the one guy I know who can tell a kid he'll hit two homers for you and you know he's good for it, and then he does it," St. Louis pitcher Adam Wainwright told the local paper.

"You always hear all these kids say hit a home run for them," Pujols said. "Obviously these days are pretty special. It's pretty special for those kids. It's pretty special for me, having a daughter with Down syndrome."

But the Cardinals' run for the wild card was at an end, as the team lost seven straight to remove any lingering questions about the possibility of a late surge. St. Louis finished the season 86–76, fourth in the division and eleven and a half games back. It was the team's lowest finish in the NL Central in nine years. In the batting race, Jones reclaimed the lead in September and went on to win his first batting title by hitting .364, with Pujols coming in second at .357. Pujols' average was tops on the team, making him the first Cardinal ever to lead the team in hitting for eight straight years (Stan Musial and Rogers Hornsby each had seven-year stretches of leading the team in batting).

Despite playing in only 148 games, the second lowest of his career, Pujols had posted MVP-caliber numbers. He hit thirty-seven homers (eight straight years of thirty-plus home runs, the only player ever to accomplish that), drove in 116 (one of only three players to begin their career with eight straight one hundred–RBI seasons), and led the league with 342 total bases. His .653 slugging percentage was easily the league best, with teammate Ryan Ludwick second at .591. He drew 104 walks, the first time for him to surpass the hundred-walk mark.

Philadelphia's Ryan Howard appeared to be Pujols' main competition for the MVP award. Howard powered forty-eight home runs and drove in 146 runs to lead a Phillies team that won the National League East and went on to win the World Series. But Howard had a full contingent of outstanding players surrounding him, while Pujols almost single-handedly kept the Cardinals—considered overachievers all year long—in playoff contention until late in the season. Pujols earned Howard's endorsement for the award, as well as support from Manny Ramirez and Derrek Lee, who lobbied for his cause.

"It's Pujols," Lee said about the league's MVP. "I think it's got to be Pujols with the numbers he's put up. A few guys have had really good years, but when you look at all the numbers and the production across the board, it's Pujols. . . . His numbers are ridiculously good."

The baseball writers who select the award's recipient agreed, giving Pujols his second career MVP—making him only the second Cardinal (Musial being the other) to win multiple awards and the first Dominican native to win the award more than once.

"It's almost like a little boy getting a toy," Pujols told the *Post-Dispatch* about winning the MVP. "You're so excited waiting for that Christmas and to find out what you got. I knew I had a pretty good chance. I think the guys who voted, the baseball writers, know what they're doing. . . . I cried like a little boy, like I did in '05."

The award wasn't the only one Pujols received in 2008. Pujols was named the winner of the annual Roberto Clemente Award, given to the player who excels on the field and who demonstrates a commitment to sportsmanship and community service. That award was even more fulfilling—and more valuable—to Pujols than the MVP.

"At the end of the day, it doesn't matter what you did on the field, it's what you did off the field and lives you touched off the field," Pujols said. "This is pretty special to me—not just because Roberto Clemente was Latin but the lives that he touched and the legacy he left behind for us to follow. Glorify God first and don't forget where we come from."

CHAPTER TWENTY-THREE

HOME IS WHERE THE HEART IS

So often, Albert was in the medical area, down on his knees wiping the tears from their eyes, speaking to them in Spanish.
—Dick Armington, Compassion International

Pujols was sixteen when he and his father Bienvenido left the Dominican Republic. Now in his thirties, Pujols' time spent in the US nearly equals that of his days in the Dominican. Even so, the old maxim rings true for Pujols—home is where the heart is—for his affections continue to burn for the people of his native land. "I don't forget where I come from," Pujols said. "That's where I learned to play the game. The people there, they have a great love for the game. That's part of me."

Flowing from Pujols' love and concern for the people of the Dominican, the mission statement of the Pujols Family Foundation says: "To improve the standard of living and quality of life for impoverished children and orphans in the Dominican Republic through education and tangible goods." Putting those words down on paper helped bring needed clarity and focus to the vision, but how would they go about implementing this? What would the plan of action look like? How could a nonprofit foundation headquartered in St. Louis, Missouri, bring to life the humanitarian dreams of a Roberto Clemente–inspired Dominican?

The first step in answering those questions involved PFF taking an exploratory trip to the island, to discern the needs within selected orphanages and to lay the groundwork for a future dental mission trip. Soaking up the firsthand experience of poverty and extreme need, Todd Perry said, "It is amazing to see people living their entire lives without running water or electricity. It really puts things into perspective."

The disciples of Jesus took delight debating with one another on the topic, "Who is the greatest among us?" But Jesus challenged their very core understanding of greatness when he said, "Whoever would be great among you must be your servant, and whoever would be first among you must be slave of all. For even the Son of Man [Jesus] came not to be served but to serve, and to give his life as a ransom for man" (Mark 10:43–45).

Jesus, the very Son of God, became flesh and blood to walk, work, sacrifice, and serve alongside people—real people with real problems. In the end, his own death and resurrection paid the death penalty of sin for all who believe in him. Although a Christian's service and sacrifice does not make atonement for sin, ministering to others does flow from a heart grateful for redemption and obedient to the Lord.

As the Pujolses lead PFF-sponsored teams to minister in the Dominican Republic, they are following Christ's pattern and example by dirtying their own hands in humble service to others.

"When we're in the Dominican, we see kids who have parasites, lice, scabies, and worse," Perry says. "But Albert and Dee Dee put themselves in a position where they love on these kids. They hug on them. It is as if they were family. When Albert is down there serving those people, you see a light come on in his eyes."

Perry remembers seeing a lady who had been bedridden for fourteen years, paralyzed from an injury she sustained working in the sugarcane fields. "She's been in this bed in this hut for fourteen or fifteen years," he says, "but seeing Albert and Dee Dee with her, you would think this woman was his grandmother, as sensitive and as gentle and as compassionate as he was."

And the Pujolses' servant spirit extended to the medical and dental teams they had brought to the country. "Each morning, the Pujolses greeted us with a motivational energy," said Joshlyn Sherman, a team member on the eyecare trip. "They stood by us throughout the day, helping to translate, providing breakfast and lunch, and to pray over us. Every night, they prepared dinner for us or took us out to dinner."

And even though Pujols (the baseball star) could receive a king's welcome every time he set foot in the DR, Pujols (the Christian) prefers a quieter approach. "I don't need my name in the paper every day," Pujols told *Post-Dispatch* reporter Joe Strauss. "That's not why I do things for people. It's enough for me to help these kids. It's not for everybody to know about."

The Pujolses bring two types of help—immediate and eternal—and give away both freely to the Dominicans they serve. Often, the act of bringing medical care, food and clean water, or education to those in need will open a door of opportunity to share the gospel of Christ.

St. Louis optician Kathy Doan remembers the time she helped an older woman be fitted with glasses, enabling the woman to see once again. "If only you were there to see how her eyes lit up after she realized she could read again," Doan said. "She called me a miracle worker and asked who I was. I explained to her that I was not a miracle worker, but an eye doctor and a Christian—sent to serve people like her. She said she liked that idea, and she, too, wanted to be a Christian, and in that instant, with the help of Martha Korman, my wonderful translator and mentor for the week, the lady committed her heart and life to Christ."

Pujols believes that his work in the Dominican can influence the young, giving them reason to hope. "I want to set an example for those kids in the Dominican because I know they look up to me and follow what I'm doing in the game," he said. "That's very important to me. People who have never been there don't know what it's like. It's not easy."

"The way Albert treats people, and the respect he has for the elderly, the silliness, the kind of giddiness he gets with the kids—it's all very, very genuine," Perry says. "It's very deep-rooted. This isn't something that he feels like he needs to do. It's truly a part of him. I think that goes back to the whole compassion thing. Albert will tell you that the Lord has called him to do that, that the Lord has put that on his heart."

One of the earliest ways the Pujolses brought the love of Christ to the Dominican Republic was to bring that love to the *Orfanato Niños de Cristo* (the Children of Christ Orphanage) in La Romana, the third-largest city in the nation. Right from the start, the orphanage began receiving much-needed funds for operation.

As of 2007, more than one hundred children called the orphanage home. The majority of them are girls who, apart from the orphanage, would have no other place to go. Once they turn eighteen and are on their own, it is imperative that they have some education or job skills. Anna Vasquez, vice president of the orphanage, knew that such skills could be obtained if the orphanage raised funds to build a vocational school.

The Bible tells us, "Religion that is pure and undefiled before God, the Father, is this: to visit orphans and widows in their affliction, and to keep oneself unstained from the world" (James 1:27). And this is where PFF stepped to the plate.

They brought Vasquez to Busch Stadium for a baseball game. There, up on the Jumbotron, PFF showed a video of the orphanage to Cardinals fans, before presenting Vasquez with a $65,000 check to pay for finishing the school building.

"It was the greatest surprise of my life, it was a dream come true overnight," Vasquez said. "I had no idea what was happening. I called Sonia Hane, the director of the orphanage, to say that the vocational school was now a reality instead of just a dream. We can only praise God."

The school opened in 2008.

Then there was the time that the orphanage needed a new bus for transporting the children. PFF had thought to buy one stateside and ship it to the orphanage, but the difficulty and cost of getting it through customs prohibited that. Instead, on one of the mission trips, Albert and Deidre showed up at a local dealership and picked out the bus themselves. "What started as a major problem with customs and taxes turned out to be a huge blessing," Perry said. "We were able to give the orphanage exactly what they needed and at the same time, help the local economy by buying the bus here."

In January 2007, less than two years after the start of PFF, the foundation sponsored a team of dentists to travel to the Dominican Republic to provide basic dental care to children and adults in various *bateys*. Long and intensive days of work combined with excellent organization and planning enabled the team to work through large numbers of children, most of whom had never received dental care.

"In one three-day stretch, I got about 10 hours of sleep," Perry said. "And right in the thick of it, though, were Albert and Deidre, overseeing the sterilization of the equipment each day. Albert was doing everything from playing baseball with the girls at the orphanage, loading and unloading trucks, calming the children in Spanish and donning gloves and helping with extractions."

After ministering to the needs of the children all day, the Pujolses served dinner to the team, before Pujols put on a display of his MVP abilities . . . in dominoes. "He's a great dominoes player," said one doctor on the team.

Because of the poor condition of their teeth and the natural fear of not knowing what to expect, many of the children needed someone to comfort and calm them. "So often, Albert was in the medical area, down on his knees wiping the tears from their eyes and speaking to them in Spanish," said Dick Armington of Compassion International.

Can you imagine having terrible eyesight, but no access to optometrists or eyeglasses? Such is the case for the poor of the Dominican Republic. On an earlier trip to the island, Dee Dee noted that none of the children wore glasses, which meant that at least 30 percent of them, according to statistics, were walking around with diminished vision.

In February 2008, PFF gathered a team of pediatricians and opticians, loaded up thousands of dollars worth of supplies, and headed to the DR. They spent long days in the villages and in the orphanage, with translation and logistical help provided by Compassion International. By the end of the week, they had helped eighteen hundred children and adults.

"The environment was less than ideal," Doan said, "but with great creativity and a strong desire to achieve the greatest in the least amount of time, we were able to successfully set up clinics and care for the less fortunate. Much of the energy was spent treating children with various ocular diseases and providing glasses to those who needed them most, in addition to swatting mosquitos and laughing at each other's poor Spanish."

Think back to a time when you struggled to get a good night's sleep. Did financial anxiety, sickness, a broken relationship, or a scary movie keep you awake? Or, perhaps you had to sleep on a dirt floor, sharing a thin blanket with vermin? Not likely. Chances are pretty good that most of us in the US have a mattress to sleep on at night. But having a bed is not something the poor take for granted in the Dominican Republic. In 2009, PFF launched Project Sound Asleep to remedy this problem for the families in Batey Aleman.

"Many families had constructed something similar to a bed out of whatever they could find," PFF's Jen Cooper said. "That would be a board on cinder blocks with sheets stacked on top to provide padding. If a family was fortunate enough to have a mattress, it was in such a state that you would not even let your dog sleep on it. And many times there would be four or five people sleeping on such a bed."

After receiving trip-preparation help from Compassion International, the seven-member PFF team arrived ready to serve. Two of the members were doctors who performed medical care while the remainder of the team distributed beds. PFF hired a Dominican company to construct frames and mattresses, benefiting the local economy.

"When we would bring a new bed into a house, the response from the family was overwhelming," Cooper said. "There were grateful thanks, big hugs, tears flowing and praises to God."

Perry recalls the special approach that Pujols took in the project. "For each one of the families and moms, he took his time, explaining to them about keeping the mattresses dry by putting them up on bricks," Perry says. "He wasn't doing this just to get it done. He was doing it because he genuinely cares about these people, and how he can make their life better and give them a chance." As an athlete, Pujols knows that sleep is as important as practice; as a Christian, he knows that rest is a gift from God.

How can you get into the lives of young men and boys from Dominican villages in order to share the gospel and give them a vision of virtuous manhood? "You do it through baseball—something they love, something that's going to get their attention. You do it with a national hero, such as Albert," Perry says. "If we create a handful of young men that want to take responsibility for their communities and their families, how do you put a price on that?"

Batey Baseball is essentially a little league system of baseball instruction and play, with the additional benefit derived from having Pujols there to instruct the players in the basics—of baseball, the gospel, and Christian masculinity.

"Albert sees these young men, and how trifling they've become with their lifestyle," Perry says. "You see these young men in these villages, and all they care about is how many babies they've had with how many women in how many different towns. There's no sense of responsibility. There's no sense of accountability to the community or their families, and it breaks his heart."

Pujols and PFF bring baseball equipment for the teams. "Those kids don't have much, but they have a passion to play the game. Equipment is hard for them to find," Albert said. Cardinals team owner David Pratt traveled with Albert one year in order to distribute fifty thousand dollars' worth of baseball gear.

"The whole thing that this *batey* baseball league is about is starting when these kids are six, seven, and eight years old, and starting to instill Christian values in them," Perry says. "Start talking about what it means to be a dad, what it means to be a man, what it means to be a husband, what it means to be a community leader, what it means to be a Christian. Share the Lord with these kids, and to get them into a position where they can make the changes they need to make in those communities."

It should come as no surprise that Pujols gets pumped up about combining two of his loves—baseball and Jesus Christ—into one opportunity for impacting future generations of men in his native country.

"That's just another way of Albert and the vision he has," says Perry. "It's something Albert's gotten excited about, and there for a while it was all he talked about. He called me from spring training, saying, 'Oh, I've got the uniform colors picked out.'"

The scope and size of the needs could crush the spirit of even the strongest person if he looks at the problems from the wrong perspective. Even as Albert and Dee Dee make the most of each opportunity to change the destiny of individual children in specific *bateys*, they also know that the mission will take more than one couple and one foundation getting involved. "There are 9.6 million people in the Dominican Republic, and I can't reach all of them," Albert said. "But I want to make sure I set an example for others to follow, for my kids, my future grandkids, and for the people of the Dominican Republic."

This is a healthy, long-term approach, refusing to either overestimate what can be done in five years or underestimating what can be done in twenty. And at the end of the day, "the King will answer them, 'Truly, I say to you, as you did it to one of the least of these my brothers, you did it to me'" (Matthew 25:40).

CHAPTER TWENTY-FOUR

DON'T BE AFRAID TO BELIEVE IN ME

I don't believe much of anything anymore. But I believe Albert Pujols.
—Bryan Burwell, St. Louis Post-Dispatch *columnist*

Tim Tepas sat in primo front row seats along the first base line at PNC Park in Pittsburgh August 7, 2009, with his son Keith, a twenty-one-year-old with Down syndrome. The Tepases are St. Louis fans from New York who had come to the game to celebrate Keith's birthday. Keith proudly sported a Cardinals hat and jersey, and watched in awe throughout the game as his hero, Pujols, played first base just a few feet away. All Keith wanted was a baseball from the game. Tim was determined to snag one for him.

In the seventh inning, Tim had his chance. With the score tied at 4, Pirates right fielder Garrett Jones grounded a foul ball that headed straight for the stands where the Tepases were sitting. Tim stood up and leaned over the railing to grab the ball, but lost his balance in the process and tumbled onto the field of play—face first—before rolling over onto his back. Dazed a bit by his mishap, Tim reached for the railing to pull himself up, with blood streaming from his forehead down his face. The next thing he knew, he felt two monstrous hands on his shoulders, as Pujols had raced from his position at first base to where Tepas lay on the field.

"Don't try to get up, sir," Pujols told him. "Please lie down."

Pujols motioned for medical personnel to come to Tepas' aid. In the meantime, he stayed there with him, talking to him, calming him, and caring for him until medical help arrived. Worried about the possibility of a neck injury, the trainers gently loaded Tepas onto a stretcher, as Keith watched with growing concern. Pujols patted Keith on the shoulder and told him his dad was going to be okay, as both Tim and Keith left the field. Tim gave fans a thumbs-up as he rode away and didn't suffer any serious injuries from his fall—just scratches and bruises. And Pujols made sure that Keith got his ball.

"It was illustrative of Albert's concern for people, and the fact that he really cares about glorifying God with his life," Cardinals broadcaster Rick Horton said of the incident. "His heart is huge. Now it's not always open, and it's not always visible by people, but that really defines him. I think that was a very sincere depiction of the real Albert Pujols."

The "real" Albert Pujols was a good description for the man who in February of 2009 was about to launch his ninth season with the Cardinals. His first eight years in the big leagues, Pujols had company anytime the best-player-in-baseball discussion came up. First it was Barry Bonds. After his departure from the game, it became Alex Rodriguez. Pujols was always in the conversation, and while many believed that title truly belonged to him, a case could always be made as to why someone else was the game's best player.

By the spring of 2009, that had changed. One of the reasons for that was A-Rod's subpar year in 2008, when he hit .302 with thirty-five home runs and 103 RBIs. While those are stats most players could only dream about, they represented a bit of a falloff for Rodriguez. Pujols, meanwhile, was busy winning the National League MVP.

But more than a statistical cause, Rodriguez's banishment from the best-player-in-the-game debate came when reports surfaced in February 2009 that his stats weren't entirely legit. He was a juicer, joining the ranks of other recent superstars like Bonds, Roger Clemens, Mark McGwire, Sammy Sosa, and others who had either been proven to have used illegal performance-enhancing drugs, or who had clouds of suspicion swirling around them.

Manny Ramirez would be outed early in the 2009 season, and would be suspended for fifty games after testing positive.

Pujols alone remained unscathed among those who could legitimately claim the title of best player in the game. In all the controversy over steroids in recent years, baseball fans had rightly become disillusioned with the game, and with the players for whom they had cheered so loyally. Was it any wonder that baseball had an image problem? Was every memorable performance chemically enhanced? Was anyone legitimate?

With all the skepticism and cynicism surrounding the game, *Sports Illustrated* ran a cover story on Pujols in the middle of March. With Pujols staring straight into the camera, a bat resting on his right shoulder, the headline on the cover read, "Albert Pujols Has a Message: Don't Be Afraid to Believe in Me." The article's message was simple: Other superstars may be tainted. Other players may be cutting corners and cheating the game. Pujols is not.

"We're in this era where people want to judge other people," Pujols told *SI*. "And that's so sad. But it's like I always say, 'Come and test me. Come and do whatever you want.' Because you know what? There is something more important to me—my relationship with Jesus Christ and caring about others. More than this baseball. This baseball is nothing to me."

In short, Albert Pujols had become baseball's indispensible ambassador. He was an unbroken hero—confident in his integrity, unflinching in his devotion to the Lord, and willing to carry the entire sport on his shoulders and prove to everyone that there was a right way to play the game. Especially with St. Louis set to host the 2009 All-Star Game, baseball needed Pujols and the honor he brought to his profession. *St. Louis Post-Dispatch* columnist Bryan Burwell echoed the sentiments of fans across the country when he wrote, "I don't believe much of anything anymore. But I believe Albert Pujols. I believe that there are plenty of clean players in baseball, and he is one of them. I think. I hope. I pray."

As the Cardinals worked their way through training camp, the season's outlook appeared a bit brighter than it had the year before. One major reason for that was the health of Chris Carpenter. The 2005 Cy Young Award–winner who'd also won fifteen games in 2006 when St. Louis won the World Series, Carpenter had been out for practically two full years with injuries. He pitched only twenty-one innings combined in 2007 and 2008, but was now deemed healthy and ready to contribute in 2009. Questions remained about the heart of the lineup and who would protect Pujols, after teams increasingly pitched around him in 2008. But other than peripheral moves, such as trading for San Diego shortstop Khalil Greene and losing players like Braden Looper, Felipe López, and César Izturis to free agency, the 2009 Cardinals looked quite similar to the 2008 team.

The Cardinals opened the season by splitting a four-game series with Pittsburgh. Pujols, who always seems to begin the season in midseason form, hit .500 in the series, including a home run and two RBIs in a 9–3 win in the second game. The Cardinals then welcomed the Astros to town by winning a 5–3 game in which Houston held Pujols hitless—but the Astros paid for that the next day. Pujols tagged Roy Oswalt with a grand slam in the fifth and connected again with a three-run homer off Wesley Wright in the seventh. His seven RBIs tied a career-best as the Cardinals roughed up Oswalt in an 11–2 trouncing.

Looking back over Pujols' career, you can see clear signs of growth, both as a player and as a person. Getting Pujols to say something positive about an opposing pitcher was nearly impossible in the early years of his career. But the longer Pujols has been around, the more willing he has been to credit excellence in the opposition.

"Oswalt is probably the best pitcher in the game," Pujols told the *Post-Dispatch* after the win. "If I'm starting an All-Star Game right now I take Oswalt from the right side. From the left side I'll take Johan Santana. They're unbelievable and so competitive. He takes the ball every fifth day. It's what I admire about him."

The Cardinals dropped two of three to the Cubs in mid-April in the rivals' first series of the year, but bounced back to win five straight, including a three-game sweep of the Mets and two-of-three in a second series with Chicago. Pujols hit .474 with three homers and eleven RBIs over that five-game stretch. In a 12–8 win over the Mets on April 23, Pujols homered twice and drove in three. Two days later, with St. Louis holding a 3–1 lead in the seventh against the Cubs, Pujols blasted his second grand slam of the season to give his team a comfortable lead. That homer gave Pujols 1,002 career RBIs, made him the eighth-youngest player in baseball history to reach the 1,000-RBI mark, and put him in the company of Stan Musial,

Enos Slaughter, Jim Bottomley, Rogers Hornsby, and Ken Boyer as the only Cardinals ever to top 1,000 RBIs.

The series finale with the Cubs was ugly, but it could have been worse. St. Louis pitcher Todd Wellemeyer beaned Alfonso Soriano in the second, and the Cubs retaliated when Rich Harden nailed Pujols in the middle of the back in the fifth after trying but failing to plunk him in the third. Pujols accepted his fate without argument.

"It's part of the game," he said. "Somebody got hit in the head. I'm just glad Soriano stayed in the game and it wasn't bad. You let the ball go and you can't control it. [Harden] did what he had to do. He did it. I'm glad the way he did it; it was professional. He tried it the first time and didn't do it. He did it the second time."

The Cardinals played superbly in April, and after a May 1 win over Washington (in which Pujols went 3-for-4 with a home run in the first that put St. Louis on top for good), held a four-game lead in the division.

Pujols unleashed one of the most damaging home runs of his career in a May 21 game against Chicago. One of the traditions at Busch Stadium focuses on the left field section of seats dubbed Big Mac Land in large, illuminated letters. That section was created during the Mark McGwire years, and anytime a St. Louis batter clubs a home run into the section, everyone in attendance gets a free Big Mac at an area McDonald's. Facing the Cubs' Sean Marshall in the first inning, Pujols unloaded a shot that smashed into the letter "i" on the Big Mac Land sign, breaking all the neon lights in that letter. After the game, Pujols responded to a question from someone wanting to know if he were expecting the Cardinals to make him pay for the damage.

"Nah," Pujols quipped. "I'm expecting a Big Mac."

Pujols continued his trend of punishing his hometown Royals in a three-game series June 19 to 21. He drove in two in a 10–5 win in the opener, and followed that with a two-run homer as the Cardinals took the second game 7–1. Pujols was just getting started. In the finale, he gave St. Louis a quick 1–0 lead in the first with an RBI single off Gil Meche. After flying out in the third, Pujols made a quick trip to the video room to analyze his at-bat. According to the *Post-Dispatch*, Pujols told assistant hitting coach Mike Aldrete that his next time up, he would hit the ball off the Royals Hall of Fame behind the visitors' bullpen in left field.

"He didn't say he might hit the Hall of Fame. He said he would hit the Hall of Fame," Aldrete said. Sure enough, the next inning with the score tied 4–4, the bases loaded and Pujols at the plate, he drove a Meche pitch off a Hall of Fame window 423 feet away. The grand slam, his third on the season and ninth in his career, tied Pujols with Stan Musial for the most career slams in team history. He went 4-for-5 on the day with six RBIs in a 12–5 victory. A pair of two-run homers against the Twins on June 27 gave him twenty-eight on the year to go along with seventy-four RBIs, both tops in the majors.

But despite Pujols' onslaught (he was the National League Player of the Month), June wasn't kind to the Cardinals, who went only 12–17 on the month. Teams were continuing to pitch around Pujols and walk him regularly, because the Cardinals didn't have a hitter behind him who could make the opposition pay for employing that strategy. Even with the poor record on the month, however, the Cardinals lost only a game in the standings. Milwaukee had a lackluster June as well, and led St. Louis by only two games. Two St. Louis wins to open July moved them back into a first-place tie and set the stage for one of the most memorable games of the season.

The Cardinals trailed the Reds 3–0 in the eighth inning July 3 in Cincinnati, when Colby Rasmus led off with a base hit. Skip Schumaker walked with one out and rookie Jarrett Hoffpauir did the same. With the bases loaded and Pujols at the plate, Reds manager Dusty Baker went to his bullpen, bringing in David Weathers—who promptly served up Pujols' fourth grand slam of the year, giving St. Louis a 4–3 lead. Cincinnati would tie the game in the bottom of the inning, but the Cardinals added three more in the ninth (one of which came on a Pujols double) to pull out the win.

As the July heat settled over St. Louis, so did the city's anticipation and excitement over the upcoming All-Star Game, which the city hadn't hosted since 1966. The midsummer classic brought escalating national attention to Pujols, almost universally acknowledged at this point as the best player in the game. As Joe Strauss of the *St. Louis Post-Dispatch* reported:

> Pujols, 29, acknowledges an increased responsibility as a team leader and even as a representative for the game. He will serve as centerpiece of attention during the festivities surrounding the upcoming All-Star Game. He will return home from a July 12 day-night doubleheader in Chicago to

accept an avalanche of media responsibilities, participate in the July 13 Home Run Derby, perhaps attend a gathering at his Westport restaurant, then start at first base in the July 14 game.

"It seems like every major magazine or newspaper wants to write something about me, either about baseball or something off the field," he said. "All that stuff has been there the last five years and they didn't want to do it. Now they do."

Once viewed as mercurial, even churlish with media, Pujols now recognizes his fame carries opportunity and obligation. But greater exposure carries a need for greater care.

"I've learned over the last three or four years this comes with it," he says. "I'm different. This came so quick. Everybody tried to approach me. I was feeling a lot of pressure. Everything came so fast. It's amazing. It's not like I'm disappointed. It's just happened very quickly."

Leading the majors with thirty-two home runs at the All-Star break, and competing in his home ballpark, Pujols was the sentimental favorite to win MLB's annual Home Run Derby preceding the All-Star Game. The St. Louis fans roared in approval at each of Pujols' homers in the competition, but Pujols made it only to the second round as Milwaukee's Prince Fielder won the crown. At the All-Star Game the next day, Pujols caught the ceremonial first pitch from President Barack Obama. He came to bat three times and grounded out three times in the National League's thirteenth straight All-Star Game without a win.

"I feel awesome," Pujols said after the leaving the game. "This is unbelievable, this is a dream come true. . . . The best fans in baseball here in St. Louis, I see this every night we have a game. These fans welcome me and my family. . . . I thank God for letting me have this opportunity."

The Cardinals led the division by two and a half games at the break, and Pujols picked up where he left off. He homered twice in a 6–1 win against Arizona in the first game of the second half. The first home run in that game, his thirty-third of the season, moved him past Hall of Famer Ralph Kiner for the most home runs ever in the first nine years of a career. But then Pujols cooled off, hitting only .235 with no homers and three RBIs over the last thirteen games in July as St. Louis clung to only a half-game lead over the Cubs. One of those three RBIs came in a crucial game with the Dodgers, who came into St. Louis for a four-game series. The Cardinals were coming off two straight losses to Philadelphia that had cost them the division lead, and now they were staring at four games with the leaders of the National League West. St. Louis took the first two against Los Angeles, and the two teams were tied in the fifteenth inning in a marathon third game.

An RBI single from Rasmus had tied the game in the bottom of the ninth, and an RBI single from Ryan Ludwick in the eleventh had extended the game again. In the fifteenth, Brendan Ryan led off with a triple and Julio Lugo walked with one out. When Mark DeRosa grounded to Rafael Furcal at short, Furcal nailed Ryan trying to score. With Lugo on at second and DeRosa at first, Pujols came up to face his old teammate Jeff Weaver. Pujols lined a single over center fielder Matt Kemp, who was playing shallow, to win the game and keep St. Louis in first place by half a game.

Despite a loss the next day that bumped the team to second place again, Cardinal Nation had reason for optimism. St. Louis general manager John Mozeliak, keenly aware of the need for another bat in the lineup, had been taking steps to rectify that shortcoming. In late June he had acquired third baseman DeRosa from Cleveland, and made an even bigger splash July 24, a week before the trade deadline, when he dealt prized prospect Brett Wallace and two other minor leaguers to Oakland in exchange for Matt Holliday. Tony La Russa had long coveted Holliday, who had excelled in Colorado before struggling a bit in his short time in Oakland. In 2007, Holliday hit .340 to win the National League batting title, while also leading the league with 137 RBIs.

St. Louis cleanup hitters had been among the league's worst in 2009. Now Mozeliak had given his team a bona fide slugger to hit in that spot and provide adequate protection for Pujols. Holliday didn't disappoint, hitting .353 with thirteen homers and fifty-five RBIs over the last two months of the season. The acquisitions of DeRosa and Holliday proved to be crucial for the Cardinals. "Albert was there and was the guy that did it all year, but I think when we got those guys around him that could kind of take a little bit of pressure off him and he might start seeing more pitches, I think that was the big turning point," St. Louis pitcher Kyle McClellan says.

Pujols busted out of his funk, which had dropped his batting average to .314, with a 4-for-5 performance against the Mets on August 4. He homered off Johan Santana in the eighth inning to pull the Cardinals to within two, and in the tenth, after Mets pitcher Sean Green plunked DeRosa with the bases loaded to give St. Louis an 8–7 lead, Pujols delivered with his fifth (and final) grand slam of the season, tying Ernie Banks for the National League record and leaving him only one short of the major league record held by Don Mattingly.

The next series against Pittsburgh proved to be a microcosm of both the season and of Pujols' character. You want compassion? Pujols demonstrated that by the way he cared for Tim Tepas when he fell over the railing and landed face-first.

What about leadership? In the series finale, the Pirates led 3–2 in the eighth when DeRosa led off with a single. Ryan grounded into a fielder's choice, and Schumaker drove a Matt Capps pitch for a two-run homer to give St. Louis the lead. Scoring ahead of Schumaker, Ryan began walking off the field as Schumaker finished his home run trot and the rest of the Cardinals poured out of the dugout. Pujols met Ryan and turned him around.

"Albert grabbed him and said, 'You congratulate him,'" Horton said. "And Brendan Ryan turned around and gave Skip a hug. Brendan just wasn't thinking, but Albert was not going to stand for that. He was flat out not going to stand for that. I mean, here's a guy in the middle of a game that's taking the time out to teach a young player like Brendan Ryan the way to play the game and the way to admire your teammates."

How about an example of self-control? Pujols provided that two pitches later. On a 0–1 count, an agitated Capps, who had just coughed up the lead to St. Louis, drilled Pujols in the ribs. The plunking wasn't an accident, and home plate umpire Mike Estabrook immediately ejected Capps from the game. Pujols, who could easily have started something with Capps, instead showed remarkable restraint and simply walked to first.

"Here's a guy who's extraordinarily emotional in one way, but he is not prone to making mistakes in the midst of that," Horton says of Pujols. "I think he was emotional when that happened, but it was the restraint that followed. I think he has some kind of internal instant check that says 'What glorifies God right here?'"

The series against Pittsburgh proved significant in the standings as well. St. Louis entered it tied with the Cubs atop the division. After sweeping the

Pirates, the Cardinals held a two-game lead they would only extend in the coming weeks. They never left first place the rest of the season, posting an incredible 20–6 record in August and cruising to the division title by a comfortable seven and a half games, after leading by as many as eleven and a half games in early September. Led by the dominant Carpenter and Wainwright, each of whom was having a season worthy of the Cy Young Award, and the offense of Pujols and Holliday, St. Louis finished the year 91–71 to return to the playoffs after a two-year absence.

Along the way, Pujols continued posting statistics that would make him the clear favorite for his third MVP award. Pujols finished the season hitting .327 with a league-leading forty-seven home runs. His 135 RBIs were only two off his personal best, set in 2006. Pujols led the league in on-base percentage (.443), slugging percentage (.658), runs (124), total bases (374), and intentional walks (44). His 115 walks were also a career best.

His value to the team went beyond his offense or defense and often showed itself in ways that don't show up in box scores. For example, in a September 11 game against Atlanta, Pujols displayed his keen baseball smarts and quick thinking that few in the game can rival. Trailing the Braves 1–0, Pujols was at second base with Holliday at first and nobody out in the seventh inning. The situation was ripe for a St. Louis rally, before Jair Jurrjens got Ludwick to ground to short for an almost certain double play. Pujols attempted to screen shortstop Yunel Escobar's view of the grounder, but didn't get out of the way in time as the ball clipped him on the leg. That meant Pujols was out, but the ball was dead and the other two runners were safe. While it's possible that Pujols did get hit accidentally, many—including Braves manager Bobby Cox—speculated that Pujols deliberately allowed the ball to hit him, to keep Atlanta from turning the double play.

"Pujols is that smart," Cox said. "I thought it was a great baserunning play by him. I thought it should have been called a double play. The ball wasn't hit that hard. But he's the guy with the glove, the arm, the bat, and the instincts to think of that. That's my opinion. I can't say for sure."

While the Cardinals had the division title locked up, their play over the final ten games of the season raised some red flags as they prepared for their National League Division Series matchup with the Dodgers, who had won the NL West. St. Louis went only 2–8 to end the season, including three straight losses to Milwaukee in the final series of the year. That nosedive cost the Cardinals home field advantage in the opening round of the playoffs and sent them out west to open the series in Los Angeles.

The Dodgers, led offensively by Matt Kemp, Manny Ramirez, and Andre Ethier, had a balanced rotation that included Randy Wolf, Chad Billingsley, and Clayton Kershaw, as well as a solid bullpen. Manager Joe Torre made his strategy clear when it came to facing Pujols—he was going to pitch around him whenever possible.

"Albert is just out there in a class by himself," Torre said. "His ability to just hit it far and hit it often does a lot of things. It may cost me . . . a three-run homer instead of a two-run homer. But I'm still going to make somebody else beat me."

Torre wasted no time in implementing his plan. When Schumaker led off game one with a walk and Ryan followed with a ground-rule double that moved Schumaker to third, Pujols came up with first base empty. Wolf gave Pujols an intentional pass.

Cleanup-hitting Holliday then set the tone for the entire series when, after taking the first two pitches for balls, he watched three straight Wolf fastballs fly by him for strikes, never taking the bat off his shoulder. Ludwick drove in one run with a base hit, but Wolf got Yadier Molina to ground into an inning-ending double play. Though the Cardinals led 1–0, the damage could have been much worse. Had the Cardinals scored multiple runs in the inning, the entire complexion of the game would have changed. The Dodgers quickly struck back in the second, with Kemp belting a two-run homer off Carpenter, and St. Louis never led again. Pujols went 0-for-3, with two intentional walks, for which the rest of the lineup couldn't punish Los Angeles.

Pujols received another intentional pass in the second game, which again paid off for the Dodgers, as Holliday couldn't capitalize behind him. The Cardinals were on the verge of tying the series, holding a 2–1 lead in the bottom of the ninth with two outs. St. Louis closer Ryan Franklin appeared to have nailed down the save when James Loney lined to left for what should have been the game's final out. Instead, Holliday lost the ball in the lights. The ball bounced off Holliday's stomach and fell to the ground, with Loney ending up at second. Franklin then imploded—walking Casey Blake, giving up an RBI single to Ron Belliard, walking Russell Martin and then coughing up the game-winning hit to Mark Loretta, as the Dodgers took a 2–0 series lead.

"This team can win three games in a row," Pujols told the *Post-Dispatch*. "This team can win 11 games in a row. This team is good enough to come back."

The team may have been good enough in Pujols' estimation, but a comeback was not in the cards. Despite two hits and an RBI from Pujols, the Dodgers took game three in St. Louis 5–1, to complete the sweep.

All that was left for Pujols was to await the MVP announcement, which came in November. For his two previous MVP awards, Pujols faced some competition. This time, the award was never in doubt. Pujols collected all thirty-two first-place votes and his 448 total points in the voting were miles ahead of Hanley Ramirez's 233. He became one of only ten players ever to win the award three times, joining Stan Musial as the only two Cardinals to accomplish that feat.

"It's pretty special to have accomplished that in just the nine years of my career," Pujols said. "All the glory goes to God because, without him, I wouldn't be standing up here."

CHAPTER TWENTY-FIVE

UNFINISHED BUSINESS

Look, I know I'm not going to play baseball forever.
But I'm never going to stop giving back.
—Albert Pujols, USA Today, November 30, 2010

During the long history of professional baseball, evolutions within the game have changed the measure and definition of what constitutes a "great player." From one era to the next, the style of play and the allowed skin color of players have transformed baseball into something much different than the game played at the formation of the National League in 1876. As a result, comparing teams and players from one generation with those of another is a tricky business. Babe Ruth hit 714 home runs without the help of video-enhanced scouting reports on opposing pitchers, but he also hit those homers without the hindrance of facing a Negro League pitcher like Satchel Paige.

Therefore, when a living legend from the past generation sings the praise of a player from the present generation—baseball fans stop and take notice. Hank Aaron kicked off Albert Pujols' 2009–2010 off-season with just such praise. "He could play in anybody's day," Aaron said in answer to the question of how Pujols compared to greats from previous eras. "And he's such a wonderful guy. He's one of the few guys in the league that you like being around." That level of praise, coming from one of the greatest of the greats, speaks volumes about Albert Pujols—the player and the man.

During the off-season, the Pujols family once again found itself in a constant motion of activity all winter long. Almost as soon as the last out was recorded in the third game of the 2009 NLDS at Busch Stadium, Albert and Dee Dee turned their attention to family vacation (and family expansion), baseball conversations, and events for the Pujols Family Foundation.

In late October, Pujols wore an arm sling to the annual PFF prom for students with Down syndrome, having recently undergone surgery on his elbow. The ailing elbow had not prevented Pujols from winning his third NL MVP in 2009, but it was obvious to many that he had been playing in spite of pain. Though there was a possibility that Pujols would need ligament reconstruction, the surgeon was able simply to remove bone spurs and chips from the elbow.

When asked about the elbow months later, Pujols said, "Only God and myself know how I feel. It's so much better. You take six bone spurs almost as big as your pinky fingernail, that's pretty huge. Some of the pieces [were so big] I remember Dr. [James] Andrews and Dr. [George] Paletta saying, 'I can't believe you could swing with those things.'" Cardinals fans breathed a collective sigh of relief that their star first baseman would not be parked on the disabled list to start the 2010 season.

In November, St. Luke's Hospital in Chesterfield, Missouri, announced that it would open the Albert Pujols Wellness Center for Adults, offering "personalized nutrition services, exercise therapy, safety instruction, and relationship-building counseling" for adults with Down syndrome. Pujols had designated a $70,000 award from the Major League Baseball Trust. "Opening a center like this is something my wife and I had talked about since we started the Pujols Family Foundation, and now to have the opportunity to do so is truly a blessing," Pujols said. "The staff at St. Luke's is one of the best, and we have no doubt this center is going to change a lot of lives."

The Pujolses hosted two large events during the holidays. First, in early December, they raised funds and awareness for the foundation's causes through another successful "O Night Divine" Christmas banquet. Then, on

January 1, Albert and Dee Dee celebrated their tenth wedding anniversary by renewing their vows in front of five hundred friends and family in Kansas City, Missouri. Given the humble financial circumstances they faced when they first said their vows, this anniversary offered a night of joy and reflection on all that had taken place during the previous decade.

Just over a month later—and only three weeks before reporting for spring training together as a family—the Pujolses rejoiced in the birth of their fourth child, a second son whom they named Ezra.

Baseball topics played a major part in Pujols' off-season conversations, as he was called to comment on the lucrative contract awarded to Matt Holliday, Tony La Russa's hiring of Mark McGwire as hitting coach, and McGwire's subsequent admission that he had used steroids during his playing career. Near-constant speculation and questions also swirled about whether the Cardinals would get Pujols re-signed to another long-term contract before he hit free agency at the end of the 2011 season.

Fans seemed quite excited to keep free-agent slugger Holliday with the team, providing protection at the plate for Pujols and further stoking predictions of great success for the 2010 team. "Now that they have their Rock under contract," *Post-Dispatch* columnist Joe Strauss said, ". . . the Cards are the prohibitive favorite to repeat as National League Central champion." Even so, when Cardinals management signed Holliday to a franchise-record, seven year, $120 million contract, many questioned whether this move would hamstring the team's financial ability to keep Pujols a Cardinal.

The end of February brought the team to Jupiter, Florida, for the start of spring training, and with it, a great amount of excitement and expectation for the coming season. Pujols and Holliday, both former batting champions, had each slugged above .500 for the past four years. Adam Wainwright and Chris Carpenter were healthy and ready to begin competing again for the NL Cy Young Award.

Only five remaining members of the 2006 World Series championship team were on the Opening Day roster (though Aaron Miles and Jeff Suppan would join the team in midseason). Would this latest edition of the Cardinals be playing for a championship in October? Veteran stars and fresh rookies alike hoped to help win an eleventh championship for the franchise. And, for yet another year, Pujols' own focus on excellence served to solidify his teammates' determination to win. "When you're around greatness, you want it too," Holliday said. "When you get a chance to watch Albert . . . it makes me want to be better."

The team won the April 5 season opener on the road with an explosion of runs against the Cincinnati Reds. After striking out the first two Cardinals, Reds' ace Aaron Harang gave up a home run to Pujols on the fifth pitch he saw that season. "You've got the crowd going in the first inning," Pujols said. "You want to find a way to calm them down. That's what we did." Pujols also hit a home run in the seventh and finished the game with four hits, four runs, three RBIs, and ten total bases. Yadier Molina bested him in the RBI department, however, by hitting his first career grand slam. This game served as a portent of the season to come, as the Cardinals easily won the battle of head-to-head matchups against the Reds, even while losing the war for the Central Division. But let's not get ahead of ourselves.

The team was already 4–2 when it rolled into St. Louis for its April 12 home opener against the yet winless Houston Astros. Home openers at Busch Stadium are always memorable events. Cardinal greats from the past—Musial, Brock, Herzog, Smith, Sutter, etc.—receive royal treatment as they don red sport coats, ride around the stadium waving at fans, and grant their regal blessing to the current team. Stan Musial, eighty-nine years old on Opening Day in 2010, serves as the godfather and living icon of the glory that is Cardinals baseball.

When Pujols was asked whether he imagines he has a future place among Cardinal Hall of Famers, he deflected the question. "Right now I am so young in my career," he said. "I know the legacy that I have to follow because of those guys. That's my job—to make sure I follow that . . . but I don't want to put that pressure on myself. I know what I'm capable of doing . . . [but] I will just try to stay healthy and let my job out there speak for itself."

Pujols' "job out there" certainly spoke for itself on that day. He went 2-for-3, with a home run off his previous nemesis Wandy Rodriguez, leading the Cardinals to a 5–0 victory. With that homer, his fifth in the first seven games of the season and the 371st of his career, Pujols broke Eddie Mathews' nearly fifty-year-old record for the most home runs hit in the first ten seasons of a career.

The Saturday, April 17, nationally televised FOX "Game of the Week" showcased the Mets versus the Cardinals at Busch Stadium. The twenty-inning contest lasted nearly seven hours, and was a marathon event few will easily forget. Holliday, struggling with a flu-like condition, went 0-for-5, and was taken out in an eleventh-inning double-switch that put the pitcher's spot in the batting order behind Pujols. As a result, the pitcher came up to bat three times with a runner in scoring position, but failed to get a hit each time. During all those extra innings, Cardinal infielders Felipe López and Joe Mather both took turns pitching; Mather took the loss as the Mets won 2–1. "That's the first time I've been part of something like that," Pujols said. "That was pretty special right there. We gave everything. It was fun." Fun and memorable.

Early in the season, it seemed as though Redbird hitters were feasting on both strikeouts and home runs. Some wondered whether the lower batting averages, higher number of strikeouts, and greater reliance on the longball were due to the influence of new hitting coach Mark McGwire. Pujols had struck out fourteen times in sixty-nine at-bats, nearly twice his career ratio for whiffs, but he remained ever confident. "If this was September, I'd worry about it. But it's too early in the season," Pujols said. Indeed, by the end of the season, Pujols had notched the ninth best strikeout-per-at-bat ratio in the NL (but his seventy-six strikeouts were his highest since his rookie year). "It's a difficult thing if you're not taking pitches," McGwire said. "When guys feel uncomfortable, the tendency is for them to swing at more than they should."

The Cardinals were 17–8 at the end of April and led the division by four and a half games, prompting Bernie Miklasz to ask, "In the National League Central, who can take this team down?" Miklasz understood that a prolonged slump would hit the team at some point, but there did not appear to be a team up to challenging the Cardinals.

Over the course of an entire season, quirky statistics often sneak into the record books and box scores. For example, Houston Astros' young pitcher Bud Norris laid down an overall losing record of 9–10 and a 4.92 ERA in 2010, but he seemed to have the Cardinals number. As he prepared for his May 13 start, he was 3–0 in three career starts, with only one earned run surrendered in twenty-six innings. This Redbird-domination led Pujols to nickname him "Chuck," in a quip to the media: "He's given us some tough times, you know, Chuck Norris . . ." By the end of the day, "Chuck" Norris once again put the hurt on the Cardinals, striking out eight batters in eight innings on his way to a 4–1 win.

The loss to Houston reduced the Cards' divisional lead to a mere half game. A few days later, the Cincinnati Reds beat the Cardinals and knocked them out of first place. "We're still in second place," Pujols said. "There's no pressure. We need to pick each other up. That's the key."

Space doesn't permit a full recap of the Cincinnati Reds 2010 season, but in brief—they far exceeded preseason expectations. As *Post-Dispatch* columnist Bryan Burwell wrote, "Every year it's someone new. It used to be the Astros, then it was the Cubbies, and now it's the Reds' turn to take the Redbirds for a little spin." Several former Cardinals filled out the roster, having been signed by former St. Louis general manager Walt Jocketty. First baseman Joey Votto led the offense and ran neck-and-neck with Pujols in the "Triple Crown" stats (HR, RBI, and AVG) all season long. Votto would go on to win the NL MVP in 2010, preventing Pujols from winning it for a third consecutive year.

Injuries also took their toll on the Cardinals. Keeping players healthy over the course of a long season is vital for a team that hopes to make it to the playoffs. During the off-season, the Cardinals had signed free-agent pitcher Brad Penny to a one-year, $7.5 million contract, assigning him the third spot in the rotation. On May 23, having pitched only fifty-five innings into the season and carrying a 3.23 ERA, Penny came to bat with the bases loaded and smashed a grand slam. Unfortunately, he also hurt a muscle in his back on the swing, and was taken out of the game. What at first appeared to be a fifteen-day trip to the disabled list turned out to be a season-ending injury.

Pujols and Holliday began to heat up at the plate in June, but they alone couldn't overturn the fair critique of the team's season, offered by Miklasz in a column titled, "Cardinals are failing to live up to ability." General manager John Mozeliak told Miklasz, "I look at what's going on, and the performance and the productivity is just not adding up to what we envisioned."

The Redbirds lost seven of eleven games as they limped into the mid-July All-Star break with a 47–41 record. One of those losses was a July 6 debacle in Colorado, wherein the Cards' bullpen surrendered nine runs in the bottom of the ninth (including a three-run walk-off homer) to lose the game 12–9. Then, the next night, the bullpen gave up four runs in the last two innings to lose 8–7. As gut-wrenching as these types of losses were, the Cards were only one game behind the Reds at the break.

Five Cardinals—Wainwright, Carpenter, Molina, Holliday, and Pujols—traveled to Anaheim to represent the team in the All-Star Game. Pujols received more than four million fan votes, the most of any NL player, and was appearing in his ninth game in ten years. Much to the relief of Cardinals fans, he opted out of the extra wear-and-tear involved in the Home Run Derby. Pujols went 0-for-2 in the game itself, but the NL still won for the first time since 1996.

Coming out of the All-Star break, the Cardinals won seven straight games, but the equally hot Reds kept pace as the teams began to trade first place back-and-forth. Fans of both clubs kept an eye on the schedule, counting down the days until August 9, when the two teams would meet for a three-game battle in Cincinnati. So far in 2010, the Redbirds had won seven of the twelve games against the Reds.

With a division title on the line, no special words were needed to motivate either club. That fact did not prevent Reds' second baseman Brandon Phillips from firing up the Cardinals, by telling the *Dayton Daily News*, "I hate the Cardinals. All they do is [expletive] and moan about everything, all of them. They're little [expletives], all of them."

The Cards won the first game 7–3 with ease. But in the first inning of the second game, Phillips approached the plate and tapped his bat against catcher Molina's shin guard. This is a common greeting in baseball, but was an unwise move given the tension between the teams. Molina knocked away Phillips' bat, and the two players exchanged heated words. A bench-emptying brawl—in baseball normally no punches are thrown—turned ugly when the mass of players smashed up against the backstop fencing. Reds' pitcher Johnny Cueto kicked up and out with his spiked cleats, landing blows to Chris Carpenter and inflicting a career-ending concussion to Cardinals' backup catcher Jason LaRue.

The Cards went on to sweep the Reds in the series, outscoring them 21–8 and moving into sole possession of first place in the division. The Redbirds' performance thrilled fans, who sensed that the full potential of the talented team might finally be realized. The remaining forty-eight games of the season also gave fans reason to be excited, because the Cardinals were scheduled to play one series after another against teams with losing records.

Things turned out very differently, though. Instead of storming out of Cincinnati full of playoff-catapulting energy, the Cards lost thirteen of the next eighteen games. Instead of mopping up on the sub-.500 teams, the Redbirds fell eight games out of first place during a span of a little more than two weeks. It was as if the team spent all its energy in Cincinnati and had nothing left from which to draw for the remainder of the season.

Off-field events also became unexpectedly complicated. On August 28, as the Cardinals prepared to open a series against the Washington Nationals (a series that started a five-game losing streak), La Russa, Albert, and Dee Dee visited the Lincoln Memorial. Sightseeing was not their mission though, for Albert came to receive the Hope Award at an event called the "Restoring Honor" rally. Radio host Glenn Beck organized the event, which included speeches by former Alaska governor Sarah Palin and Alveda King, the niece of Martin Luther King Jr. La Russa introduced Pujols to the immense crowd gathered at the Mall and watching online. Pujols received the medal and spoke a few words of thanks and an explanation of the work of his foundation.

Given the highly contested nature of politics in the United States, it came as no surprise that La Russa and Pujols were praised as well as vilified for their participation at the event.

In his best-selling book, *Three Nights in August: Strategy, Heartbreak, and Joy Inside the Mind of a Manager*, author Buzz Bissinger offered an inside profile of La Russa and also devoted numerous pages to Pujols. To say that Bissinger has long admired them both is not overstating things. Nonetheless, he could not hide his disgust at their presence alongside Beck. "The whole thing with TLR [Tony La Russa] and the Beck rally makes me very sad," Bissinger wrote on his Twitter account. "We will no longer be friends. He will resent what I have said. Life goes on."

Pujols defended his participation, saying, "I wasn't out there trying to be political. I was out there because somebody wanted to honor me for the things I've done through my foundation."

Pujols also took joy in knowing the rally raised millions to support families of fallen Special Forces troops. As Matthew Leach of MLB.com reported, Pujols said, "Now, they [Special Operations Warrior Foundation] have like $30 million, where they can support families, and if people have a problem with that, they need to look themselves in the mirror and say, 'You know what? I'm the one that has a problem.' It is what it is. I can't control what people say. If I'm going to take some heat about the things that I believe and who I represent, then you know what? I take the heat. Just the same way that [Jesus] died on the cross for our sins to give us eternal life, he took a lot of heat. That doesn't bother me at all."

Pujols devoted three hours in August to showing up at an event that allowed him to share his life's mission with millions of his fellow citizens. The fact that his participation brought fierce criticism did not seem to faze him, demonstrating once again his principled approach to life. "They can say and do whatever they want. It's a free country," Pujols said. "I don't play for people. I don't live for people. I live to represent Jesus Christ."

Returning to the baseball diamond, the Cardinals desperately needed to get hot again, while also hoping the Reds would fall into a late summer swoon. The Reds did their part, going 12–15 in September—their worst month of the season. Unfortunately, the Cards also played poorly, going 14–15 in the month, and were officially eliminated from playoff contention on September 28. They ended the season with a five-game win streak and pushed their season record to a respectable 86–76, three wins better than the 2006 team.

In the end, expectations for the Cardinals' 2010 season were not realized. The Holliday-Pujols duo on offense and the Carpenter-Wainwright duo on the mound did not match up to the play of the resurgent Reds. Interestingly, in preseason speculation, *Baseball Prospectus* crunched team and player statistics through its computers and predicted the Cardinals would win the division with an 87–75 record. As far as wins and losses, this prediction was only one game short of reality. Therefore, the unexpected fact of the 2010 season was that another team from the Central Division stood up and played good baseball too.

The 2010 season ended with the sense that this talented team was walking away from unfinished business that would need to be attended to in the coming year.

In a USA Today column on November 30, 2010, Pujols wrote about his other "unfinished business," his Christian mission in the world:

This isn't only about being a baseball player. It's about having the opportunity to change lives.

God has given me a gift in the ability to play baseball. And baseball has given me a platform to give back to the community and put a smile on kids' faces.

It's nice what I do on the baseball field, but I don't want to be remembered for being a very good baseball player. I want to be remembered as a man who helped people and had an impact on their lives. That's what makes me proud.

Look, I know I'm not going to play baseball forever. But I'm never going to stop giving back. It means everything to me. People say the bigger the name, the more responsibility you have. I'm a big believer that I had a responsibility as soon as I put on a uniform. I want to keep moving, keep going to different places, helping as many people as I can.

. . . It's really humbling what we've been able to do, but there's so much more work left.

CHAPTER TWENTY-SIX

THE ST. LOUIS SWAN SONG

We're world champions.
—Albert Pujols

Albert Pujols wasn't supposed to be at the plate staring down Texas Rangers pitcher Darren Oliver in game three of the 2011 World Series. The Cardinals weren't supposed to be leading the game 15–7, and they weren't supposed to be tied with the Rangers at one game apiece in the series. And Pujols wasn't supposed to have two homers already in the game.

The mere suggestion in August would have elicited chuckles and laughs. As late as August 27, the Cardinals were 10 games behind Atlanta in the National League wild card race, with San Francisco also in front of them. Everybody had written off their playoff hopes. Everybody.

But baseball sometimes has a funny way of sticking it to suppositions. And sure enough, the Cardinals began charging, and the Braves began choking. Fast-forward almost two months later, and here Pujols stood, already 4–for–5 on the day with five RBIs. It was already his best World Series game ever, but Pujols wasn't done. With nobody on base, two outs, two balls, and two strikes, Pujols drove an Oliver pitch over the left field fence for his third homer of the game. In doing so, he joined elite company—only Babe Ruth and Reggie Jackson had ever homered three times in a single World Series game. With five hits and six RBIs, Pujols' game was arguably the greatest offensive performance in World Series history.

"It truly is an honor for me," Jackson said in the *St. Louis Post-Dispatch* about Pujols' historic game. "It makes it a little more special for me. Nobody understands how great Ruth was. It was too long ago, a different game. Ruth hit more homers than most teams. This makes it relative for today's fan. When it's Pujols, who is the undisputed best in the game, it shows how special it is."

It was indeed a game for the ages, in a series for the ages, in the final days of a St. Louis Cardinals career for the ages.

The main question lingering throughout the months leading up to the 2011 season was whether the Cardinals and Pujols would be able to agree on a contract extension. Pujols' contract with St. Louis would expire after 2011 and lead to free agency, but both he and the Cardinals had publicly expressed their desire to come to a mutual agreement that would keep Pujols in a St. Louis uniform for the rest of his career.

Despite such insistence from both sides, however, contract talks reached an impasse. Pujols and his agent had set a mid-February deadline for negotiating the extension, because they said they didn't want the issue to be a distraction during the season. The deadline came and went with no resolution, and with Pujols rejecting what was reported as an offer of more than $200 million over nine or ten years from Cardinals owner Bill DeWitt and general manager John Mozeliak.

"Once the 2011 season is over, we hope to revisit those talks," Pujols said in a released statement about the contract negotiations. "I have the utmost respect for Mr. DeWitt, Mo, and the rest of the Cardinals organization, and the path that these negotiations have taken, will not impact our relationship moving forward in any way. I also would like to take this opportunity to reassure the Cardinal Nation, that my effort both on and off the field will never change. I am devoted to giving 100 percent on the field, every single day, just as I have done the last 10 years.

"We're all working together toward a common goal and that is to win a world championship for the city of St. Louis," Pujols continued. "The last thing anyone in this clubhouse needs to worry about, is what's going to happen to me after the season. Let's focus on winning in 2011 and prepare each day to accomplish our goals as a team. I'm feeling strong, healthy, and excited to be at spring training in what I hope to be the start of a world championship season. I can't wait to get started, and God bless."

But Cardinals fans were worried about the team's ability to sign Pujols once the season ended. And they were worried about the team's chances in 2011, especially when ace starter Adam Wainwright went down with a season-ending elbow injury during spring training, only a few days after the Pujols contract drama had ended. Wainwright had won twenty games for St. Louis in 2010 and finished second in Cy Young Award voting—and teams typically don't lose a pitcher of that caliber and still hope to compete.

In April, Pujols and his foundation were the subject of a major story aired on *60 Minutes*. Though it was light on Pujols' faith and reduced it to a snippet in which Pujols said he didn't smoke, didn't drink, and rarely cursed, the story did tell a compelling story of the work Pujols does with children with Down syndrome and in the Dominican Republic. Reporter Bob Simon traveled with Pujols on one of the foundation's mission trips to Pujols' native land.

"Here you are in a pretty messy place. Why do you do it?" Simon asked Pujols.

"This is my passion, and I believe this is what God is calling me to do," Pujols replied.

Both Pujols and the Cardinals started the season slowly, with the Cardinals falling four games out of the division lead in mid-April and Pujols struggling to keep his average above .200. It was the slowest start of Pujols' career. But his bat came to life over a span of four straight Cardinals wins April 13–16, and by April 20, St. Louis had moved into a first-place tie. Pujols homered against Cincinnati in a losing effort on April 23, beginning a homerless drought that lasted a month—the longest such stretch in Pujols' career.

"When it rains, it pours," Pujols told the *Post-Dispatch* during the slump. "But why is this happening? Only God knows. If this is the year that I'm going to struggle, then it is. It is what it is, man. I'm telling you at the end of the year, the numbers will be there."

The power outage from Pujols seemed to have little effect on the team, as others in the lineup were contributing in big ways, especially Lance Berkman, the former star of the Houston Astros who had signed with the

Cardinals prior to the 2011 season. Berkman's bat, in the middle of the St. Louis lineup, was a potent force all year long. Over the month that Pujols went without a homer and drove in only eight runs, Berkman went deep five times and collected 20 RBIs. By the time Pujols homered on May 23 in a 3–1 St. Louis win over San Diego, the Cardinals had moved to a three-and-a-half-game lead in the division.

By the end of May, Pujols was hitting an uncharacteristic .267, with only nine homers and 31 RBIs on the year. He had also grounded into 16 double plays. But he started coming to life in June. He homered in a 6–1 win to open a series against the Cubs June 3, and he was just getting started. The next day, with the score tied at 4 in the bottom of the 12th inning, Pujols smashed a Jeff Samardzija pitch over the left field wall for a game-winning homer (his second home run of the game, to go along with four RBIs). He repeated his heroics in the series finale, slamming another homer in the 10th inning to give the Cardinals a 3–2 win. He went deep for the fourth game in a row June 7, in another St. Louis win against Houston.

The slump was certainly over. But the season took a dark turn starting on June 10 when St. Louis lost the first of seven straight games. The losing streak dropped the Cardinals to second place until they rebounded for two straight wins against Kansas City and moved back into a first-place tie. The second of those wins came at a great cost. Pujols left the June 19 game after a collision at first base with Wilson Betemit. X-rays revealed a small fracture in Pujols' left forearm, with a prognosis that he would be sidelined for up to six weeks.

The news was a serious blow to the gut for the Cardinals. Though they had lost their best pitcher before the season started, they had still managed to stay in the thick of things in the National League Central. Now they were faced with the loss of their star first baseman until August. How would the team respond? Could they hang in there until Pujols returned to the lineup?

Early indications weren't promising. The Cardinals dropped five of their next six to fall three games behind Milwaukee. The offense had been sluggish even before Pujols' injury, and the bullpen had been ineffective. But then St. Louis peeled off four straight wins to recapture the division lead. And a few days later, after only missing 16 games, Pujols came off the disabled list and returned to the lineup much earlier than anyone expected.

"I knew that hopefully it would be less than six weeks," Pujols said. "I told everybody around that I was looking forward to coming off (the DL) in two weeks, and here I am. . . . I have faith in God, training, and working hard. That's the easy way to explain it."

Even with Pujols back in the lineup, the Cards couldn't get much traction. They hovered near the division lead for all of July, closing out the month only a couple of games behind the Brewers. August, however, was another story. Milwaukee got hot and went 21–7 over the month, and St. Louis couldn't keep up, posting a record of only 15–13 and falling as far as ten and a half games behind the Brewers and effectively ending the team's chances of winning the division.

The Cardinals' wild card hopes also seemed slim. With St. Louis trailing Atlanta by 10 games in late August, the only question that seemed to remain was whether Pujols could get hot enough to extend his streak of 10 straight seasons with a .300 batting average, 30 home runs, and 100 RBIs. He ended August hitting .286 with 32 home runs and 79 RBIs, so the home runs weren't the problem. The average and RBIs were going to be close.

Twelve hits in the first seven games of September raised Pujols' average to .295 as the Cardinals welcomed Atlanta to town for a key three-game series. St. Louis had overtaken the Giants in the wild card race but still remained a distant seven and a half games behind the Braves. That was about to change.

Atlanta led the opener 3–1 with two on base and two outs in the bottom of the ninth inning when Pujols singled to drive in two and tie the game. St. Louis won it in the 10th. The next day, Pujols drove in a run in the first inning, and David Freese doubled in Pujols to give the Cardinals a quick 2–0 lead in a game they won 4–3. Pujols added another RBI in the series finale, a 6–3 St. Louis win that left the Cards only four and a half games out of the wild card lead. By September 21, the Braves' lead had shrunk to only a game and a half.

Pujols hit safely in eight straight games from September 16 to September 23. He went 4–for–4 against the Phillies September 16 and scored one of two St. Louis runs in the 11th inning that won the game. He added four more hits in an 11–6 win against the Mets September 20, and two more the following day in another win to raise his average to a season-high .305.

With Atlanta idle on September 22, the Cardinals seemed likely to pick up even more ground that day, especially when they carried a 6–2 lead into the ninth against the Mets. But then the unthinkable happened—the bullpen imploded and the defense struggled. St. Louis gave up six runs in the ninth inning to lose in an 8–6 heartbreaker, and then lost again the next day against the Cubs to fall to three games back in the wild card hunt with only five left to play. It had been a great run, but once again, the outlook seemed dim.

If one trait characterized the Cardinals in 2011, however, it was resilience. Pujols went 0–for–7 over the next two games, but St. Louis won them both. The Cards got help from the continuing collapse of the Braves, who lost two straight to the Nationals, and who clung to a wild card lead of just one game. Fans in St. Louis gave Pujols a standing ovation in his final plate appearance September 25, not knowing if they'd ever get another chance to show their appreciation to their favorite slugger as the Cardinals prepared to head to Houston for the season's final series.

The Cardinals lost another painful game September 26, 5–4 in ten innings against the Astros, and fell behind 5–0 after three innings the next day. But again St. Louis bounced back, erupting for 13 runs in a come-from-behind win and cheering as the Braves lost their fourth straight game. The wild card race was tied with one game left.

Pujols was hitting an even .300 with 37 homers and 98 RBIs. His streak was in jeopardy. He needed a couple of hits and RBIs to keep his .300–30–100 streak alive, and it looked like he'd get it. In the first inning against Houston in the season finale, Pujols singled to drive in Jon Jay as the Cards exploded for five runs. But he went hitless the rest of the game, leaving him with a .299 batting average and 99 RBIs. St. Louis rode the arm of Chris Carpenter, who tossed a two-hitter as the Cardinals cruised to an 8–0 lead and headed into the clubhouse to watch the ending of the Braves-Phillies game, which had gone into extra innings after Philadelphia scored a run in the top of the ninth to tie the score at 3.

An Atlanta win would mean a one-game playoff between the Cardinals and Braves to determine the wild card winner. The stats from that game would count toward season totals, meaning Pujols would still have another shot to extend his streak. But Philadelphia's Hunter Pence drove in the go-ahead run in the top of the 13th inning and the Braves failed to score in the bottom of the 13th. Pujols' streak may have been over, but that mattered little to him—the Cardinals were playoff bound. They had completed an impossible comeback, one of the greatest comebacks in baseball history.

"We were 10 ½, 9 ½ out. But we kept telling ourselves we had a good chance," Pujols told the *Post-Dispatch*. "This is probably the best group of guys we've had and adding those guys brought a little different energy we needed in the clubhouse. We just went out there and had fun."

Opposing St. Louis in the National League Division Series were the Philadelphia Phillies, with Roy Halladay, Cliff Lee, and Cole Hamels anchoring the league's best rotation. Few expected the Cardinals to pose much of a threat to the Phillies, but St. Louis quickly jumped out to a 3–0 lead in the first inning of game one when Rafael Furcal singled, Pujols walked, and Berkman hammered a three-run homer off Halladay. The Phillies rallied, however, to win 11–6. In game two, Pujols broke a 4–4 tie in the sixth with an RBI single that proved to be the game-winner as the Cardinals evened the series.

Pujols stroked four hits the next game in a 3–2 loss that put St. Louis on the brink of elimination. Though Pujols went hitless in game four, the Cards prevailed 5–3 to force a decisive fifth game in Philadelphia, a classic matchup between Carpenter and Halladay. St. Louis quickly jumped on top with an RBI double by Skip Schumaker in the first that proved to be the game's only run. Carpenter hurled a masterpiece and the Cards squeaked by 1–0 and into the National League Championship Series against the Milwaukee Brewers, their division rivals.

After losing 9–6 in the opener, Pujols and the Cardinals exploded in game two. Pujols cranked a two-run homer in the first, the first of his four hits on the night. He drove in five runs in a 12–3 thrashing of the Brewers. Pujols added another two hits and an RBI in game three, when St. Louis scored four runs in the first and held on for a 4–3 win. Milwaukee evened the series in game four, but the Cardinals erupted for nineteen runs over the next two games to win the series in six.

For the third time in his career, Pujols was headed for the World Series, this time against the Texas Rangers, who were making a repeat appearance in the Fall Classic. The series proved to be one of the greatest in baseball history. St. Louis took the opener, 3–2, and seemed poised to grab a commanding 2–0 series lead, carrying a 1–0 lead into the ninth in game two. But the Rangers rallied for two runs, thanks in part to a botched cutoff attempt from Pujols that allowed the go-ahead run to move into scoring position, and the Cardinals couldn't answer in the bottom of the inning. The series was tied 1–1.

Pujols was heavily criticized by the media after the game, when he quickly showered and left the clubhouse without talking to reporters. The loss was a difficult one for the Cardinals, after Jaime Garcia had thrown seven shutout innings and given up only three Texas hits, and Pujols' absence left the team's younger players to talk about it to the media. But as he has done so many times in his career, Pujols took the criticism and turned it into fuel. The next game, he made history.

The offensive output in game three was slow at the start. St. Louis held a 1–0 lead until the Cardinals scored four times in the fourth inning to extend their lead to 5–0. Texas responded with three runs in the bottom of the inning, but St. Louis again padded its lead to 8–3 in the fifth. After Texas scored three times in the bottom of the inning to pull back to within two, Pujols took over.

With Furcal and Ryan Theriot on base, Pujols jacked a three-run homer off Alexi Ogando. He was just getting warmed up. The next inning, with St. Louis holding a 12–6 lead, he took Mike Gonzalez deep for a two-run shot. When Pujols came to the plate in the ninth with the Cardinals comfortably on top 15–7, he got the hat trick—his third home run of the game, earning his place in World Series lore.

Though the win gave the Cardinals a 2–1 series lead, the Rangers weren't done. Derek Holland hurled a gem in game four to tie things at 2–2, and then Texas edged St. Louis 4–2 in game five to put the Cardinals in a 3–2 hole, setting the stage for one of the greatest games in World Series history.

Late in game six, the Rangers seemed in control and on the verge of winning their first World Series title. Texas held a 7–4 lead in the eighth in a game that had been marred by errors and missed opportunities for the Cardinals. Allen Craig homered to pull St. Louis within two.

With the Cardinals down to their final three outs in the bottom of the ninth, Theriot led off the inning and struck out. St. Louis fans again gave Pujols a standing ovation as he came to the plate—just in case they'd never get another opportunity. Pujols responded by lining a double and keeping the Cardinals' hopes alive. Berkman walked, and after a Craig strikeout, Freese tripled in both runners to tie the score and send the game to extra innings.

Josh Hamilton hit a two-run homer in the top of the 10th to give Texas the lead again, but again the Cardinals rallied in the bottom of the inning to tie the game. Freese led off the 11th with a game-winning homer that sent the series to a seventh and final game in St. Louis. In that decisive game seven, though Texas quickly grabbed a 2–0 lead in the first, Freese tied the game in the bottom of the inning with a two-run double, scoring Pujols and Berkman. St. Louis added four more runs, and Carpenter and the bullpen held the Rangers scoreless the rest of the way to give the Cardinals their 11th World Series championship, and Pujols' second. The unlikeliest of post-season runs had concluded with Pujols and the Cardinals as victors.

"It's incredible what the Cardinals were able to do from August on, when they were ten and a half games out," Cardinals broadcaster Rick Horton said. "I would venture a guess that you couldn't find one person at that time who would have said it was possible for them to be World Series winners. I don't believe that a baseball team in the major leagues has had that kind of miraculous, one after another, nail-biting finishes in the history of the game."

"We had a 5 percent chance [to reach the playoffs] with 35 games left in the season," Pujols said. "We knew we had to play great. The first five months of the season were pretty bad. But it doesn't matter. We're world champions."

EPILOGUE

On December 8, 2011, one day after the day that lives in infamy, St. Louis Cardinals fans and Los Angeles Angels fans alike marked another day that will live in baseball infamy: when Albert Pujols left the Cardinals for California.

Pujols became a free agent at the end of the 2011 season, after he and the Cardinals were unable to come to terms prior to the season's start. Although St. Louis had exclusive negotiating rights with him during a five-day window at the season's end, talks didn't start heating up until baseball's winter meetings in Dallas the first week of December. Though hotly pursued by the Miami Marlins, all indications seemed that Pujols and the Cardinals would come to an agreement that would have kept him a Cardinal for life.

But at the last moment, Angels owner Arte Moreno swooped in and made an offer the Cardinals couldn't come close to matching: ten years, $254 million—an offer too good for Pujols to refuse. After accepting the Angels' offer and announcing his exit from St. Louis, Pujols and his wife, Deidre, wrote a letter to Cardinals fans in a full-page ad in the *St. Louis Post-Dispatch*:

> To the City of St. Louis and Cardinal Nation,
>
> I want to thank each and every one of you sincerely from the bottom of my heart for the love and support you have shown me and my family for the past 11 years. In my time with the Cardinals, I have been fortunate enough to play on championship teams, and in front of championship

fans. This community has reached out and embraced me, and for that I am truly humbled and grateful.

My decision to leave has been incredibly difficult, and your support is the biggest reason why. While I am excited about this new chapter in my life, it was very important to me to let you know that St. Louis has been, and will always remain in my heart. I have been honored to be able to wear the Cardinal uniform the last 11 seasons, and I want to thank the entire Cardinals organization, my teammates, coaches, managers and staff for everything they have given to me as well.

We call St. Louis home and my family and I are so blessed to have made lifelong relationships in St. Louis that we look forward to continuing for many years to come, and words cannot fully express our gratitude to you all.

Thank You and God Bless,

Albert and Deidre

Pujols' departure marked an end of an era in St. Louis. Over eleven years with the Cardinals, Pujols amassed statistics that rival the best in baseball history over the same time frame: 445 home runs, 1,329 RBIs; 2,073 hits; a .328 batting average. He led the Cardinals to seven playoff appearances, three World Series, and two World Series titles. His name will forever be linked, as far as stats go, to the best players in St. Louis history.

But Pujols also left behind an opportunity to establish a lasting legacy in St. Louis and to be forever embraced as a hero there. Most fans were hoping he'd be another Stan Musial, playing his entire career with the Cardinals before entering the Hall of Fame, with the adulation and admiration of the entire city for the rest of his life.

Pujols chose a different path for himself and his legacy. Barring some unforeseen circumstance, he'll spend the rest of his career as an Angel, doing his best to establish and build a new legacy in Anaheim. Whatever team's name he wears on the front of his uniform, Pujols remains committed to what he sees as his most important work—his Christian mission in the world. As he wrote in a 2010 column in *USA Today*:

This isn't only about being a baseball player. It's about having the opportunity to change lives.

God has given me a gift in the ability to play baseball. And baseball has given me a platform to give back to the community and put a smile on kids' faces.

It's nice what I do on the baseball field, but I don't want to be remembered for being a very good baseball player. I want to be remembered as a man who helped people and had an impact on their lives. That's what makes me proud.

Look, I know I'm not going to play baseball forever. But I'm never going to stop giving back. It means everything to me. People say the bigger the name, the more responsibility you have. I'm a big believer that I had a responsibility as soon as I put on a uniform. I want to keep moving, keep going to different places, helping as many people as I can.

. . . It's really humbling what we've been able to do, but there's so much more work left.

APPENDIX

SEASON-BY-SEASON STATS

Year	G	AB	R	H	2B	3B	HR	RBI	SB	CS	BB	SO	BA	OBP	SLG
2001	161	590	112	194	47	4	37	130	1	3	69	93	.329	.403	.610
2002	157	590	118	185	40	2	34	127	2	4	72	69	.314	.394	.561
2003	157	591	**137**	**212**	**51**	1	43	124	5	1	79	65	**.359**	.439	.667
2004	154	592	**133**	196	51	2	46	123	5	5	84	52	.331	.415	.657
2005	161	591	**129**	195	38	2	41	117	16	2	97	65	.330	.430	.609
2006	143	535	119	177	33	1	49	137	7	2	92	50	.331	.431	**.671**
2007	158	565	99	185	38	1	32	103	2	6	99	58	.327	.429	.568
2008	148	524	100	187	44	0	37	116	7	3	104	54	.357	.462	**.653**
2009	160	568	**124**	186	45	1	**47**	135	16	4	115	64	.327	**.443**	**.658**
2010	159	587	**115**	183	39	1	**42**	**118**	14	4	103	76	.312	.414	.596
Career Totals	1558	5733	1186	1900	426	15	408	1230	75	34	914	646	.331	.426	.624
Bold = Led league															

NOTES

CHAPTER 1

3. *There was too much Albert Pujols today*: Derrick Goold, "Pujols hits 3 home runs on Down Syndrome Awareness Day," *St. Louis Post-Dispatch*, September 3, 2006.
6. *Among all major leaguers who ever played*: general statistical information about Major League Baseball gleaned from www.baseball-reference.com.
8. *If Pujols plays only nine more*: Kevin Baxter, "Albert Pujols leaves no doubt," *Los Angeles Times*, August 19, 2009.
9. *embarrassed and disappointed*: Mel Antonen, "Focus of Cardinals first baseman Pujols: higher power," *USA Today*, April 1, 2009.
9. *I hung it, and he banged it*: Goold, "Pujols hits 3."
10. *faith, family, others*: Pujols Family Foundation, "About Us," www.pujolsfamilyfoundation.org/about/, accessed July 10, 2010.
10. *People have said to me*: Pujols Family Foundation, "A Message of Faith from Albert Pujols," www.pujolsfamilyfoundation.org/faith, accessed July 10, 2010.
10. *God's only son, [who] lived*: Ibid.
10. *The answer simply is because our faith*: Ibid.
11. *At the end of the day*: Andrew Knox, "Albert Pujols: A Hero's Worship," *The 700 Club*, www.cbn.com/entertainment/sports/700club_albertpujols080206.aspx, accessed July 10, 2010.
11. *The highway's jammed with broken heroes*: Bruce Springsteen "Born to Run," 1975.
11. *The kids look at me*: Knox, "A Hero's worship."

CHAPTER 2

15. *I always liked to go*: Mike Eisenbath, "Man oh man! Albert makes his mark in the lineup for the Cardinals," *St. Louis Post-Dispatch*, May 20, 2001.
17. *Can you imagine*: Bryan Burwell, "Are Cards fans not getting the message?" *St. Louis Post-Dispatch*, May 6, 2007.

13, 17. *God made*: Joe Posnanski, "The Power to Believe," *Sports Illustrated*, March 16, 2009.

17. *My dad always*: Mel Antonen, "Slugger's focus: Higher power; Faith compels Pujols to help less fortunate," *USA Today*, March 31, 2009.
18. *He showed me*: author interview with Todd Perry.
19. *They had (Fred) McGriff*: Antonen, "Slugger's focus."

CHAPTER 3

21. *He was an absolute*: author interview with Ryan Stegall.
21. *He hit a ball*: Ibid.
21. *It hasn't gone away*: Ibid.
21. *That was one of those*: author interview with Dave Fry.
22. *He didn't hardly say*: Ibid.
22. *Albert says that*: Ibid.
23. *I go up there*: Ibid.
23. *You're coming from another*: author interview with Chris Francka.
23. *Albert's the type of guy*: Ibid.
24. *He had to work extra hard*: author interview with Scott Hanna.

24. *When it came to the baseball*: Fry.
25. *He really got mad*: Ibid., Fry.
25. *It was an older car*: Ibid.
25. *a poor man's version*: Paul Coro, "Fits with a glove: Dominican player joins Fort Osage," *Kansas City Star*, April 4, 1997.
25. *I remember down at state*: Hanna.
20, 26. *He wasn't the normal*: Francka.
26. *A lot of the other coaches*: Fry.
26. *He was so driven*: Ibid.

CHAPTER 4

Note: material from author interview with Dee Dee Pujols was originally used in "Deidre Pujols: Living for God," by Tim Ellsworth, *HomeLife*, April 2006.

27. *I just felt that God*: *HomeLife*, April 2006.
28. *I really enjoyed it*: Ibid.
28. *She did not come from*: author interview with Jeff Adams, November 16, 2009.
28. *The day I gave birth to Isabella*: *HomeLife*, April 2006.
29. *I think Deidre's maturity*: *HomeLife*, April 2006.
29. *I call Albert my earthly savior*: from "Albert and Dee Dee Pujols: Giving Honor To God," an interview with James Dobson for *Focus on the Family* radio program, originally aired August 15–16, 2006.
29. *It's been a slow process*: Ibid.
29. *Albert and I are on such a platform*: Ibid.
29. *Dee Dee is really the one*: Adams.
30. *Albert didn't want her*: Ibid.
30. *There are also times when*: *HomeLife*, April 2006.
30. *Next to the Lord*: *HomeLife*, April 2006.
30. *Here's a woman with two*: *HomeLife*, April 2006.
30. *My immediate reaction*: "Giving honor to God."
31. *We can get so worn out*: Dee Dee Pujols.
31. *We're going to have problems*: Ibid.
31. *I could sit here*: Ibid.

CHAPTER 5

33. *That kind of got*: author interview with Marty Kilgore, November 17, 2009.
32, 33. *This kid had a work*: Ibid.
33. *We would always take*: author interview with Landon Brandes, December 28, 2009.
34. *So we went down there*: Kilgore, November 17, 2009.
34. *He was always helping*: Ibid.
35. *The other players were*: Ibid.
36. *You knew that hurt*: Ibid.
35. *With him coming in*: Brandes, December 28, 2009.
36. *It was more of an*: Ibid.
36. *I'll never forget our talks*: Kilgore, November 17, 2009.
37. *He wanted to hang out*: Ibid.
37. *It really means a lot*: Ibid.

CHAPTER 6

38. *I'm the pastor of*: author interview with Jeff Adams, November 16, 2009.
39. *I feel a long way*: Bono (lyrics), "Bullet the Blue Sky," U2, 1987.
39. *to be serious with God*: from "Albert and Dee Dee Pujols: Giving Honor To God,"

an interview with James Dobson for *Focus on the Family* radio program, originally aired August 15–16, 2006.

39. *I went to church probably once*: Ibid.
39. *After a couple of weeks*: Ibid.
39. *Her Spanish was not that good*: Adams, November 16, 2009.
40. *One Sunday, she just invited*: authors' transcription of video clip "Albert gives testimony at Family Christian Day at Busch Stadium in 2007," www.youtube.com/watch?v=wX6_6MtaA1o&feature=related, accessed July 11, 2010.
40. *From that time forth*: Adams, November 16, 2009.
40. *I had no idea he played baseball*: Ibid.

CHAPTER 7

42. *He could really hit*: Scott Carter, "The one that got away," *Tampa Tribune*, June 17, 2005.
42. *But he had some things*: author interview with Dave Karaff, February 1, 2010.
42. *just an ugly workout*: Marc Topkin, "Pujols a Ray: Yes, it could have happened," *St. Petersburg Times*, October 27, 2004.
43. *Karaff was sitting at home*: author interview with Dave Karaff
44. *He wasn't like he is now*: author interview with Marty Kilgore, November 17, 2009.
44. *Here's the thing about Albert*: Karaff, February 1, 2010.
44. *I was really excited*: Bob Luder, "Cards draft Fort Osage player," *Kansas City Star*, July 15, 1999.
44. *He was a very mature*: author interview with Frank Leo, January 31, 2010.
45. *And it wasn't a soft*: Ibid.
45. *Someday I'm going to be watching*: Ibid.
45. *He was so polite*: Ibid.
46. *I didn't get what*: Dave Reynolds, "Big stick, good glove for chiefs—Peoria's 20-year-old Dominican 3B bonus on this season's roster," *Peoria Journal Star*, April 21, 2000.
46. *How can you draft*: Mike Dodd, "Cards' Pujols blasts off; St. Louis slugger says he doesn't play for numbers, but opposing pitchers can count, and totals are high," *USA Today*, May 23, 2006.
46. *I never once said*: Karaff, February 1, 2010.
47. *It's just an unfortunate*: Ibid.

CHAPTER 8

49. *I've been enjoying*: Marlon W. Morgan, "Redbirds postgame," *Commercial Appeal* (Memphis), September 7, 2000.
49. *The people in Memphis*: author interview with Allie Prescott.
50. *That first day*: author interview with Dave Reynolds.
50. *While he's laying there*: Dave Reynolds, "Basebrawl erupts as Chiefs beat Lugnuts," *Peoria Journal Star*, May 1, 2000.
51. *We were truly living*: Pujols Family Foundation, "Deidre Pujols," www.pujolsfamilyfoundation.org/about/deidre-pujols.htm, accessed July 11, 2010.
51. *He was very humble*: Reynolds.
51. *That was nice*: Dave Reynolds, "Chiefs' lead West to All-Star victory," *Peoria Journal Star*, June 21, 2000.
48, 51. *He was sort of*: author interview with Dave Reynolds.
52. *I didn't try to do*: Jeff Seidel and Todd Jacobson, "Rust belts 2-run double for Baysox," *Washington Post*, August 12, 2000.

52. *We needed another bat*: author interview with Galen Pitts.
53. *It was impressive*: Ibid.
53. *He wasn't here long*: author interview with Woody Galyean.
53. *It's nice to see*: Ibid.
54. *Some of the things*: author interview with Mike Maroth.
54. *Playing with him before*: Ibid.
54. *He's not afraid to share*: Ibid.
54. *Even with that work ethic*: Ibid.
55. *He's really excited about*: Mike Eisenbath, "Man Oh Man! Albert makes his mark in the lineup for the Cardinals," *St. Louis Post-Dispatch*, May 20, 2001.

CHAPTER 9

57. *That's beautiful*: Rick Hummel, "Time is short for the players trying to make Cardinals roster," *St. Louis Post-Dispatch*, March 28, 2001.
57. *It was an unbelievable: Bernie Miklasz*, "Balls hit buildings, jaws hit floor as Pujols comes up swinging," *St. Louis Post-Dispatch*, March 1, 2001.
58. *He was the most*: Rick Hummel, "Hermanson is slated to start in Cards' first exhibition game," *St. Louis Post-Dispatch*, February 25, 2001.
58. *Everybody wants to make*: author interview with Ben Zobrist.
58. *He has presence*: Miklasz, "Balls hit buildings."
58. *This guy is going*: David Waldstein, "Boras changes Sheffield's tune," *Star-Ledger* (Newark, NJ), March 18, 2001.
59. *Only a few guys*: Chuck Johnson, "Pujols a Card-carrying star 21-year-old rookie impresses with his power and his poise," *USA Today*, May 22, 2001.
59. *I don't think you*: Rick Hummel, "Paquette maintains his position at third, regardless of spot in batting order," *St. Louis Post-Dispatch*, March 25, 2001.
61. *There are so many*: Rick Hummel, "Try this on for openers: Pujols makes team," *St. Louis Post-Dispatch*, April 2, 2001.
61. *I'm still working hard*: Ibid.

CHAPTER 10

66. *It was big*: author interview with Woody Williams.
66. *Strong kid*: Mike Eisenbath, "McGwire heads fan club for Pujols: Rookie slugger makes Johnson pay for mistake," *St. Louis Post-Dispatch*, October 11, 2001.
66. *Just try to be*: Ibid.
66. *He's gotten so many*: Eisenbath, "McGwire heads fan club."
67. *More seasoning at Memphis*: "Cardinals player capsules," *St. Louis Post-Dispatch*, April 1, 2001.
68. *[Pujols] is a winning*: Rick Hummel, "Cards get it done without big guns," *St. Louis Post-Dispatch*, April 8, 2001.
68. *These guys love*: Rick Hummel, "Cards bring Rockies down to earth," *St. Louis Post-Dispatch*, April 10, 2001.
65, 68. *a new hero*: Steven A. Riess, *Encyclopedia of Major League Baseball Clubs*, Vol. 1 (Santa Barbara, CA: Greenwood Publishing Group, 2006), 435.
68. *It was kind of amazing*: author interview with Rick Horton.
69. *He seemed to be*: Ibid.
69. *I'm just trying*: Rick Hummel, "Light hitters fuel NY's comeback," *St. Louis Post-Dispatch*, April 29, 2001.
71. *As I sat there*: author interview with Dave Fry.
71. *That's great*: Rick Hummel, "As expected, Pujols and Morris are named to the All-Star team," *St. Louis Post-Dispatch*, July 5, 2001.

72. *It was amazing that*: author interview with Doug Glanville.
76. *I'm excited, I'm glad*: Jack Curry, "Pujols and Suzuki win, but there is a surprise," *New York Times*, November 13, 2001.

CHAPTER 11

78. *Thanks for your patience*: Ed Price, "Girardi recalls Kile's death," *Star-Ledger* (Newark, NJ), June 22, 2008.
79. *Please be respectful*: Price, Ibid.
79. *Darryl was always there*: Joe Strauss, "Cards still are grieving but try to regain focus," *St. Louis Post-Dispatch*, June 25, 2002.
80. *I was totally surprised*: Joe Strauss, "Trading places: Pujols goes to left, Polanco to third," *St. Louis Post-Dispatch*, March 25, 2002.
80. *If there's such a thing*: Bernie Miklasz, "Pressure mounts on the Cardinals to make it a Redbird October," *St. Louis Post-Dispatch*, March 31, 2002.
81. *This is a team*: Joe Strauss, "Stephenson's back woes resurface; DL is likely," *St. Louis Post-Dispatch*, April 18, 2002.
81. *I have a lot*: Strauss, Ibid.
81. *I'm a little upset*: Joe Strauss, "Astros believe they stand alone as division champs," *St. Louis Post Dispatch*, April 14, 2002.
82. *There's no excuse*: Stu Durando, "Pujols drops opportunity to beat Reds," *St. Louis Post-Dispatch*, June 30, 2002.
85. *If Darryl and Jack Buck*: Joe Strauss, "Pity by the bay; Cardinals waste Morris' gem as season ends," *St. Louis Post-Dispatch*, October 15, 2002.

CHAPTER 12

86. *The thing I appreciate about*: Allen Palmeri, "3rd MVP lifts Pujols to Musial's level," Baptist Press, November 24, 2009.
87. *God has given them all*: author interview with Todd Perry.
87. *These guys are espousing faith*: author interview with Rick Horton.
87. *Sometimes baseball players will get*: author interview with Kyle McClellan.
87. *Pastor Hunter developed a system*: Lee Warren, "Getting faith past first base," *Living Light News*, 2006.
88. *The year he made it*: author interview with Walt Enoch.
88. *You can do any book*: author interview with Grant Williams.
88. *A lot of times Albert will*: McClellan, October 27, 2009.
88. *When Albert was in his rookie*: author interview with Jeff Adams.
89. *When Mike Matheny was on our*: from "Albert & Dee Dee Pujols: Giving Honor To God," an interview with James Dobson for *Focus on the Family* radio program, originally aired August 15–16, 2006.
89. *We used to get together*: Ibid.
89. *In the baseball world, it is hard*: Horton, August 11, 2009.
89. *I wouldn't trade places*: Perry, October 23, 2009.
89. *Albert has had his struggles*: Ibid.
90. *He thinks about his game*: Daniel G. Habib, "Albert the Great," *Sports Illustrated*, June 30, 2003.
90. *We're all guilty of taking the game*: author interview with Woody Williams.
90. *Albert is a strong follower*: McClellan, October 27, 2009.
90. *Sometimes he really gets*: Ibid.
90. *Albert has a faith that appears*: Adams, November 16, 2009.
90. *You know, we're just sold out*: Jen Collins's KJSL radio interview with Deidre Pujols, June 22, 2009.

CHAPTER 13

91. *If it doesn't work*: Dan O'Neill, "Cards cash in on La Russa's gamble to play Pujols in left," *St. Louis Post-Dispatch*, April 26, 2003.
92. *He can make*: Ibid.
93. *toughest kick in the gut*: Joe Strauss, "La Russa ranks NLCS loss as his most profound disappointment as a manager," *St. Louis Post-Dispatch*, January 28, 2003.
94. *It's good money*, $900,000: Joe Strauss, "Pujols is taking a relaxed approach to long-term deal," *St. Louis Post-Dispatch*, March 12, 2003.
94. *Without a doubt*: Dan O'Neill, "Cardinals keep feasting on AL teams," *St. Louis Post-Dispatch*, June 7, 2003.
95. *He's a great player*: Joe Strauss, "Pujols says Sosa has remained 'my hero,'" *St. Louis Post-Dispatch*, June 6, 2003.
96. *complacent . . . flat*: Bernie Miklasz, "Cards should drop complacent attitude," *St. Louis Post-Dispatch*, June 1, 2003.
96. *It's a helluva compliment*: Bernie Miklasz, "Pujols' approach puts him at the top of La Russa's list," *St. Louis Post-Dispatch*, June 14, 2003.
96. *I went to Tony*: Ibid.
96. *He walks around*: Bernie Miklasz, "Sosa over Pujols? Some All-Star voters are big hypocrites," Bernie Miklasz, *St. Louis Post-Dispatch*, June 29, 2003.
97. *He recognizes that God*: author interview with Jeff Adams, November 16, 2009.
97. *Albert doesn't do anything*: Ibid.
98. *He hit the hell*: R. B. Fallstrom, "Pujols punches catcher in win over Padres," Associated Press, July 13, 2003.
98. *I threw the punch*: Rick Hummel, "Suspension appears likely for Pujols," *St. Louis Post-Dispatch*, July 15, 2003.
99. *It's 100 home runs*: Joe Strauss, "Redbirds overpower Dodgers in homer fest," *St. Louis Post-Dispatch*, July 21, 2003.
99. *There was nothing*: Buzz Bissinger, *Three Nights in August*, (Houghton Mifflin, 2005), 150–151.
102. *Certainly, no player*: William Gildea, "A search for superlatives; Cardinals' Pujols is a hitter who evokes sense of awe," *Washington Post*, August 24, 2003.
102. *It's amazing these last*: Joe Strauss, "Brewers pep up Cardinals," *St. Louis Post-Dispatch*, September 17, 2003.

CHAPTER 14

106. *In that moment*: Joe Strauss, "The Redcaps are coming," *St. Louis Post-Dispatch*, October 22, 2004.
107. *This is business*: Joe Strauss, "Pujols plan to make Cardinals pay up," *St. Louis Post-Dispatch*, January 19, 2004.
107. *This is what I dreamed*: Joe Strauss, "Historic deal sets Cardinals' cornerstone," *St. Louis Post-Dispatch*, February 21, 2004.
107. *I'm pretty sure people*: Ibid.
109. *I was excited for him*: Rick Hummel, "Pujols is helping Luna adjust to life in the major leagues," *St. Louis Post-Dispatch*, April 24, 2004.
110. *We can get on*: Joe Strauss, "Redbirds rock the house," *St. Louis Post-Dispatch*, May 30, 2004.
111. *The best thing about*: Joe Strauss, "Wondrous at Wrigley: Cubs gum it up; Birds stick it to 'em," *St. Louis Post-Dispatch*, July 21, 2004.
111. *It's great if I*: Derrick Goold, "Pujols makes history with his 30th home run," *St. Louis Post-Dispatch*, August 4, 2004.
112. *It bothers me*: Rick Hummel, "Pujols' 5 RBIs propel the Redbirds," *St. Louis Post-Dispatch*, August 17, 2004.

113. *Forty and 100 is*: Rick Hummel, "Pujols deals another winning hand," *St. Louis Post-Dispatch*, August 30, 2004.
113. *[I'd be] hard pressed*: author interview with Woody Williams.
115. *So far, I'd say*: Bernie Miklasz, "Like Clark in 1985, Pujols delivers a jolt," *St. Louis Post-Dispatch*, October 11, 2004.
116. *On Pujols' play*: Rick Hummel, "Big hits aside, Cards do little things well," *St. Louis Post-Dispatch*, October 15, 2004.
116. *It's just a blessing*: Mike Dodd, "Cards' Pujols showing why he's considered one of best," *USA Today*, October 26, 2004.
117. *That's the way*: Tyler Kepner, "Red Sox erase 86 years of futility in 4 games," *New York Times*, October 28, 2004.

CHAPTER 15

119. *Deidre and I have always*: Albert Pujols, "Letter from Albert," *Pujols News*, vol. 1, no. 1 (Summer 2005).
119. *I want to hit a grand slam*: David Wilhelm, "The Pujols family create new foundation," *Belleville News-Democrat*, May 6, 2005.
119. *Going into our fifth year*: Ibid.
120. *Albert had just signed, and remainder of narrative about the origins of PFF*: author interview with Todd Perry, October 23, 2009.
122. *To live and share our commitment*: Pujols Family Foundation, "Mission Statement," www.pujolsfamilyfoundation.org/about/, accessed July 14, 2010.
122. *Our faith in Jesus Christ*: http://www.pujolsfamilyfoundation.org/faith/.
123. *We wish the best*: Perry, October 23, 2009.
123. *When everything is stripped away*: Ibid.
123. *The Pujols Family Foundation, an IRS 501(c)3*: Pujols Family Foundation, "Purpose," www.pujolsfamilyfoundation.org/about/, accessed July 14, 2010.
123. *in lieu of flowers: St. Louis Post-Dispatch obituaries.*
123. *Each year she gives up*: "Leah Hammann does it again," *Pujols News*, vol. 3, no. 1 (Summer 2007).
124. *I've really been amazed at the public's perception*: Perry, October 23, 2009.
124. *There was a guy talking to Albert*: author interview with Dr. Jan Mueller.

CHAPTER 16

127. *"If it comes to"*: Derrick Goold, "Still nursing foot, Pujols eases into camp," by Derrick Goold, *St. Louis Post-Dispatch*, February 21, 2005.
127. *I think the main thing*: Joe Strauss, "Pujols: Young man, old eyes," *St. Louis Post-Dispatch*, April 3, 2005.
127. *I want to help those*: Ibid.
128. *It's like winning*: Tom Timmermann, "Cereal slugger 'Breakfast of Champions' adds Pujols to its lineup," *St. Louis Post-Dispatch*, April 8, 2005.
129. *It doesn't matter*: Derrick Goold, "Pujols delivers in the clutch: Two-run double in sixth keys come-from-behind victory," *St. Louis Post-Dispatch*, May 24, 2005.
130. *I told him I*: author interview with Woody Williams.
132. *I wasn't even trying*: Ibid.
132. *Can we pull off*: Bryan Burwell, "Things are tight, but Cards are hanging loose," *St. Louis Post-Dispatch*, October 17, 2005.
133. *Just give me the strength*: Bernie Miklasz, "For Houston, Pujols' HR is a wrecking ball," *St. Louis Post-Dispatch*, October 18, 2005.
133. *When I hit it*: Joe Strauss, "Homecoming king Pujols crowns Astros with dramatic blast, sends series back to Busch," *St. Louis Post-Dispatch*, October 18, 2005.
133. *It's tough to lose*: Bernie Miklasz, "Determined Oswalt turns out the lights at Busch Stadium," *St. Louis Post-Dispatch*, October 20, 2005.

134. *Last season, Deidre Pujols*: Bernie Miklasz, "Number 5 is the charm as Pujols gets his due," *St. Louis Post-Dispatch*, November 16, 2005.
134. *I slept two hours*: Joe Strauss, "MVP Albert Pujols: No more worrying for Pujols: prize is his," *St. Louis Post-Dispatch*, November 16, 2005.
134. The thing I want to: Joe Strauss, "Mulder celebrates birthday with 13th victory," *St. Louis Post-Dispatch*, August 6, 2005.

CHAPTER 17

135, 137. *Baseball is simply my platform*: Pujols Family Foundation, "A Message of Faith from Albert Pujols," www.pujolsfamilyfoundation.org/faith/, accessed July 15, 2010.
135. *more important than anything I could*: "My Story: Albert Pujols," *Sharing the Victory*, October 2006.
135. *a thousand copies of the Pujols piece*: Roger Garfield, "Pujols family pays tribute to teen," *Daily News Journal* (Murfreesboro, TN), September 23, 2007.
136. *joined Pujols, the Frizzells and Riverdale*: Roger Garfield, "Jordan's night," *Daily News Journal* (Murfreesboro, TN), July 1, 2008.
136. *Make sure that you stand up for Christ*: Ibid.
136. *Evangelism is just one*: D. T. Niles (1908–1970), Sri Lankan evangelist and hymn writer, is credited for this great quote.
137. *As conditioned as we are to hear the word*: Jeff Passan, "Pujols is a faith-based mystery," Yahoo Sports, July 14, 2009, www.sports.yahoo.com/mlb/news?slug=jp-pujols071409, accessed July 15, 2010.
137. *God has given me the ability to succeed*: PFF, "A Message of Faith."
137. *It is a wonderful paradox that*: Todd Perry, "From the director's desk," *Pujols News*, vol. 2, no. 3 (Winter 2006).
137. *He's very vocal and very simple*: author interview with Grant Williams, October 23, 2009.
137. *How do I know that I will spend eternity*: PFF, "A Message of faith."
138. *As a Christian, I am called to live*: Scott Lamb and Tim Ellsworth, "Holy hitter," *World Magazine*, February 27, 2010.
138. *I can't think of a greater place to celebrate*: Ibid.
138. *He is, by far, one of the most*: Bob Costas MLB.com interview with Mark McGwire, January 11, 2010, quoted in Lamb and Ellsworth, "Holy hitter."
138. *In baseball, every night there are*: Lamb and Ellsworth, "Holy hitter."
138. *Many men come to hear Albert*: *Pujols News* Vol. 2 Issue No. 3 (Winter 2006).
139. *Albert and Deidre Pujols have become*: author interview with Judy Boen.
139. *The first year, Albert came out*: Ibid.
139. *He was a relatively new Christian*: Ibid.
139. *This is an opportunity to share*: Tim Townsend, "Two religions converge at Busch: baseball and Christianity," *St. Louis Post-Dispatch*, June 24, 2007.
140. *Mark told him, 'You have*: author interview with Mike Maroth, November 3, 2009. The name of the book that influenced Pujols is *One Thing You Can't Do in Heaven*, by Mark Cahill.
140. *What do you think is going to happen*: Chad Bonham, "Albert Pujols' field of faith," *Charisma* Magazine, February 27, 2009.
140. *Here you're playing a game*: Maroth, November 3, 2009.
140. *There were some that would say*: Bonham, "Albert Pujols' field."
140. *One funny thing about Albert is*: Williams, October 23, 2009.
140. *You'd be surprised how many people I witnessed to*: Bonham, "Albert Pujols' field."
140. *Being one of the star players*: Williams, October 23, 2009.
140. *I've seen him share himself*: author interview with Walt Enoch.

141. *One of your greatest thrills*: from "Albert and Dee Dee Pujols: Giving honor to God," an interview with James Dobson for *Focus on the Family* radio program, originally aired August 15–16, 2006.
141. *Definitely—that was better than anything*: Ibid.
141. *I thanked God that He had opened*: Ibid.
141. *He's always going to be there for you*: Ibid.
141. *Albert said that his personal highlight*: Todd Perry, "From the director's desk," *Pujols News*, vol. 2, no. 2 (Autumn 2006).
142. *Every time I step on the field*: "Albert Pujols' testimony at the '2007 Christian Day at the Ballpark.'" author's transcription of the YouTube video of the event: http://www.youtube.com/watch?v=0Y8Axr1m7Ys&p=2FCF13193E59D05E&playnext=1&index=32.

CHAPTER 18

145. *This is a great opportunity*: Joe Strauss, "Pujols embraces chance to fill void," *St. Louis Post-Dispatch*, February 26, 2006.
146. *For the fans in*: Rick Hummel, "Notebook," *St. Louis Post-Dispatch*, April 18, 2006.
146. *They sense a teammate*: Bernie Miklasz, "Fans ripping Pujols make no sense at all," *St. Louis Post-Dispatch*, April 22, 2006.
146. *I went to the video*: Joe Strauss, "No dancing zone," *St. Louis Post-Dispatch*, April 25, 2006.
147. *It's difficult for Pujols*: Miklasz, "Fans ripping."
147. *Pujols has done to*: Nate Silver, "Baseball's most valuable players," ESPN.com, sports.espn.go.com/espn/page2/story?page=silver/060418_2, accessed August 25, 2010.
149. *I see it this way*: Dionisio Soldevila, "Pujols says MVP should come from playoff team," Associated Press, November 30, 2006.
149. *I was a little hurt*: Tom Finkel, "Pujols remarks lost in translation?" *Riverfront Times*, November 30, 2006.
149. *I feel so bad because*: "Pujols feels his MVP message was lost in translation," December 4, 2006, ESPN.com news services, sports.espn.go.com/mlb/news/story?id=2685770, accessed July 27, 2010.
150. *He wasn't good*: Murray Chass, "Not everybody is happy in St. Louis," *New York Times*, October 15, 2006.
150. *The real shame*: John Harper, "Albert's no prince," *New York Daily News*, October 14, 2006.
150. *Pujols, considered by many*: Chass, "Not everybody."
150. *For some odd reason*: Bryan Burwell, "Surly Pujols mirrors Bonds at his worst," *St. Louis Post-Dispatch*, October 17, 2006.
151. *I still close my eyes*: Bryan Burwell, "Pujols mourns death of his beloved uncle," *St. Louis Post-Dispatch*, October 18, 2006.
151. *I told him that whenever*: Ibid.
151. *Life's too short*: Ibid.
152. *Who of us wants*: author interview with Rick Horton, August 11, 2009.
154. "*He pitched a good*: Joe Strauss, "Tigers freeze out Cards," *St. Louis Post-Dispatch*, October 23, 2006.
154. *I said when I won*: Bernie Miklasz, "Loss in '04 intensifies Pujols' hunger for ring," *St. Louis Post-Dispatch*, October 26, 2006.

CHAPTER 19

155. *This is what it is all about*: quoted in "Albert's hitters and splitters," *Pujols News*, vol. 2, no. 1 (Summer 2006).

155. *"Fredbird!" Tim exclaimed, pointing toward*: Tim Ellsworth, "A prom to remember," Baptist Press, October 30, 2009.
156. *This is heaven-sent*: Ibid.
156. *promote awareness, provide hope and meet*: Pujols Family Foundation, "Vision statement," www.pujolsfamilyfoundation.org/about/, accessed July 27, 2010.
157. *Through the PFF, we want to showcase*: "Spotlight: Pujols Foundation," a video from Fox Sports, multimedia.foxsports.com/m/video/25928454/spotlight-pujols-foundation.htm?q=%22Albert+Pujols%22, accessed July 27, 2010.
157. *God is using Bella's life in such a major way*: Jen Collins' radio interview (KJSL) with Deidre Pujols, June 22, 2009.
157. *Nobody could have set that up*: Ibid.
157. *According to the* New York Times: "Prenatal Test Puts Down Syndrome in Hard Focus" by Amy Harmon, accessed here: http://www.nytimes.com/2007/05/09/us/09down.html.
157. *In "A Letter from Deidre Pujols" in 2006*: "A Letter from Deidre Pujols," *Pujols News*, vol. 1, no. 3 (Winter 2005).
158. *The fact that 92 percent of women who are told*: R. Albert Mohler, "Will babies with Down Syndrome just disappear?" (blog post), September 18, 2009, www.albertmohler.com/2009/09/18/will-babies-with-down-syndrome-just-disappear/, accessed July 27, 2010.
158. *intended to take him home*: George Will, "Golly, what did Jon do?" *One Man's America: The Pleasures and Provocations of Our Singular Nation* (NY: Three Rivers Press, 2009), 366.
158. *Because Down syndrome is determined at conception*: George Will, "Jon Will's aptitudes," *The Leveling Wind: Politics, the Culture, and Other News 1990–1994* (Penguin, 1995), 446.
158. *Jon experiences life's*: Ibid.
159. *PFF has served as a bridge*: This story is told in "Carli Maucher update," *Pujols News*, vol. 2, no. 4 (Spring 2007).
159. *My goal for the year*: "A letter from Deidre Pujols."
159. *With only two full-time staff members*: Anna Jones, "O' Night Divine Christmas Celebration, December 15, 2007," *Pujols News*, vol. 3, no. 3 (Winter 2007).
159. *Learning to ride a bike is an important*: This story is told in "Lose the training wheels bike camp," *Pujols News*, vol. 4, no. 1 (Summer 2008).
160. *They had so much girly stuff to do*: This story is told in Anna Jones, "High tea at the Chase Park Plaza," *Pujols News*, vol. 1, no. 2 (Fall 2005).
160. *For you formed my inward parts*: Psalm 139:13–14.
161. *Ten Hummers at a time took off*: This story is told in Anna Jones, "Lynch Hummer / Pujols Family Foundation Off Road Event," *Pujols News*, vol. 3, no. 4 (Spring 2008).
161. *We are all confronted with needing*: Jen Cooper, "Batter Up! Family cooking experience," *Pujols News* (Summer 2009).
161. *I'm bowling 300 but hitting .220*: Allen Barra, *Yogi Berra: Eternal Yankee*, xv.
162. *It was obvious to anyone who attended that*: "Albert's 'Hitters and Splitters' bowling event," *Pujols News*, vol. 2, no. 1 (Summer 2006).
162. *This is what it is all about*: Ibid.
162. *We told our players*: Anna Jones, "The perfect game," *Pujols News*, vol. 4, no. 1 (Summer 2008).
162. *That's what a day like today*: Ibid.
163. *To see how athletic the All-Stars*: Ibid.
163. *You have these dads*: Ibid.
163. *As great as he is on the field*: Ibid.

163. *There is a light that goes on inside of Albert*: author interview with Todd Perry, October 23, 2009.
163. *It is a great blessing*: author interview with Kevin Garrett.

CHAPTER 20

164. *There's no crying in baseball*: Bernie Miklasz, "Cards psyche takes lickin', but somehow keeps tickin'," *St. Louis Post-Dispatch*, September 2, 2007.
164. *I can't forget the sound*: Joe Strauss, "A season of upheaval," *St. Louis Post-Dispatch*, September 9, 2007.
165. *Just pray for him*: Derrick Goold, "Career in jeopardy?" *St. Louis Post-Dispatch*, September 2, 2007.
165. *There was an empty feeling*: Joe Strauss, "At last, La Russa has filled the void," *St. Louis Post-Dispatch*, January 11, 2007.
165. *You build a fan base*: Philip Dine, "Cards paint the White House red," *St. Louis Post-Dispatch*, January 17, 2007.
166. *anyone who is close to me*: Joe Strauss and Derrick Goold, "La Russa is contrite after arrest," *St. Louis Post-Dispatch*, March 23, 2007.
167. *I think something is either good*: Joe Strauss and Rick Hummel, "Pujols strongly backs La Russa 'like a father'," *St. Louis Post-Dispatch*, March 24, 2007.
167. *He cares about everybody*: Ibid.
167. *He commands that kind of respect*: author interview with Adam Wainwright.
168. *Despite the negativity, the Cards*: Jeff Gordon, "'Experts' say Cards won't even win NL Central title," *St. Louis Post-Dispatch*, April 2, 2007.
168. *We're going to get frustrated*: Rick Hummel, "Cards Notes," *St. Louis Post-Dispatch*, April 22, 2007.
168. *I wish the report had reflected*: Joe Strauss, "Cards change alcohol policy," *St. Louis Post-Dispatch*, May 5, 2007.
169. *Believe me, if I had*: Bryan Burwell, "Are Cards fans not getting the message?" *St. Louis Post-Dispatch*, May 6, 2007.
169. *He's not making enough*: Joe Strauss, "Pujols woes," *St. Louis Post-Dispatch*, May 15, 2007.
169. *You can write that I'm lost*: Ibid.
169. *I told the guys*: Joe Strauss, "Cardinals locate missing power," *St. Louis Post-Dispatch*, June 4, 2007.
169. *It could have been a lot worse*: Bryan Burwell, "Cards need to figure out their identity," *St. Louis Post-Dispatch*, July 10, 2007.
170. *I look at it as an honor*: Joe Strauss, "Cards one and only All-Star: Pujols," *St. Louis Post-Dispatch*, July 2, 2007.
170. *Go ask the manager*: Rick Hummel, "La Russa understands fans' questions," *St. Louis Post-Dispatch*, July 12, 2007.
170. *just for the drama of the All-Star Game*: Ibid.
170. *People want to start World War III*: Derrick Goold, "Pujols, La Russa deny any friction," *St. Louis Post-Dispatch*, July 13, 2007.
171. *Do I want to hit a home run*: Rick Hummel, "Cards Notes," *St. Louis Post-Dispatch*, July 6, 2007.
171. *When the home runs come*: Ibid.
171. *I don't feel good yet*: Derrick Goold, "Cards Notes," *St. Louis Post-Dispatch*, July 17, 2007.
171. *It's a good strategy to use*: Joe Strauss, "La Russa has pitcher bat 8th," *St. Louis Post-Dispatch*, August 5, 2007.
171. *I don't want a day off*: Derrick Goold, "Pujols plays despite aches," *St. Louis Post-Dispatch*, August 11, 2007.

171. *The next 14 games will determine*: Ibid.
171. *We never give up*: Joe Strauss, "Pujols warns doubters: never count out Cards," *St. Louis Post-Dispatch*, August 19, 2007.

CHAPTER 21

174. *Anytime anybody puts up*: "Bob Costas interview of Albert Pujols," MLB.com, July 14, 2009, mlb.mlb.com/video/play.jsp?content_id=5571709, accessed August 25, 2010.
174. *People marvel at how much louder*: Joe Posnanski, "The power to believe," *Sports Illustrated*, March 16, 2009.
174. *That's part of being on top*: author interview with Rick Horton, August 11, 2009.
175. *We're living in this dark cloud*: Bryan Burwell, "Pujols' new job: the face of baseball," *St. Louis Post-Dispatch*, February 27, 2009.
175. *On your present pace*: "Bob Costas interview."
175. *I don't think so*: Ibid.
175. *I'm really proud of Mark*: http://www.ksdk.com/video/default.aspx?bctid=62201778001
175. *If I accuse you [of] something*: "Bob Costas interview."
176. *Let's say I retire 15 years from now*: Posnanski, "The power to believe."
176. *People just have to make up*: Ibid.
176. *He was so disciplined*: Richard Jerome, "League of his own," *People*, October 11, 2004.
177. *Major League Baseball had named former*: Tom Goldman, "Baseball seeks to fix Dominican troubles" (transcript), *All Things Considered*, NPR News, March 12, 2010, www.npr.org/templates/story/story.php?storyID=124628534, accessed July 28, 2010.
178. *To find prospects, Major League Baseball*: Joe Strauss, "Agents rule over players," *St. Louis Post-Dispatch*, November 28, 2005.
178. *I believe in the Lord Jesus Christ*: Scott Lamb and Tim Ellsworth, "Holy hitter," *World Magazine*, February 27, 2010.
179. *It would be easy to go out and do*: Ibid.
179. *I fear God too much to do*: Posnanski, "The power to believe."
179. *You know what, I forgive those people*: "Bob Costas interview."
180. *My focus is on God*: Ibid.
180. *Albert is a man very concerned about purity*: Horton, August 11, 2009.
181. *I've known Albert since*: Wright Thompson, "Trainer for Pujols says he's not linked to Grimsley case," *The Kansas City Star*, June 9, 2006.
181. *above reproach*: 1 Timothy 3:2 says, "Therefore [a leader] must be above reproach, the husband of one wife, sober-minded, self-controlled, respectable, hospitable, able to teach."
181. *They can test me every day*: Derrick Goold, "Pujols to world: I'm clean," *St. Louis Post-Dispatch*, May 18, 2006.
181. *Now that they do the testing*: Ibid.
182. *Everything that I earn in this game*: "Bob Costas interview."
182. *I challenged whoever who wants*: Ibid.
182. *He works harder*: Eric Velazquez, "Swing king," *Muscle and Fitness*, May 2007.
182. *He's one of those guys that leads*: author interview with Mike Maroth, November 3, 2009.
183. *I grew up in the Dominican Republic*: Velazquez, "Swing king."
183. *He was around 205 pounds*: Ibid.
183. *From my first year that we lifted*: Ibid.
183. *We took small steps*: Ibid.

183. *We're always going heavy with legs*: Ibid.
184. *He watches video on his swing*: Ibid.
184. *On any given day*: author interview with Walt Enoch.
184. *I believe in work*: Velazquez, "Swing king."
184. *They would be embarrassed*: Mel Antonen, "Focus of Cardinals first baseman Pujols: Higher Power," *USA Today*, April 1, 2009.
184. *I made that commitment to follow God*: "Bob Costas interview."
184. *He's very careful to honor his family*: author interview with Todd Perry, October 23, 2009.
184. *If he ever got involved in that stuff*: Posnanski, "The power to believe."
184. *To our fans and to the millions*: "Bob Costas interview."
185. *He really cares*: Wright Thompson, "Trainer for Pujols says he's not linked to Grimsley case," *The Kansas City Star*, June 9, 2006.
185. *This is my job*: ESPN.com, "A conversation with Albert Pujols," February 24, 2010, espn.go.com/video/clip?id=4941241, accessed July 28, 2010.
185. *He cares what every little kid thinks*: Thompson, "Trainer for Pujols."
185. *I don't want to be called that*: Bernie Miklasz, "Camp puts smile on Pujols' face," St. *Louis Post-Dispatch*, February 27, 2010.
185. *Of course, Stan and Albert are a lot*: Posnanski, "The power to believe."
186. *Todd Perry was sitting*: author interview with Toddy Perry.
187. *People just have to make up their own minds*: Ibid.
187. *You know how I want people*: Ibid.

CHAPTER 22

189. *a great guy: Joe Strauss, "Pujols*: 'It did bother me,'" *St. Louis Post-Dispatch*, May 23, 2008.
189. *He was bleeding*: Ibid.
190. *Just a class act*: Jay Posner, "Young out indefinitely with multiple fractures," *San Diego Union Tribune*, May 24, 2008.
190. *In all my years*: "Sound off," *St. Louis Post-Dispatch*, May 27, 2008.
190. *We're getting ready*. Joe Strauss, "Pujols sounds off. Star slugger welcomes Cardinals' youth movement, expects a better showing this season," *St. Louis Post-Dispatch*, March 3, 2008.
191. *The last thing he needs*: Derrick Goold, "Astro alarm awakens Albert," *St. Louis Post-Dispatch*, April 10, 2008.
192. *You need to take*: Derrick Goold, "A dashing victory: Pujols scores the winning run with a mad spring from second on an infield grounder," *St. Louis Post-Dispatch*, May 6, 2008.
192. *Albert has a knack*: author interview with Woody Williams.
192. *I play the game*: Joe Strass, "Redbirds run into trouble in Milwaukee," *St. Louis Post-Dispatch*, May 12, 2008.
193. *You can't do that*: Derrick Goold, "Cards notes," *St. Louis Post-Dispatch*, May 7, 2008.
193. *Just a home run*: Derrick Goold, "Cards notes," *St. Louis Post-Dispatch*, July 5, 2008.
195. *Us mere mortals*: Bernie Miklasz, "Fans who rip Pujols are laughably off base," *St. Louis Post-Dispatch*, August 25, 2008.
195. *I don't care when*: Joe Strauss, "Late antics fire up Cardinals," *St. Louis Post-Dispatch*, August 28, 2008.
196. *I guess he did*: Ibid.
196. *He's the one guy*: Derrick Goold, "On special day, Pujols makes home run a 'Walk in the Park,'" *St. Louis Post-Dispatch*, September 8, 2008.

196. *You always hear*: Ibid.
197. *It's Pujols*: Joe Strauss and Derrick Goold, "Cards notes," *St. Louis Post-Dispatch*, September 22, 2008.
197. *It's almost like*: Joe Strauss, "MVP 2008 National League: Pujols wins his second award, putting him in a select group," *St. Louis Post-Dispatch*, November 18, 2008.
197. *At the end of*: Rick Hummel, "Pujols is Clemente winner," *St. Louis Post-Dispatch*, October 26, 2008.

CHAPTER 23

198. *So often, Albert was in the medical area*: Anna Jones, "Dental trip to the Dominican Republic," *Pujols News*, vol. 2, no. 3 (Winter 2006).
198. *I don't forget where I come from*: Joe Strauss, "Pujols maintains a strong bond with Dominican," *St. Louis Post-Dispatch*, November 29, 2005.
198. *To improve the standard of living*: Pujols Family Foundation, "Vision Statement," www.pujolsfamilyfoundation.org/about/, accessed July 29, 2010.
199. *It is amazing to see people living*: "The Pujols Family Foundation visits the Dominican Republic," *Pujols News*, vol. 2, no. 2 (Autumn 2006).
199. *When we're in the Dominican*: author interview with Todd Perry, October 23, 2009.
199. *She's been in this bed in this hut*: Ibid.
200. *Each morning, the Pujolses*: Kathy Doan, "Showing compassion in the Dominican Republic," *Pujols News*, vol. 3, no. 4 (Spring 2008).
200. *I don't need my name in the paper*: Strauss, "Pujols maintains."
200. *If only you were there to see*: Doan, "Showing compassion."
200. *I want to set an example*: Strauss, "Pujols maintains."
200. *The way Albert treats people*: Perry, October 23, 2009.
201. *It was the greatest surprise*: Anna Jones, "Foundation helps to build school in DR," by *Pujols News*, vol. 2, no. 4 (Spring 2007).
201. *What started as a major problem*: "PFF buys new bus for Dominican orphans," *Pujols News*, vol. 2, no. 4 (Spring 2007).
202. *In one three-day stretch*: Jones, "Dental trip."
202. *So often, Albert was in the medical*: Ibid.
202. *He's a great dominoes player*: Ibid.
202. *The environment was less than ideal*: Doan, "Showing compassion."
203. *Many families had constructed something*: Jen Cooper, "2009 project sound asleep," *Pujols News*, vol. 4, no. 2 (Winter 2008).
203. *When we would bring a new bed*: Ibid.
203. *For each one of the families and moms*: Perry, October 23, 2009.
203. *You do it through baseball*: Ibid.
204. *Albert sees these young men*: Ibid.
204. *Those kids don't have much*: Strauss, "Pujols maintains."
204. *The whole thing that this batey baseball*: Perry, October 23, 2009.
204. *That's just another way of Albert*: Ibid.
204. *There are 9.6 million people*: Brandy Campbell, "To whom much is given," *Compassion Magazine*, vol. 3, no. 2 (Summer 2009).

CHAPTER 24

207. *It was illustrative of*: author interview with Rick Horton, August 11, 2009.
208. *We're in this era*: Joe Posnanski, "The power to believe," *Sports Illustrated*, March 16, 2009.

208. *I don't believe much*: Bryan Burwell, "Pujols' new job: the face of baseball," *St. Louis Post-Dispatch*, February 27, 2009.
209. *Oswalt is probably*: Joe Strauss, "Pujols' blasts fuel Cardinals' 19-hit attack," *St. Louis Post-Dispatch*, April 12, 2009.
210. *It's part of the*: Joe Strauss, "Cards notebook: Time is on Pujols' side," *St. Louis Post-Dispatch*, April 28, 2009.
210. *Nah*: Bryan Burwell, "How quickly things change," *St. Louis Post-Dispatch*, May 22, 2009.
211. *He didn't say he*: Joe Strauss, "Slam is a KO in KC as Pujols calls shot," *St. Louis Post-Dispatch*, June 22, 2009.
211. *Pujols, 29, acknowledges*: Joe Strauss, "Pujols checks his swings on issues," *St. Louis Post-Dispatch*, June 21, 2009.
212. *I feel awesome*: Dan Caesar, "Fox telecast recovers after missing catch of Obama's first pitch," *St. Louis Post-Dispatch*, July 15, 2009.
213. *Albert was there*: author interview with Kyle McClellan, October 27, 2009.
214. *Albert grabbed him*: Horton, August 11, 2009.
214. *Here's a guy who's*: Ibid.
215. *Pujols is that smart*: Rick Hummel, "Cox wins No. 2,400, is awed by Pujols," *St. Louis Post-Dispatch*, September 12, 2009.
216. *Albert is just out there*: Dan Caesar, "KMOX would get Sunday's Game 4," *St. Louis Post-Dispatch*, October 10, 2009.
217. *This team can win*: Joe Strauss, "Ninth-inning nightmare," *St. Louis Post-Dispatch*, October 9, 2009.
217. *It's pretty special*: Rick Hummel, "The Man pours on the praise for Pujols," *St. Louis Post-Dispatch*, November 25, 2009.

CHAPTER 25

218. *He could play in anybody's day:* Rick Hummel, "Aaron shows he's a big fan of Pujols," *St. Louis Post-Dispatch*, November 2, 2009.
219. *Only God and myself know:* Joe Strauss, "Pujols, Holliday arrive at Cardinals training camp," *St. Louis Post-Dispatch*, February 22, 2010.
219. *Opening a center like this:* "St. Luke's adult Down syndrome center named for Albert Pujols," accessed at http://www.ksdk.com/news/local/story.aspx?storyid=183598
220. *Now that they have their:* Joe Strauss, "Cards now are clear-cut Central pick," *St. Louis Post-Dispatch*, January 10, 2010.
220. *had each slugged above .500:* Derrick Goold, "Cards have only Nos. 3–4 hitters who were both batting champs," *St. Louis Post-Dispatch*, April 4, 2010.
220. *Only five remaining members of*: Rick Hummel, "Josh Kinney looking for spot in Cardinal bullpen," *St. Louis Post-Dispatch*, February 28, 2010.
221. *When you're around greatness:* Ibid., "Cards have only Nos. 3–4."
221. *You've got the crowd going:* Joe Strauss, "Pujols, Carpenter lead Cardinals to opening day win at Cincinnati," *St. Louis Post-Dispatch*, April 6, 2010.
221. *Right now I am so:* Bryan Burwell, "Pujols is 'just amazing,'" *St. Louis Post-Dispatch*, April 13, 2010.
222. *That's the first time I've:* Joe Strauss, "20 and done for Cards," *St. Louis Post-Dispatch*, April 18, 2010.
222. *If this was September:* "Redbirds have words but no runs," *St. Louis Post-Dispatch*, April 26, 2010.
222. *It's a difficult thing if*: Joe Strauss, "McGwire: Cards will be more balanced," *St. Louis Post-Dispatch*, April 22, 2010.

222. *In the National League:* Bernie Miklasz, "Cards look like runaway winners," *St. Louis Post-Dispatch*, May 3, 2010.
222. *He's given us some tough:* Derrick Goold, "Cardinals have tough times against Astros pitcher," *St. Louis Post-Dispatch*, May 13, 2010.
223. *We're still in second place:* Joe Strauss, "Reds bump St. Louis Cardinals out of first place," *St. Louis Post-Dispatch*, May 17, 2010.
223. *Every year it's someone new:* Bryan Burwell, "Cards' bats heat up for Reds," *St. Louis Post-Dispatch*, June 1, 2010.
223. *Cardinals are failing to live:* Bernie Miklasz, "Cardinals are failing to live up to ability," *St. Louis Post-Dispatch*, June 14, 2010.
224. *I hate the Cardinals:* Hal McCoy, "Phillips: 'I hate the Cardinals, hate 'em,'" *Dayton Daily News*, August 9, 2010.
225. *The whole thing with TLR:* Buzz Bissinger, accessed at http://twitter.com/buzzbissinger/status/22303915864.
225. *I wasn't out there trying:* Matthew Leach, "Pujols defends decision to attend rally," accessed http://stlouis.cardinals.mlb.com/news/print.jsp?ymd=20100828&content_id=14037398&vkey=news_stl&fext=.jsp&c_id=stl.
225. *Now, they have like $30 million:* Ibid., Matthew Leach.
226. *They can say and do:* Joe Strauss, "Game Update: Cards vs. Nationals," *St. Louis Post-Dispatch*, August 28, 2010.
226. *Baseball Prospectus crunched team:* Bernie Miklasz, "Cardinals can win NL Central if they stay healthy," *St. Louis Post-Dispatch*, March 28, 2010.
227. *This isn't only about being:* Albert Pujols, "Giving back means everything," *USA Today*, November 30, 2010.

CHAPTER 26

229. *It truly is an honor for me*: Derrick Goold, "Reggie Jackson welcomes Pujols to elite club," *St. Louis Post-Dispatch*, October 24, 2011.
229. *Once the 2011 season is over*: "Statements released Wednesday," St. Louis Post-Dispatch, February 17, 2011.
230. *When it rains, it pours*: Derrick Goold, "Pujols equals his longest homerless run," *St. Louis Post-Dispatch*, May 18, 2011.
231. *I knew that hopefully it would be less than six weeks*: Derrick Goold, "16 days later, the injured Pujols returns and is expected to play tonight," *St. Louis Post-Dispatch*, July 6, 2011.
234. *We were 10 ½, 9 ½ out*: Joe Strauss, "Wild Cards complete comeback for the ages," *St. Louis Post-Dispatch*, September 29, 2011.
236. *It's incredible what the Cardinals*: author interview with Rick Horton, December 13, 2011.
236. *We had a 5 percent chance*: Joe Strauss, "11TH HEAVEN: Wild Cards win World Series!" *St. Louis Post-Dispatch*, October 28, 2011.
238. "This isn't only about being": Albert Pujols, "Albert Pujols: 'Giving back means everything,'" *USA Today*, November 30, 2010.

ACKNOWLEDGEMENTS

SCOTT AND TIM WOULD LIKE TO THANK:

A number of people were so generous with their time, granting us interviews and providing helpful information about Albert and Deidre Pujols. Those interviewees included Jeff Adams, Debra Babor, Judy Boen, Landon Brandes, Phil Caldarella, Jen Cooper, Karen Cunningham, Miki Cunningham, Walt Enoch, Morgan Ensberg, Chris Francka, Dave Fry, Woody Galyean, Doug Glanville, Scott Hanna, Blake Hawksworth, Jan Hennicke, Rick Horton, Ron Hoskin, Dave Karaff, Marty Kilgore, Alan M. Klein, Frank Leo, Mike Maroth, Kyle McClellan, Don Mitchell, Jan Mueller, Luis Ortiz, Todd Perry, Galen Pitts, Allie Prescott, Dave Reynolds, Ryan Stegall, Adam Wainwright, Grant Williams, Woody Williams, and Ben Zobrist.

Others who helped in various ways included Joel Akridge, Craig Davis, Becky Ding, Sylvia Ellsworth, Derrick Ford, Tricia Latham, Matthew Leach, Devin Maddox, Tyler Miller, Michael Nowlin, Jim and Marge Pearson, Chad Quinn, Steve Rataj, Terry Reeder, Jeff Robinson, Joe Strauss, Timothy Wallis, Steve Weaver, Scott Gladin, and Christy Young. We appreciate each of their contributions and help.

Our agent, Andrew Wolgemuth, of Wolgemuth and Associates, Inc. Thanks for your wise counsel and for shepherding us through the whole process with the book. We almost forgive you for cheering for a Kansas City Royals team that stole the 1985 World Series from St. Louis.

The entire Thomas Nelson team, including Joel Miller, Kristen Parrish, Heather Skelton, Jason Jones, David Schroeder, and others. Thank you for your expertise and energy in making the book a reality. It's been a pleasure.

TIM WOULD LIKE TO THANK:

My co-author Scott Lamb for his vision and diligent work on the project. Who knew that our time years ago as college roommates would yield such fruit?

Union University President David S. Dockery and my Union colleagues provided tremendous encouragement throughout this project. It's a high honor to labor with them each and every day.

My Cornerstone Community Church family prayed for me and for my family regularly throughout the process of writing the book. We are truly blessed to be part of such a caring body of believers.

And last, but certainly not least, a huge word of gratitude to my wife Sarah and my kids Daniel, Emmalee, and Noah. Thank you for your support, love, and patience. I love each of you deeply.

SCOTT WOULD LIKE TO THANK:

Tim Ellsworth for being a loyal friend and a talented writer through all the twists and turns of this project. I have immense respect for you as a man of deep integrity, faith, and gifting.

Albert Mohler, President of The Southern Baptist Theological Seminary and the human instrument for bringing so much good into the lives of so many people. It is an honor and a joy to labor alongside you in your ministry of proclaiming the glories of God.

Matt Hall and Jason Allen, Christian leaders who know how to get things done the right way. You guys are an invaluable resource for wise counsel.

Friends who pray for me and have spoken timely words I needed to hear: Klay Aspinwall, Melvin Clark, Don Hinkle, Don Kirby, Josh Manley, Luther Powell, Clay Smith, and Steve Weaver.

Providence Baptist Church of St. Louis, a congregation that honors Christ and continues to pray for the Lambs. I love you guys and "do not cease to give thanks for you, remembering you in my prayers." Also, Immanuel Baptist Church of Louisville—a house of bread for my family.

My parents, Walter and Rexanna Lamb, for pointing me to Christ, early and often. And J.D. and Gail Clanton who gave me their Pearl and give us their prayers. My sister Jennifer Quinn and my brother Matthew who always believe (or at least listen to) my big plans and ideas . . . and will always be my "big sis" and "baby brother." I love you all.

Finally, I am so very grateful to my wife Pearl and my children—Josiah, Nathanael, Isaac, Benjamin, and Savannah. They have been without me on countless days of "Pujols work" and have never complained. Thanks for making this book possible. Pearl, I stand taller because of your love for me. Children, I will always be your biggest fan. I love you all.

ABOUT THE AUTHORS

Tim Ellsworth is director of news and media relations at Union University in Jackson, Tennessee, and author of *God the Whirlwind: Stories of Grace from the Tornado at Union University*. He is also a frequent contributor to Baptist Press. He previously worked as an editor, reporter, and high school social studies teacher. He and his wife, Sarah, have three children and are actively involved at Cornerstone Community Church.

Scott Lamb is director of research for the President of The Southern Baptist Theological Seminary. A native of St. Louis, Scott has pastored churches in Alabama and Missouri, and and is the pastor of Victory Memorial Baptist Church in Louisville, Kentucky. He and his wife, Pearl, have four sons and a daughter.

INDEX